FROMMER'S

COMPREHENSIVE TRAVEL GUIDE

MIAMI '93-'94

by Dan Levine

PRENTICE HALL TRAVEL

NEW YORK • LONDON • TORONTO • SYDNEY • TOKYO • SINGAPORE

FROMMER BOOKS

Published by Prentice Hall General Reference
A division of Simon & Schuster Inc.
15 Columbus Circle
New York, NY 10023

ISBN 0-671-84681-7
ISSN 1047-790X

Design by Robert Bull Design
Maps by Geografix Inc.

FROMMER'S EDITORIAL STAFF

Editorial Director: Marilyn Wood
Senior Editors: Alice Fellows, Lisa Renaud
Editors: Charlotte Allstrom, Thomas F. Hirsch, Peter Katucki, Sara Hinsey
  Raveret, Theodore Stavrou
Assistant Editors: Margaret Bowen, Lee Gray, Chris Hollander, Ian Wilker
Managing Editor: Leanne Coupe

Special Sales

Bulk purchases of Frommer's Travel Guides are available at special discounts. The publishers are happy to custom-make publications for corporate clients who wish to use them as premiums or sales promotions. We
can excerpt the contents, provide covers with corporate imprints, or create
books to meet specific needs. For more information write to Special Sales,
Prentice Hall Travel, Paramount Communications Building, 15 Columbus
Circle, New York, NY 10023.

Manufactured in the United States of America

CONTENTS

INDEX 190

LIST OF MAPS

INVITATION TO THE READER

In this guide to Miami, I have selected what I consider to be the best of the many fine establishments I came across while conducting my research. You, too, in the course of your visit to Miami and its environs, may come across a hotel, restaurant, shop, or attraction that you feel should be included here; or you may find that a place I have selected has since changed for the worse. In either case, let me know of your discovery. Address your comments to:

Dan Levine
Frommer's Miami '93–'94
c/o Prentice Hall Travel
15 Columbus Circle
New York, NY 10023

A DISCLAIMER

(1) I have made every effort to obtain up-to-the-minute prices and to ensure the accuracy of the other information contained in this guide. But even the most conscientious research cannot keep up with the changes that frequently occur in prices, as well as in some of the other information herein, as a result of the various volatile factors affecting the travel industry. Nevertheless, even if prices have risen above those quoted, I feel sure that the selections described in these pages still represent the best value for the money.

(2) The author and the publisher cannot be held responsible for the experiences of the reader while traveling.

SAFETY ADVISORY

Whenever you are traveling in an unfamiliar city or country, stay alert. Be aware of your immediate surroundings. Wear a moneybelt and keep a close eye on your possessions. Be especially careful with cameras, purses, and wallets—all of which are favorite targets of thieves and pickpockets.

CHAPTER 1

INTRODUCING MIAMI

recently met a woman who told me that although she was born and raised in Miami, she no longer considered the city her own. "It's changed," she lamented. "It's been invaded by foreigners and it's not the same Miami I was attached to." She is absolutely right. Florida's second-largest city, and unofficial capital of the state's "Gold Coast," is not the same place it used to be. Through a series of stunning international events—primarily during the last decade—the city has experienced startling changes in demographics as well as a miraculous spurt of economic growth. An enormous influx of refugees, predominantly from Cuba and Haiti, has swelled the city's Caribbean population and influenced all aspects of living, from art and architecture, and food and music to fashion, theater, and dance. Miami is now the Latin-American regional headquarters for over 120 multinational corporations, and it is the second-largest banking center in the United States. Encompassing both the mainland and the barrier islands of Miami Beach, Greater Miami now boasts almost 2 million residents and hosts over 8 million visitors annually.

South Florida's climate, ocean, and location have always been its top draws, and, fortunately, the evolution of America's southernmost metropolitan region—from a simple playground to a vibrant cosmopolitan city—has not been achieved at the expense of the area's celebrated surf and sand. Despite Miami's quick transformation, the almost complete absence of heavy industry has left the air and water as clear, clean, and inviting as ever. But Miami is no longer *just* a beach vacation. Recent trends, along with an enormous assortment of high-quality hotels, distinctive restaurants, unusual attractions, and top shopping opportunities have helped Miami become one of America's newest world-class cities. Relaxing days on the water are now complemented by cultural nights that include choice theater opportunities, top opera, a hopping club scene, and a lively café culture.

The unique influence of Miami's complex mix of cultures creates excellent and unusual opportunities that are exciting to explore. For

WHAT'S SPECIAL ABOUT MIAMI

Beaches
□ Over a dozen miles of white sandy beaches, edged with coconut palms on one side and a clear, turquoise-blue ocean on the other.

Nightlife
□ Music choices include everything from rock to reggae, and Latin influences mean irresistible rhythms.

Food
□ America's freshest citrus and seafood are prepared so uniquely that Miami regional cooking has its own name.

Architecture
□ Miami Beach's art deco district—the largest collection of buildings on the National Register of Historic Places.
□ The cityscape of Downtown Miami, one of the prettiest in the world.

Festivals
□ From Calle Ocho to Goombay, Miamians know how to party.

Water sports
□ Parasailing, jetskiing, sailing, boating, windsurfing . . . it's all here.

the weary, Miami continues to offer the same soothing sands that originally made the city famous. But, for the adventurous, this book is your guide to the wonders of one of America's freshest, most dynamic and vibrant cities.

DATELINE

- **1513** Juan Ponce de León is first European to land in Florida.
- **1600** Spanish colonization continues.
- **1763** England trades Havana for Florida. British plantations established.
- **1776** Florida fights on England's side during American Revolution.

(continues)

1. HISTORY & PEOPLE

Astonishly, just 100 years ago Miami didn't even exist. Until the final years of the 19th century, much of the Florida peninsula remained unsurveyed, inhabited only by a few remaining Native American Seminoles. To most Americans, southern Florida was arduously remote, visited only by enterprising explorers and hunters. Some adventurers attempted the journey south on horseback, following ancient Native American trails. Others went by sea, on one of the open sloops that carried the coastal trade. Either way, the voyage down Florida's east coast was both long and dangerous.

Despite the fact that an unescorted woman traveling alone was nothing short of scandalous, in 1891, Julia Tuttle, the widow of a wealthy Cleveland industrialist, arrived in a small town in southeast Florida with determination and a dream. At that time, the town consisted of little more than a couple of plantations, a small trading post, and the ruins of a U.S. Army camp once known as Fort Dallas. But sensing the economic and social potential of America's most tropical land, Tuttle set out to transform it into a full-blown town. Realization of her dream depended on easier access to the area, but the northern railroad magnates were less than enthusiastic. Fate intervened, however, in the winter of 1895, when a gripping freeze practically destroyed the state's northern citrus crop. With a shipment of fresh orange blossoms as evidence of southern Florida's ability to rebound quickly from severe cold and its agricultural ability, Tuttle again courted America's rail barons. The following year, Henry Flagler's first train steamed into town, and Tuttle became the only woman in American history to start a major city.

It wasn't long before Miami's irresistible combination of surf, sun, and sand prompted America's wealthy to build elaborate winter retreats overlooking Biscayne Bay (one of these mansions, Villa Vizcaya, remains and is open to the public; see Chapter 7). Miami became chic and, following World War I, widespread middle-class interest in the region prompted spectacular growth. The newcomers discovered that hefty windfalls could be made in real-estate speculation, and tales of million-dollar profits drove the population of Miami up from 30,000 to 100,000 in just 5 years. Over 300,000 vacationers visited Miami in the winter of 1924–25 alone.

The building boom of the Roaring Twenties is directly responsible for the city's distinctive neighborhoods of today. Coral Gables, the single largest real-estate venture of the time, became one of the most beautiful and exclusive residential areas in Miami. The towns of Hialeah, Miami Springs, and Opa-Locka were planned and built by the

DATELINE

- **1783** England returns Florida to Spain in exchange for the Bahamas and Gibraltar.
- **1785** Border disputes occur between Spain and America.
- **1821** U.S. acquires Florida. Andrew Jackson appointed first governor.
- **1835–42** Seminole War; some 300 remaining natives deported to reservations.
- **1845** Florida becomes the 27th U.S. state.
- **1881** Philadelphia industrialist Hamilton Disston buys million acres of Everglades, paving the way for South Florida's development.
- **1896** Henry M. Flagler extends railroad to Miami.
- **1898** Spanish-American War; army camps based in Miami.
- **1900** Florida's population 530,000.
- **1915** Carl Fisher dredges Biscayne Bay to build Miami Beach.
- **1921** President-elect Warren Harding spends winter in Miami.
- **1926** Hurricane swamps Miami.

(continues)

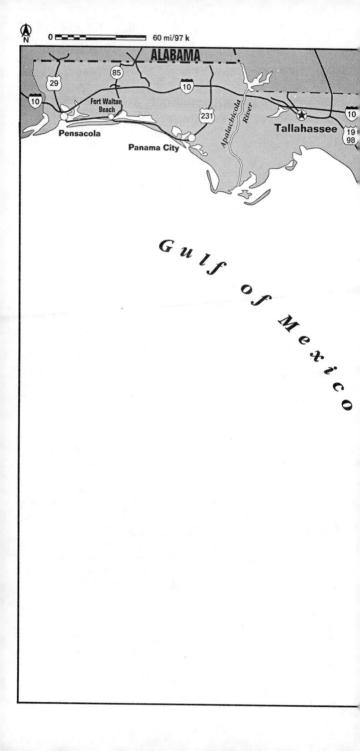

DATELINE

- **1930s** Hundreds of art deco hotels built in South Miami Beach.
- **1945** Thousands of American service personnel are based in Miami.
- **1947** Everglades National Park dedicated by President Harry S Truman.
- **1950** Frozen citrus concentrate becomes a major industry.
- **1954** Fontainebleau Hotel opens on Miami Beach.
- **1958** First jet passenger service between Miami and New York.
- **1959** Fidel Castro assumes power in Cuba; a mass exodus to South Florida follows.
- **1968** Richard Nixon nominated for president at the Republican national convention in Miami Beach.
- **1973** Miami Dolphins win Super Bowl VII, boasting the only undefeated season in NFL history.
- **1977** Orange juice spokesperson Anita Bryant leads fight against equal rights ordinance for gays. Dade County rejects rights bill.
(continues)

entrepreneur Glenn H. Curtiss as winter-home sites for upper-middle-class northerners. Opa-Locka, his most celebrated development, was designed around an Arabian Nights theme, complete with domes, parapets, and minarets. Another fanciful developer, Carl Fisher, dredged Biscayne Bay and built up the islands of Miami Beach for his opulent hotels, tennis courts, golf courses, and polo fields.

The Great Depression slowed Miami's boom and changed the nature of the city's buildings, exemplified primarily by the art deco styles of South Miami Beach. The buildings are at the same time austere and whimsical, reflecting both a stark reality and the promise of better times. Regarded as architectural masterpieces today, these pastel-colored structures offered budget-minded visitors an attractive alternative to the luxurious accommodations up the beach.

Miami's belt-tightening days were short lived. The end of World War II brought a second boom and another development frenzy. Again entire communities were built and sold wholesale. Miami Beach's megahotels were redesigned and rebuilt as resorts, and some television shows, like Arthur Godfrey's in the 1950s and Jackie Gleason's in the '60s, began to be telecast coast to coast from Miami.

Tourism waned again in the 1960s, but, at the same time, Miami began welcoming a new wave of dreamers. With a desire for a better life, and a steadfast belief in the American Dream, Cuban refugees and other sunbelt settlers started Miami's transformation from a resort community to a city of international stature. Most of the original 265,000 Cuban freedom-seekers came with little more than their entrepreneurial skills and a desire to build a new life. Their overwhelming accomplishments in constructing a strong educational, economic, and cultural base is one of America's greatest success stories.

In the early 1980s, Miami underwent its biggest building boom yet. Fantastically beautiful and unique skyscrapers sprang up downtown and along the boulevards flanking Biscayne Bay. The city's harbor became the biggest cruise-ship port in the world, and Miami International Airport grew to be America's second-busiest international gateway. Hundreds of multinational corporations, banks, and insurance firms opened offices, and a futuristic, billion-dollar Metrorail system whisked its way into the city. Suddenly Miami wasn't just booming; it was stylish. The hit TV series *Miami Vice* put the city on the fashion map, the world's top models and photographers seduced by the region's climate and colors.

Today, Miami is a unique American polyglot. There are almost 2 million residents in Dade County, of which 39% are non-Latin white, 19% black, and 42% Latin. The city's heterogeneous mix includes over 550,000 Cubans, 90,000 Haitians, 80,000 Jamaicans and Bahamians, 52,000 Puerto Ricans, and 28,000 Dominicans. Add to this a 1991 total of 8.2 million visitors from all around the world and it's easy to understand why this is truly an international city.

DATELINE

- **1980** Four ex-Miami policemen acquitted of killing black insurance executive Arthur McDuffie; riots leave 16 dead, 370 wounded. 140,000 Cubans enter South Florida when Castro opens port of Mariel.
- **1984** Miami's $1-billion Metrorail opens.
- **1991** Greater Miami's population reaches 1.8 million.

Miami is just now discovering its own identity. A vibrant, brash young adult of a city, it is continually testing and molding its own limits and capabilities. The air here is electric with the excitement of growth, change, and expansion. Especially in newly developing South Miami Beach, there is an overwhelming sense of being in the right place at the right time. To those who live here, and those who are lucky enough to visit, there is no doubt that what goes on in today's malleable Miami will have lasting effects long into the city's future.

2. ARCHITECTURE

Miami's flamboyant, surprising, and fanciful architecture is one of the city's greatest treasures. This young city's various building styles are too close together in time to classify them in "eras," but three distinct forms, indigenous to specific periods, are clearly in evidence.

The best of the "old" buildings were constructed between 1914 and 1925 by Miami's first developers. Designed primarily in an Italian Renaissance style are such structures as Villa Vizcaya, the Biltmore Hotel, and the Venetian Pool. Other monuments in and around Coral Gables and Coconut Grove, including George Merrick's wonderful plazas and fountains, are timeless examples of tasteful wealth and beauty. See "Driving Tour 2" in Chapter 8 for more in-depth descriptions.

Miami's second distinct building style is its most famous. The celebrated art deco district in South Miami Beach is a remarkable dreamlike foray into fashion and art on a grand scale. For the casual observer, the best buildings are the recently rehabilitated ones fronting the Atlantic on Ocean Drive. Until recently, South Beach, as the area is also called, had fallen into massive decay. But, thanks to strong community involvement and support, the district is now protected by a 1979 listing on the National Register of Historic Places. Continuously undergoing intensive revitalization, South Beach's hotels are now some of the best in Miami. See "A Walking Tour" in Chapter 8 for more in-depth information.

The sleek, 21st-century skyline of downtown Miami represents the city's newest building wave. Almost every structure in the small bayfront cluster is a gem. Designed with independence, creativity, and a flamboyant flair, the skyscrapers in and around Brickell Avenue stand sharp and proud, like exotic entrants in a futuristic design competition. From across the bay, the cluster of shining buildings creates one of the most awesome cityscapes in the world. Miamians are always proud to take visitors on a driving tour downtown, both during the day and at night. When the sun sets, the tall, twinkling towers are artfully illuminated in a spectacular and graceful dance of light. (See "Driving Tour 2" in Chapter 8.)

FAMOUS MIAMIANS

Bob Marley [1945–81] Perhaps one of the most influential figures in Jamaican history, Bob Marley was more than just a reggae musician. He was a spokesman for his people—a cultural leader of millions. Marley spent a lot of time in Miami, and eventually died in a Miami hospital. Some members of Marley's family still live in the city, along with an estimated 40,000 other Jamaicans.

Roy Cohn [1927–86] Disbarred just before he died, Roy Cohn is best known as the chief counsel for the "red-baiting witch hunts" organized by Senator Joseph McCarthy in the 1950s. Cohn was raised in Miami Beach, where he was a childhood friend of television journalist Barbara Walters.

Muhammad Ali [1942–] Like many other boxers who hit the big time, Muhammad Ali (Cassius Clay) lived in Miami and trained in South Miami Beach's Fifth Street Gym. The gym, at the corner of Washington Avenue, is still around, training the next generation of hopeful contenders.

The Bee Gees The English Gibb brothers are best known for their *Saturday Night Fever* soundtrack, produced in the disco days of the 1970s. They have always spent a lot of time in Miami and now own a mansion and recording studio in the city. The singing group is immortalized with their own suite on the top floor of Miami Beach's Fontainebleau Hotel.

Al Capone [1899–1947]   In the late 1920s, Chicago's most infamous gangster moved his operations to Miami and settled into a white stucco mansion on Palm Island.

Don Johnson [1950–]   New episodes of *Miami Vice* are no longer being produced, but Don Johnson, one of the show's stars, still likes to kick around the city that made him famous. Appropriately, Johnson bought a home on Star Island, a fancy parcel in the middle of Biscayne Bay.

Amelia Earhart [1897–1937]   The world's most famous aviatrix began her ill-fated flight around the world from Miami. She is immortalized by a city park named in her honor.

Richard M. Nixon [1913–]   Richard Nixon made Key Biscayne his "Winter White House" during his years as president of the United States. Subsequent owners have remodeled the property extensively, making it unrecognizable as the ex-president's ex-residence.

3. FOOD & DRINK

One of the best things about traveling is the taste of new foods. South Florida boasts a host of outstanding regional specialties that will definitely please your palate.

Miami's regional cooking is the result of the city's unique location, climate, and ethnic composition. Miami regional cooking is based on the California model, exemplified by creatively prepared dishes using fresh, local ingredients. Many of the presentations are health-oriented fish and vegetable dishes, highlighted by delicate dashes of color. Fruity sauces topping succulent seafood are common, as are jazzed-up versions of traditional meat and poultry dishes. Local citrus fruits are widely used as garnishes, in sauces, and as the primary ingredient in recipes such as Key lime pie.

Miami's ethnic edibles are as rich and diverse as the city's brilliant blend of cultures. In addition to the many straightforward rice-and-beans dishes served in traditional South and Central American restaurants (see "Little Havana" in Chapter 6 for details), you'll find Latin and Caribbean influences on even the most conservative menus. Cuban fried yucca, Bahamian conch fritters, tropical Caribbean preserves, creole-style blackened fish, Spanish arroz con pollo, and all kinds of tapas are available all over town.

Here's a short list of readily available, unique local specialties:

Florida alligator is not an endangered species, and it appears on many menus, often as an appetizer. Many people compare it to chicken, but a bird it's not. Slightly tough, and superbly subtle, gator meat is best as fried finger food, or broiled and eaten between bread like a hamburger.

✪ **Florida alligator is not an endangered species, and it appears on many menus.**

Conch, pronounced "conk," is a chewy shellfish that comes in those huge shells you blow as horns and put next to your ear to "hear" the ocean. This Bahamian specialty is usually served as an appetizer, either plain, in chowder, or battered and fried as "fritters."

Florida lobster is smaller and somewhat sweeter than the Maine variety, and the bulk of the meat is in the body, not the claws. Once you try this succulent shellfish, you'll find yourself ordering it again and again.

Dolphin fish has nothing to do with the marine mammal. This Florida specialty is a plump, white-meat, saltwater fish that seems to find its way onto more "chef's special" lists than any other dish. Try it.

Stone crabs are to Miami what the Eiffel Tower is to Paris. The crab's claws are the only part of the animal you eat, and they are ecologically collected; crabbers clip just one claw, then toss the crustacean back in the water to grow another one. The resulting meals are huge, meaty, and out-of-this-world delicious.

Key lime pie is the region's most famous dessert. The citrus fruits that flavor the filling are small and yellow, and indigenous to South Florida and the Florida Keys. The most authentic pie will have a yellow meringue filling and a graham-cracker crust.

Citrus fruits are the area's largest legal cash crop, accounting for the lion's share of Florida's $12 billion agricultural industry. The state produces more than 80% of the nation's limes, 50% of the world's grapefruits, and 25% of the world's oranges. Needless to say, citrus juice is the drink of choice in these parts. Try starting your day with a cool glass of the freshest orange or grapefruit juice you've ever had. At night, get a sense of the city's close Caribbean connections by mixing that juice with rum from one of the nearby islands.

A wide selection of bottled waters are available in Miami. And although designer brands are popular, the local tap supply is perfectly safe to drink.

4. RECOMMENDED BOOKS & FILMS

Dozens of books about Miami and South Florida can give you a more in-depth perspective on one of America's most unique regions. Here is a short list to get you started:

BOOKS

NONFICTION

Miami, by Joan Didion (Pocket Books, 1988), is a highly acclaimed book about the region's intimate Cuban connection. *Miami: City of the Future,* by T. D. Allman (Atlantic Monthly Press, 1988), takes a wider look at the many forces that have shaped Miami. *Deco Delights,* by Barbara Baer Capitman (E. P. Dutton, 1988), is an excellent documentation of the art deco district by the area's greatest champion. The book features colorful, coffee table–quality photographs by Steven Brooke.

FICTION

James Michener's *Caribbean* (Random House, 1989), devotes two chapters to Miami, the "capital of the Caribbean." *The True Sea,* by F. W. Belland (Holt, Rinehart & Winston), is a well-written novel about the difficulties encountered in the construction of Henry Flagler's railroad to the Florida Keys.

FILM

Dozens of top full-length feature films have been set against Miami's beautiful backdrop. Some of the best include:

Absence of Malice, starring Paul Newman and Sally Field; *Body Heat,* with William Hurt and Kathleen Turner; *Caddyshack,* starring Bill Murray and Rodney Dangerfield; *Hole in the Head,* starring Frank Sinatra; *Goldfinger,* the 1964 James Bond film; *Married to the Mob,* by director Jonathan Demme; *The Mean Season,* with Kurt Russell and Mariel Hemingway; *Miami Blues,* featuring Alec Baldwin; *Police Academy,* starring Jim Belushi; and the numerous *Porky's.*

IMPRESSIONS

The sun and fun capital of the world.
—JACKIE GLEASON

CHAPTER 2

PLANNING A TRIP TO MIAMI

Although it is possible to land in Miami without an itinerary or reservations, your trip will be much more rewarding with a little bit of advance planning.

1. INFORMATION

In addition to the data and sources listed below, foreign visitors should see Chapter 3 for entry requirements and other pertinent information.

The **Greater Miami Convention and Visitors Bureau,** 701 Brickell Ave., Miami, FL 33131 (tel. 305/539-3063 or toll free 800/283-2707), is the best source of any kind of specialized information about the city. Even if you don't have a specific question, be sure to phone ahead for their free magazine, *Destination Miami,* which includes several good, clear maps. The office is open Monday through Friday from 9am to 5:30pm.

For information on traveling in the state as a whole, contact the **Florida Division of Tourism (FDT),** 126 W. Van Buren St., Tallahassee, FL 32399 (tel. 904/487-1462; open Monday to Friday 8am to 5pm). Europeans should note that FDT maintains an office in England at 18/24 Westbourne Grove, 4th floor, London W2 5RH (tel. 071/727-1661).

In addition to information on some of South Miami Beach's better hotels, the **Miami Design Preservation League,** 1244 Ocean Dr. (P.O. Bin L), Miami Beach, FL 33119 (tel. 305/672-2014), offers a free, informative guide to the art deco district, and several books on the subject. They're open Monday to Saturday from 10am to 7pm.

Greater Miami's various chambers of commerce also send maps and information about their particular parcels. These include: **Coconut Grove Chamber of Commerce,** 2820 McFarlane

Rd., Miami, FL 33133 (tel. 305/444-7270); **Coral Gables Chamber of Commerce,** 50 Aragon Ave., Coral Gables, FL 33134 (tel. 305/446-1657); **Florida Gold Coast Chamber of Commerce,** 1100 Kane Concourse (Bay Harbor Islands), Miami, FL 33154 (tel. 305/866-6020). This office represents Bal Harbour, Sunny Isles, Surfside, and other North Dade waterfront communities; **Greater Miami Chamber of Commerce,** Omni International, 1601 Biscayne Blvd., Miami, FL 33132 (tel. 305/539-3063 or toll free 800/283-2707); and **Miami Beach Chamber of Commerce,** 1920 Meridian Ave., Miami Beach, FL 33139 (tel. 305/672-1270).

The following organizations represent dues-paying hotels, restaurants, and attractions in their specific areas. These associations can arrange accommodations and tours, as well as provide discount coupons to area sights: **Miami Beach Resort Hotel Association,** 407 Lincoln Rd., Miami Beach, FL 33139 (tel. 305/531-3553 or toll free 800/531-3553) and **Sunny Isles Beach Resort Association,** 3909 Sunny Isles Blvd., Suite 307, Sunny Isles, FL 33160 (tel. 305/947-5826 or toll free 800/327-6366).

WHAT THINGS COST IN MIAMI	U.S. $
Taxi from Miami Airport to a Downtown hotel	16.00
Local telephone call	.25
Double room at the Grand Bay Hotel (Deluxe)	265.00
Double room at the Cavalier Hotel (Moderate)	120.00
Double room at the Driftwood Resort Motel (Budget)	65.00
Lunch for one at The Caribbean Room (Moderate)	13.75
Lunch for one at the News Café (Budget)	8.50
Dinner for one, without wine, at The Pavillon Grill (Deluxe)	45.00
Dinner for one, without wine, at Versailles (Budget)	12.00
Pint of beer	2.75
Coca-Cola in a restaurant	1.25
Cup of coffee	.85
Roll of ASA 100 film, 36 exposures	5.65
Admission to Miami Metrozoo	8.25
Movie ticket	7.00

2. WHEN TO GO

Miami's tourist season, lasting from October through May, is more reflective of the weather up north than it is of climatic changes in South Florida. It's always warm in Miami. No matter what time of year you visit you'll find that indoor spaces are always air conditioned, cafés always have tables out on the sidewalk, and the beaches are always full. Terrific weather has always been Miami's main appeal and is a particular delight during the winter, when the rest of the country is shivering. When it's winter in Wisconsin it's still summer in the Sunshine State. Christmas is a particularly good time to visit, since prices haven't yet reached the heights they will by the middle of the season.

HURRICANE ANDREW

In August 1992, Hurricane Andrew, one of the strongest Atlantic storms on record, struck southern Florida and parts of Louisiana. With winds of up to 164 mph, it swept across Dade County, south from Miami, and most of Monroe County, causing extensive damage. The storm's total destruction was estimated at $30 billion, making Andrew the costliest natural disaster in American history.

Downtown Miami and Miami Beach survived relatively intact, but other areas in and around Miami suffered varying damage. Among the places severely hit were the **Miami Metrozoo,** near Coral Gables, and **Monkey Jungle,** in Greater Miami South; both closed for repairs. Also badly damaged was the 740-acre **Dade County Zoo,** with its popular rare-bird collection. Other major tourist attractions, however, remained largely unaffected by the storm, as did most of the hotels in the Greater Miami area.

Don't overlook traveling to Miami during the "off" seasons, when vacationing can be every bit as rewarding. The weather is still great, and hotel prices are significantly less than at other times of year. In addition, restaurants, stores, and highways are less crowded.

CLIMATE

South Florida's unique climate is extremely tropical. Hot, sometimes muggy summers are counterbalanced by wonderfully warm winters. Winds are strong and clouds move fast across the sky. It's not uncommon for a sudden shower to be followed by several hours of intense sunshine. For most natives, "winter" is too cold for swimming; for the rest of us, however, 70-degree January afternoons are welcome miracles of nature. But don't be misled: There are occasional cold snaps and even one short tropical rain shower can ruin a day at the beach.

Finally, a word about Florida's tropical storms and hurricanes. Most occur between August and November. For local property owners, the tumultuous winds that sweep in from the Atlantic Ocean can be devastating. In August 1992, for example, Hurricane Andrew—one of the fiercest storms ever recorded in Florida—caused extensive damage to residential and business districts in Dade and Monroe counties. More than 250,000 people were left homeless.

For tourists, the high winds and incessant rains *usually* mean little more than a delayed vacation. Visitors to Miami who stayed through Hurricane Andrew found that most hotels and major tourist attractions suffered relatively little damage. But three popular places that were severely hit were the Miami Metrozoo, Monkey Jungle, and the Dade County Zoo, all of which closed for repairs.

Meteorologists know far in advance when a storm is brewing off the Atlantic coast and can determine pretty accurately what force it will have; the information is then broadcast nationwide. With respect to Andrew, the National Hurricane Center, located in Coral Gables, gave due warning of the storm and tracked it closely as it approached Florida.

Note: If there are reports of an impending storm before you leave for your trip to Florida, you may want to postpone your trip.

Miami's Average Temperatures and Rainfall

	Jan	Feb	Mar	Apr	May	June	July	Aug	Sept	Oct	Nov	Dec
Avg. High (°F)	75	76	79	82	85	87	89	90	88	84	80	76
Avg. Low (°F)	59	60	64	68	72	75	76	77	76	72	66	61
Avg. Rain (in.)	2.0	2.0	2.3	3.6	6.3	8.6	6.7	7.2	8.6	6.9	2.9	1.9

MIAMI CALENDAR OF EVENTS

Of the many special events scheduled throughout the year, the bulk are staged from October through May. This reflection of the close relationship between tourism and festivals in no way means that Miami's special events are canned tourist traps; in fact, the truth is quite the contrary. Miamians have an innate talent for presenting and attending outdoor festivals, and although the success of city festivals often relies on tourist dollars, the inspiration and creativity that goes into them is 100% homegrown. The list below highlights Miami's most important annual events, and contact numbers are provided with each. For more information on these, and on other seasonal activities, call or write the Greater Miami Convention and Visitor's Bureau (see above).

JANUARY

☐ **Art Deco Weekend** Held along the beach between 8th and 13th streets, this festival celebrates the whimsical architecture that has made South Beach one of America's most unique neighborhoods with bands, food stands, and other festivities. A weekend mid-month.

☐ **Taste of the Grove Food and Music Festival** This is an excellent chance for visitors to sample menu items from some of the city's top restaurants. The party is a fund-raiser held in the Grove's Peacock Park. For details, call 305/444-7270. A weekend mid-month.

☐ **The Key Biscayne Art Festival** brings more than 200 artists together in a high quality, adjudicated show—all for charity. It is held in Cape Florida State Park. Call 305/361-0775 for more information. Late January.

⊙ *THE ORANGE BOWL Featuring two of the year's toughest college teams, this football match kicks off the month with a game in the stadium of the same name. Other activities include a marathon, a powerboat regatta, and the Three Kings Parade.*

*Where: Miami **When:** New Year's Day **How:** Tickets are available starting March 1, through the Orange Bowl Committee, Box 350748, Miami, FL 33135 (tel. 305/371-4600).*

FEBRUARY

⊙ *MIAMI FILM FESTIVAL This festival has made an impact as an important screening room for Latin American cinema. Fashioned after the San Francisco model, this annual event is relatively small, well priced, and easily accessible to the general public.*

*Where: Miami **When:** 10 days in mid-February **How:** Contact the Film Society of Miami, 7600 Red Rd., Miami, FL 33157 (tel. 305/377-FILM).*

☐ **Coconut Grove Art Festival** This is the state's largest art festival, and the favorite annual event of many locals. Almost every medium is represented including, unofficially, the culinary arts. For details call 305/447-0401. Mid-month.

☐ **The Grand Prix of Miami** An auto race that rivals the big ones in Daytona this is a high-purse, high-profile event that attracts the top Indy car drivers and large crowds. For information and tickets contact Miami Motorsports, 7254 SW 48th St., Miami, FL 33155 (tel. 305/662-5660). Late February.

MARCH

☐ **Calle Ocho Festival** One of the world's biggest block parties and Miami's answer to Carnival. Over one million people attend this salsa-filled blowout which is held along 23 blocks of Little Havana's SW 8th Street. For information call 305/644-8888.

☐ **The Italian Renaissance Festival** Stage plays, music, and period costumes complement Vizcaya's neo-Italian architectural style. Call 305/579-2767 for more information. A mid-month weekend.

☐ **Dade County Youth Fair and Exposition** A huge, 2-week carnival-style romp featuring dozens of rides, over 100 food booths, and more than 350 shows including dancers, magicians, and clowns. For more information call 305/223-7060. Late March.

MAY

☐ **The Miami International Festival** features food, folklore, and dance from around the world. It is held in Coconut Grove's Exhibition Center. Call 305/279-1538 for more information.

JUNE

✪ *COCONUT GROVE GOOMBAY FESTIVAL A Bahamian bacchanalia with dancing in the streets, this bash is billed as the largest black-heritage festival in America. It celebrates Miami's Caribbean connection.*

*   **Where:** Coconut Grove, Miami **When:** June **How:** Call 305/372-9966 for festival details.*

JULY

☐ **Independence Day** (July 4) is celebrated on the beaches. Parties, barbecues, and fireworks flair all day . . . and night.

AUGUST

☐ **Miami Reggae Festival** Jamaica's independence is celebrated with a dozen top bands playing for much of the city's sizable Rastafarian community. The first Sunday in August.

SEPTEMBER

☐ **Festival Miami,** sponsored by the University of Miami, is a 3-week program of performing and visual arts centered in and around Coral Gables. For a schedule of events contact the University of Miami's School of Music, Box 248165, Coral Gables, FL 33124 (tel. 305/284-6477).

☐ **The Miami Boat Show** draws almost a quarter of a million boat enthusiasts to the Coconut Grove Convention Center, conveniently located right on the water. Call 305/579-3310 for details. Second or third week of September.

NOVEMBER

☐ **Miami Book Fair International** One of the city's leading cultural attractions. Last year's show drew hundreds of thousands of visitors, including foreign and domestic publishers, and authors from around the world. For more information call 305/347-3000.

DECEMBER

☐ **The King Mango Strut** parades from Commodore Plaza to Peacock Park in Coconut Grove. This fun-filled march encourages everyone to wear wacky costumes and join the floats in a spoof on the King Orange Jamboree Parade, which is held the following night. Comedians and musical entertainment follow in the park. December 30.

✪ *THE KING ORANGE JAMBOREE PARADE Ending the year, this special New Year's Eve event may be the world's largest nighttime parade, and is followed by a long night of festivities.*

*   **Where:** Along Biscayne Boulevard **When:** December 31 **How:** For information and tickets (which cost $7.50 to $13) call 305/642-1515 or contact the Greater Miami Convention and Visitors Bureau (see above).*

3. WHAT TO PACK

If you're renting a car and staying in a deluxe hotel, pack as much as you like—porters are everywhere. Other travelers, however, should be aware that most smaller hotels, including those in South Beach's art deco district, do not have porters, and Miami International Airport is one of the few in the country without luggage-cart rentals. In general, it's unwise to bring more than you can carry. Don't worry if you forget something, or need an emergency item—everything you could possibly want can be purchased in Miami.

Warm weather translates into informal dress. Few places require jackets and ties, and if you're on vacation, you'll rarely feel out of place without these business staples. The city is particularly hot and humid during summer, but ample air conditioning (often too ample) means you should take pants and a light sweater even in the hottest months. During winter, plan for cold snaps and cool nights with clothes appropriate to more northerly climates. Of course you should bring shorts, a bathing suit, and sunglasses.

With the exception of an umbrella, keep your rain gear at home.

During winter, rain showers rarely last long and may be over by the time you've reached for your poncho. During summer, the humidity will discourage you from wearing plastic no matter how hard it's raining.

Exposure to the sun's rays is healthy only in moderation. Over a long period of time, too much can be detrimental, and can even cause cancer. Protect yourself with a high Sun Protection Factor (SPF) lotion or screen, and don't expose yourself to too much in one day—especially if you've been out of the sun for months. If you burn easily, a product with an SPF of at least eight is recommended. Also, wear sunglasses—the kind that block out ultraviolet rays—and bring a hat with a wide bill or rim. When you're walking on the beach in the middle of the afternoon, or driving west in the early evening, you'll be glad you did.

4. TIPS FOR SPECIAL TRAVELERS

FOR THE DISABLED

Several hotels offer special accommodations and services for wheelchair-bound and other physically challenged visitors. These include large bathrooms, ramps, and telecommunication devices for the deaf. The Greater Miami Convention and Visitors Bureau (see "Information" above) has the most up-to-date information. The City of Miami Department of Parks and Recreation, 2600 S. Bayshore Dr. (Coconut Grove), Miami, FL 33133 (tel. 305/579-3431; TTY 305/579-3436), maintains many programs for the disabled at parks and beaches all around the city. Call or write for a listing of special services. They're open Monday to Friday from 8am to 5pm. Primarily a referral service, the Deaf Services Bureau, 4800 W. Flagler St., Suite 213, Miami, FL 33134 (tel. 305/444-2266; TTY 24 hours 305/444-2211), may be contacted for any special concerns you may have about traveling in and around Miami. Hours are Monday to Friday from 9am to 5pm. The Division of Blind Services, 401 NW 2nd Ave., Suite 700, Miami, FL 33128 (tel. 305/377-5339), offers similar services as the bureau above but to the visually impaired. The office is open Monday to Friday from 8am to 5pm.

FOR SENIORS

Miami is well versed when it comes to catering to seniors. Ask for discounts everywhere: at hotels, movie theaters, museums, restaurants, and attractions. The worst the cashier will say is "no," and more often than not the answer will be "yes."

You may wish to pick up a copy of *Travel Easy: The Practical Guide for People over 50*, by Rosalind Massow, published by the American Association of Retired Persons (AARP), 1909 K St. NW, Washington, DC 20049 (tel. 202/872-4700).

FOR STUDENTS

Students will find their valid high school or college I.D. will mean discounts at museums and attractions, as well as at many bars during "college nights." When student prices are available, they are noted in this book under the appropriate listing.

5. GETTING THERE

Miami is easy to get to, but not all transportation options are created equal. Shopping around will ensure that you get there the best way at the best price.

BY AIR

More than 80 scheduled airlines service Miami International Airport, including almost every major domestic and foreign carrier. The city is so well connected that the problem isn't getting there, but rather deciding what service and fare to select. Your air transportation options run the gamut from courier flights to the Concorde (including a courier flight *on* the Concorde). Following are the major American carriers offering regular flights to Miami, along with their local sales office addresses and telephone numbers (where available): **American Airlines,** 150 Alhambra Plaza, Coral Gables (tel. 358-6800 or toll free 800/433-7300); **Continental,** 38 Biscayne Blvd., Downtown (tel. 871-1400 or toll free 800/525-0280); **Delta Airlines,** 201 Alhambra Circle, Suite 516, Coral Gables (tel. 448-7000 or toll free 800/221-1212); **Northwest Airlines,** 150 Alhambra Plaza, Coral Gables (toll free 800/447-4747); and **United Airlines,** Miami International Airport (tel. 377-3461 or toll free 800/521-4041).

TYPICAL REGULAR FARES

Florida destinations are often at the heart of "fare wars" that airlines wage; flights to the city are usually pretty reasonable, if not downright cheap. Sometimes a ticket to Miami is so inexpensive that it's not worth it to travel agents to dig for information. I usually do the leg work and make the reservation myself, and then visit my travel agent for ticketing. Check the newspapers for advertisements and call a few of the major carriers before committing yourself to a fare.

The cheapest standard **economy-class** fare usually comes with serious restrictions and steep penalties for altering dates and itineraries. When requesting this kind of ticket, don't use the terms *APEX, excursion,* or other airline jargon; just ask for the lowest fare. If you are flexible with dates and times, say so. Ask if you can save money by staying an extra day or by flying mid-week. Most airlines won't volunteer this information. At the time of this writing, the lowest round-trip fare from New York was $178; from Chicago, $298; and from Los Angeles, $398. You may even find it cheaper. **Business**

Class seats can cost twice that of coach. You should know that airlines sometimes offer "free" business-class upgrades to passengers who purchase an unrestricted coach-class ticket. Unrestricted fares are the most expensive, but may still be less than a business-class seat. Ask about this when purchasing your ticket. Many domestic flights to Miami don't even carry a **first-class** section. When they do, they're predictably expensive. Before buying, see if your airline offers a first-class upgrade with a full-fare business-class ticket.

OTHER GOOD-VALUE CHOICES

Alternatives to the traditional travel-agent ticket have their advantages (usually price), and their drawbacks (usually freedom). Don't overlook a **consolidator,** or "bucket shop," when hunting for domestic fares. By negotiating directly with the airlines, the "buckets" can sell tickets at prices below official rates. On the minus side, consolidators usually don't offer travel counseling or reserve accommodations or rental cars. Like the most heavily restricted tickets, these often carry heavy penalties for changes or cancellations.

The lowest-priced bucket shops are usually local operations with low profiles and low overheads. Look for their advertisements in the travel section or the classifieds of your local newspaper. Nationally advertised businesses are usually not as competitive as the smaller operations, but they do have toll-free telephone numbers and are easily accessible. One well-known concern is **Unitravel,** 1177 N. Warson Rd. (P.O. Box 12485), St. Louis, MO 63132 (tel. 314/569-0900 or toll free 800/325-2222). **Courier flights** are primarily long-haul jobs and are not usually available for short domestic hops. But if you are crossing the country or an ocean, becoming a mule might be for you. Companies that hire couriers will use your luggage allowance for their business's baggage, but in return, you'll get a deeply discounted ticket. Flights are often offered at the last minute, and you may have to arrange a pretrip interview to make sure you're right for the job.

Now Voyager, Inc. (tel. 212/431-1616 from 11:30am to 6pm) flies from New York, and sometimes has flights to Miami for as little as $99 round-trip. **I.B.C. Pacific** (tel. 310/607-0125 from 9am to 4pm Pacific time) offers flights from Los Angeles to Florida for around $200 round-trip. Travelers may stay in Miami from 7 to 19 days.

BY TRAIN

Train travel is slow and it usually costs as much, or more, than flying. But if you don't like to fly or if you want to take a leisurely ride through America's countryside, Amtrak may be a good option. Two trains leave daily from New York—the *Silver Meteor* at 8:40am and the *Silver Star* at 4:30pm—and take 26½ hours to complete the journey. At press time, the lowest-priced round-trip ticket from New York to Miami cost $152, climbing to a whopping $417 for a sleeper (based on double occupancy).

If you are planning to stay in South Florida for some time, you might think about taking your car on Amtrak's East Coast Auto Train. The 16½-hour ride, connecting Lorton, Virginia (near Washington, D.C.) with Sanford, Florida (near Orlando), has a glass-domed viewing car, and includes breakfast and dinner in the ticket price. Round-trip fares are only a few dollars higher than one-way—about $170 for adults, $85 for children under 12, and $300 for your car. One-way fares are discounted as much as 50% when most traffic is going in the opposite direction. Call toll free 800/USA-RAIL for more information about these and other Amtrak services.

BY BUS

Bus travel is often an inexpensive and flexible option. Greyhound/Trailways can get you to Miami from virtually anywhere, and they offer several money-saving multiday bus passes. Round-trip fares vary depending on your point of origin, but few, if any, exceed $200. Greyhound/Trailways no longer operates a single nationwide telephone number, so consult your local directory for the office nearest you.

BY CAR

Florida is well connected to the rest of the United States by three interstates: I-10, which originates in Los Angeles and terminates in Jacksonville; I-75, which begins in north Michigan and runs through the center of Florida; and I-95, which begins in Maine and follows the eastern seaboard to its end in Downtown Miami.

Car is a great way to go if you want to become intimate with the countryside, but after adding in food, lodging, and automobile expenses, it may not be your cheapest option. For tips on getting around Miami by car, see "Getting Around" in Chapter 4.

Before taking a long car trip you should seriously consider joining a major **automobile association.** Not only do they offer travel insurance and helpful information, but they can also perform vacation-saving roadside services, including towing. The American Automobile Association (AAA), 1000 AAA Dr., Heathrow, FL 32746 (tel. 407/444-7000), is the nation's largest auto club with over 850 offices. Membership ranges from about $20 to $60, depending on where you join.

Other recommendable auto clubs include the Allstate Motor Club, Allstate Place, Northbrook, IL 60062 (tel. 312/402-5461); and the Amoco Motor Club, P.O. Box 9046, Des Moines, IA 50369 (tel. toll free 800/334-3300).

FOR FOREIGN VISITORS

American fads and fashions have spread across Europe and other parts of the world. Although America, in consequence, may seem like familiar territory to you when you arrive, there are still many peculiarities and uniquely American situations that every foreign visitor will encounter. This chapter is meant to clue you in on what they are. International visitors should also read carefully Chapter 1, "Introducing Miami."

1. PREPARING FOR YOUR TRIP

NECESSARY DOCUMENTS

Canadian nationals need only proof of Canadian residence to visit the United States. Citizens of Great Britain and Japan need only a current passport. Citizens of other countries, including Australia and New Zealand, usually need two documents: a valid **passport** with an expiration date at least six months later than the scheduled end of their visit to the United States, and a **tourist visa** available at no charge from a U.S. embassy or consulate.

To get a tourist or business visa to enter the United States, contact the nearest American embassy or consulate in your country; if there is none, you will have to apply in person in a country where there *is* a U.S. embassy or consulate. Present your passport, a passport-size photo of yourself, and a completed application, which is available through the embassy or consulate. Visa applications are also distributed by many airline offices and travel agents.

You may be asked to provide information about how you plan to finance your trip or show a letter of invitation from a friend with whom you plan to stay. Those applying for a business visa may be asked to show evidence that they will not receive a salary in the United States.

Be sure to check the length of stay on your visa; usually it is six months. If you want to stay longer, you may file for an extension with the Immigration and Naturalization Service once you are in the country. If permission to stay is granted, a new visa is not required unless you leave the United States and want to reenter.

MEDICAL REQUIREMENTS

No inoculations are needed to enter the U.S. unless you are coming from, or have stopped in, areas known to be suffering from epidemics, especially of cholera or yellow fever. Applicants for immigrants' visas (and only they) must undergo a screening for AIDS.

If you have a disease requiring treatment with medications containing a controlled substance, carry a valid, signed prescription from your physician to allay any suspicions that you are smuggling drugs. Ditto for syringes.

TRAVEL INSURANCE

All such insurance is voluntary in the U.S.; however, given the very high cost of medical care, I cannot too strongly advise every traveler to arrange for appropriate coverage before setting out. There are specialized insurance companies that will, for a relatively low premium, cover the loss or theft of your baggage; trip-cancellation costs; guarantee of bail in case you are sued; sickness or injury costs (medical, surgical, and hospital); and costs of an accident, repatriation, or death. Such packages (for example, "Europe Assistance" in Europe) are sold by automobile clubs at attractive rates, as well as by insurance companies and travel agencies.

2. GETTING TO THE U.S.

In addition to the domestic American airlines listed in Chapter 2, dozens of international carriers including Air Canada, Air France, British Airways, El Al, Iberia, and Lufthansa also serve Miami International Airport. Icelandair usually offers attractive fares from Luxembourg to Orlando, while Continental and Virgin Atlantic are often the price-leaders directly into Miami. At the time of this publication, several airlines were offering a round-trip fare of £198 from London to Miami. For the best rates, compare fares and be flexible with the dates and times of travel.

For information on travel to and around Miami, see "Getting There" in Chapter 2 and "Getting Around" in Chapter 4.

Some large airlines (for example American Airlines, Northwest, and Delta) offer travelers on their transatlantic or transpacific flights special discount tickets under the name **Visit USA,** allowing travel between any U.S. destinations at minimum rates. They are not on sale in the U.S. and must therefore be purchased before you leave your foreign point of departure. This system is the best way of seeing the U.S. at low cost. You should obtain information well in advance from your travel agent or the office of the airline concerned, since the conditions attached to these discount tickets can be changed without advance notice.

European visitors can also buy a **USA Railpass,** good for unlimited train travel on Amtrak. The pass is available through some airlines and travel agents, including Thomas Cook in Britain and Cuoni on the Continent. Various itinerary options are available for $299 and up. Amtrak officials suggest you make route reservations as soon as possible, as many trains are often sold out.

With a foreign passport and airline ticket you can also buy the passes at Amtrak offices in Seattle, San Francisco, Los Angeles, Chicago, New York, Miami, Boston, and Washington, D.C. For further information write Amtrak Distribution Center, P.O. Box 7717, 1549 W. Glen Lake Ave., Itasca, IL 60143; in the U.S. call toll free 800/USA-RAIL.

FAST **FOR THE FOREIGN TRAVELER**

Accommodations Some of the major hotels listed in this book maintain overseas reservation networks and can be booked either directly, or through travel agents. Some hotels are also included in tour operators' package tours. Since tour companies buy rooms in bulk, they can often offer them at a discount. Discuss this option with your travel agent, and compare tour prices to those in this guide. For accommodations in Miami, see Chapter 5.

Automobile Rentals If you plan on renting a car in the U.S., you will probably not need the services of an auto organization. If you are planning to buy or borrow a car, however, automobile association membership is recommended. The American Automobile Association (AAA), 1000 AAA Dr., Heathrow, FL 32746 (tel. 407/444-7000), is the country's largest auto club, supplying members with maps, insurance, and most importantly, emergency road service. The cost of joining runs from $20 to $60, but if you are a member of a foreign auto club with reciprocal arrangements, you can enjoy free AAA service in America. See "Getting There" in Chapter 2 for more information.

Business Hours See "Fast Facts: Miami" in Chapter 4.

Climate See "When to Go" in Chapter 2.

Currency and Exchange The U.S. monetary system has a decimal base: one **dollar** ($1) = 100 **cents** (100¢).

The most common **bills** (all green) are the $1 ("a buck"), $5, $10, and $20 denominations. There are also $2 (seldom encountered), $50, and $100 bills (the last two are not welcome when paying for small purchases).

There are six denominations of **coins:** 1¢ (one cent or "penny"); 5¢ (five cents, or "nickel"); 10¢ (ten cents, or "dime"); 25¢ (twenty-five cents, or "quarter"); 50¢ (fifty cents, or "half dollar"); and the rare, and prized by collectors—$1 piece (both the older, large silver dollar and the newer, small Susan B. Anthony coin).

Foreign exchange bureaus are rare in America and most banks are not equipped to handle **currency exchange.** Miami's money changing offices include: BankAmerica International, Concourse E, at Miami International Airport (tel. 377-6000; open 24 hours); Abbot Foreign Exchange, 255 E. Flagler St., Downtown (tel. 374-2336; open Monday to Friday 8am to 5pm, Saturday 8am to 2pm); and Deak International, in the Fontainebleau Hilton Hotel, 4441 Collins Ave., Miami Beach (tel. 674-1907; open Monday to Friday 8:30am to 4:30pm, Saturday 9am to 1pm).

Traveler's checks are widely accepted, but make sure they are denominated in U.S. dollars, as foreign currency checks are difficult to exchange.

After cash, the method of payment most widely used in the United States is the **credit card:** VISA (BarclayCard in Great Britain), MasterCard (EuroCard in Europe, Access in Great Britain, Diamond in Japan), American Express, Diners Club, and Carte Blanche, in descending order of acceptance. You can save yourself trouble by using "plastic money" rather than cash or traveler's checks, in 95% of all hotels, motels, restaurants, and retail stores (except for those selling food or liquor). A credit card can serve as a deposit for renting a car, as proof of identity (often carrying more weight than a passport), or as a "cash card," enabling you to withdraw money from banks that accept them.

Customs and Immigration   Every visitor over 21 years of age may bring in, free of duty: one liter of wine or hard liquor; 200 cigarettes or 100 cigars (but *no* cigars from Cuba) or three pounds of smoking tobacco; $400 worth of gifts. These exemptions are offered to travelers who spend at least 72 hours in the U.S. and who have not claimed them within the preceding six months. It is altogether forbidden to bring into the country food stuffs (particularly cheese, fruit, cooked meats, and canned goods) and plants (vegetables, seeds, tropical plants, and so on.) Foreign tourists may bring in or take out up to $10,000 in U.S. or foreign currency with no formalities; larger sums must be declared to Customs on entering or leaving.

The wait to have your passport stamped at Miami International Airport can be frustratingly long. Plan on an hour (sometimes more) to get through Customs and immigration proceedings.

Electric Current   U.S. wall outlets give power at 110–115 volts, 60 cycles, compared to 220 volts, 50 cycles in most of Europe. Besides a 110-volt converter, small appliances of non-American manufacture, such as hairdryers or shavers, will require a plug adapter with two flat, parallel pins.

Embassies and Consulates   All embassies are located in the national capital, Washington, D.C.; some consulates are located in major cities, and most nations have a mission to the United Nations in New York City.

Listed here are the embassies and the nearest consulates of the major English-speaking countries—Australia, Canada, the Republic of Ireland, New Zealand, and the United Kingdom. If you're from a country other than one of these, you can get the telephone number of your embassy by calling "Information" in Washington, D.C. (tel. 202/555-1212).

Australia The embassy is located at 1601 Massachusetts Ave. NW, Washington, D.C. 20036 (tel. 202/797-3000). A consulate is maintained in New York, at 636 Fifth Ave. (tel. 212/245-4000).

Canada The embassy is located at 501 Pennsylvania Ave. NW, Washington, D.C. 20001 (tel. 202/682-1740). Consulates are maintained in Atlanta, at One CNN Center, Suite 400 South Tower, GA 30303 (tel. 404/577-6810); in Boston, at 3 Copley Plaza, Suite 400, MA 02116 (tel. 617/536-1731); in Buffalo, at One Marine Midland Center, Suite 3550, NY 14203 (tel. 716/825-1345); and in New York, at 1251 Ave. of the Americas, NY 10020 (tel. 212/586-2400).

Republic of Ireland The embassy is located at 2234 Massachusetts Ave. NW, Washington, D.C. 20008 (tel. 202/462-3939). Consulates are maintained in Boston, in the Chase Building, at 535 Boylston St., MA 02116 (tel. 617/267-9330); and in New York, at 515 Madison Ave., NY 10022 (tel. 212/319-2555).

New Zealand The embassy is located at 37 Observatory Circle NW, Washington, D.C. 20008 (tel. 202/328-4800).

United Kingdom The embassy is located at 3100 Massachusetts Ave. NW, Washington, D.C. 20008 (tel. 202/462-1340). Consulates are maintained in Atlanta, at 245 Peachtree Center Ave., Suite 912, GA 30303 (tel. 404/524-5856); in Miami, at Coconut Grove Office Tower, Suite 2110, 1001 S. Bayshore Dr., FL 33131 (tel. 305/374-1522); and in New York, at 845 Third Ave., NY 10022 (tel. 212/752-8400).

Emergencies In all major cities you can call the police, an ambulance, or the fire department through the single emergency telephone number **911.** Another useful way of reporting an emergency is to call the telephone company operator by dialing **0** (zero, *not* the letter O). Outside major cities, call the county sheriff or the fire department directly at the number you will find in the local telephone book.

If you encounter such travelers' problems as sickness, accident, or stolen baggage, call **Travelers' Aid,** an organization that specializes in helping distressed travelers, American and foreign. Check the local telephone book for the nearest office, or dial *0* and ask the telephone operator.

Gasoline Prices vary, but expect to pay anywhere between $1.15 and $1.40 for one U.S. gallon of "regular" unleaded gasoline (petrol). Higher-test fuels are also available at most gas stations for slightly higher prices. Taxes are already included in the printed price.

Holidays On the following legal national holidays, banks, government offices, post offices, and many stores, restaurants, and museums are closed:

New Year's Day January 1
Martin Luther King Day Third Monday in January
Presidents Day Third Monday in February
Memorial Day Last Monday in May
Independence Day July 4
Labor Day First Monday in September
Columbus Day Second Monday in October
Veterans (Armistice) Day November 11
Thanksgiving Day Last Thursday in November
Christmas Day December 25

Election Day, which falls on the Tuesday following the first Monday in November, is a national holiday during presidential-election years.

Information See Chapter 2.

Legal Aid The foreign tourist, unless positively identified as a member of the Mafia or of a drug ring, will probably never become involved with the American legal system.

If you are pulled up for a minor infraction (for example, of the highway code, such as speeding), never attempt to pay the fine directly to a police officer; you may wind up arrested on the much more serious charge of attempted bribery. Pay fines by mail, or directly into the hands of the clerk of the court.

If accused of a more serious offense, it is wise to say and do nothing before consulting a lawyer. Under U.S. law, an arrested person is allowed one telephone call to a party of his or her choice. Call your embassy or consulate.

Liquor Laws See "Fast Facts: Miami" in Chapter 4.

Mail If you want your mail to follow you on your vacation, you need only fill out a change-of-address card at any post office. The post office will also hold your mail for up to one month. If you aren't sure of your address, your mail can be sent to you, in your name, **c/o General Delivery** at the main post office of the city or region where you expect to be. The addressee must pick it up in person, and produce proof of identity (driver's license, credit card, passport, and so on).

Generally found at street intersections, mailboxes are blue and carry the inscription "U.S. Mail." If your mail is addressed to a U.S. destination, don't forget to add the five-figure ZIP Code, after the two-letter abbreviation of the state to which the mail is addressed (FL for Florida).

Measurements See "The American System of Measurements" at the end of this chapter.

Medical Emergencies See "Emergencies," above. For a list of hospitals and other emergency information, see "Fast Facts: Miami" in Chapter 4.

Newspapers and Magazines Most magazine racks at drugstores, airports, and hotels include a good selection of foreign periodicals like *Stern, The Economist,* and *Le Monde.* Spanish-language newspapers and magazines are particularly abundant. For information on local literature, see "Fast Facts: Miami" in Chapter 4.

Post See "Mail," above.

Radio and Television Audiovisual media, with four coast-to-coast networks—ABC, CBS, NBC and the Fox network—joined in recent years by the Public Broadcasting system (PBS) and the cable network CNN, play a major part in American life. In the big cities, televiewers have a choice of about a dozen channels (including the UHF channels), most of them transmitting 24 hours a day, without counting the pay-TV channels showing recent movies or sports events. In smaller communities the choice may be limited to four TV channels (there are 1,200 in the entire country), and a half dozen local radio stations (there are 6,500 in all), each broadcasting a particular kind of music—classical, country, jazz, pop, gospel—punctuated by news broadcasts and frequent commercials. Spanish-language newscasts are common in Miami, particularly on the AM dial. For stations in Miami see "Fast Facts: Miami" in Chapter 4.

Safety In general, the U.S. is safer than most other countries, particularly in rural areas, but there are "danger zones" in the big cities that should be approached only with extreme caution.

As a general rule, isolated areas such as parks and parking lots should be avoided after dark. Elevators and public-transport systems in off-hours, particularly between 10pm and 6am, are also potential crime scenes. You should drive through decaying neighborhoods with your car doors locked and the windows closed. Never carry valuables like jewelry or large sums of cash; traveler's checks are much safer.

Taxes In the United States there is no VAT (Value-Added Tax), or other indirect tax at a national level. Every state, and each city in it, is allowed to levy its own local tax on all purchases, including hotel and restaurant checks, airline tickets, and so on. It is automatically added to the price of certain services such as public transportation, cab fares, phone calls, and gasoline. It varies from 4% to 10% depending on the state and city, so when you are making major purchases such as photographic equipment, clothing, or high-fidelity components, it can be a significant part of the cost.

For information on the sales tax in and around Miami, see "Fast Facts: Miami" in Chapter 4.

Telephone, Telegraph, and Telex Pay phones are an integral part of the American landscape. You will find them everywhere: at street corners, in bars, restaurants, public buildings, stores, service stations, along highways. Outside the metropolitan areas, public telephones are more difficult to find. Stores and gas stations are your best bet. In Miami local calls cost 25¢.

Phones do not accept pennies, and few will take anything larger than a quarter. Some public phones, especially those in airports and large hotels, accept credit cards like MasterCard, VISA, and American Express. These are especially handy for international calls; instructions are printed on the phone.

For **long-distance or international calls,** stock up with a supply of quarters; a recorded voice will instruct you when and in what quantity you should put them into the slot. For direct overseas calls, first dial 011, followed by the country code (Australia, 61; Republic of Ireland, 353; New Zealand, 64; United Kingdom, 44; and so on), and then by the city code (for example, 71 or 81 for London, 21 for Birmingham) and the number of the person you wish to call. For long-distance calls within Canada and the U.S., dial 1 followed by the area code and the number you want.

Before calling from a hotel room, always ask the hotel phone operator if there are any telephone surcharges. These are best avoided by using a public phone, calling collect, or using a telephone charge card.

For **reversed-charge or collect calls,** and for **person-to-person calls,** dial 0 (zero, *not* the letter "O") followed by the area code and number you want; an operator will then come on the line, and you should specify that you are calling collect, or person-to-person, or both. If your operator-assisted call is international, ask for the overseas operator.

For local **directory assistance** ("Information"), dial 411; for long-distance information in Canada or the U.S. dial 1, then the appropriate area code and 555-1212.

Like the telephone system, **telegraph and telex** services are provided by private corporations like ITT, MCI, and above all, Western Union. You can bring your telegram in to one of the hundreds of Western Union offices across the U.S. or dictate it over the phone (a toll-free call, 800/325-6000). You can also telegraph money, or have it telegraphed to you, very quickly over the Western Union system. In Miami a conveniently located office is located at 9500 NW 27th Ave., near Downtown (tel. 691-7912). Most copy shops also offer fax services.

Telephone Directory America's telephone directories are divided into white and yellow pages. The former lists subscribers alphabetically, while the latter lists services and businesses by activity.

Greater Miami's phone books come in two volumes; the first covers the letters A through K, the second encompasses L through Z. Schools, parks, police, and other local government offices are listed in the white pages of Volume 1, under the heading "Dade County." Post offices and other national government offices are listed in the white pages of Volume 2, under the heading "United States."

America's phone books are also a good source for other general information such as sight-seeing, maps, local "hotline" telephone numbers, and other interesting facts and figures. Miami's "Community Interest Pages," as they are called, are located in the center of Volume 1.

Time   The United States is divided into six time zones. From east to west, these are: eastern standard time (EST), central standard time (CST), mountain standard time (MST), Pacific standard time (PST), Alaska standard time (AST), and Hawaii standard time (HST). Miami is on eastern standard time. Always keep changing time zones in mind if you are traveling (or even telephoning) long distances in the U.S. For example, noon in New York City (EST) is 11am in Chicago (CST), 10am in Denver (MST), 9am in Los Angeles (PST), 8am in Anchorage (AST), and 7am in Honolulu (HST).

Daylight saving time is in effect from 1am on the first Sunday in April until 2am on the last Sunday in October except in Arizona, Hawaii, part of Indiana, and Puerto Rico.

Tipping   The amount that you tip should depend on the service you have received. Good service warrants the following tips:

Bartenders 15%
Bellhops $2–$4
Cab drivers 15%
Cafeterias, fast-food restaurants No tip
Chambermaids $1 per person per day
Cinemas No tip
Checkroom attendants 50¢–$1 (*unless they charge*)
Gas-station attendants No tip
Hairdressers 15%–20%
Parking valets $1
Redcaps (*in airports and rail stations*) $2–$4
Restaurants, nightclubs 15%

Toilets   Public toilets can be hard to find. There are none on the streets, and few small stores will allow you access to their facilities. You can almost always find a toilet in restaurants and bars, but if you are not a customer, you should ask permission to use their facilities. Large hotels and fast-food restaurants are probably the best bet for good, clean facilities. Museums, department stores, shopping malls, and, in a pinch, gas stations all have public toilets.

Yellow Pages   The *Yellow Pages* telephone directory lists all local services, businesses, and industries by category; it also has an index for quick reference. Categories range from automobile repairs (listed by make of car) and drugstores, or pharmacies, to places of worship and restaurants (listed according to cuisine and geographical location). The *Yellow Pages* directory is also a good source for information of particular interest to the traveler; among other things, it has maps of the city, showing sights and transportation routes, "hotline" telephone numbers, and interesting facts about local attractions.

THE AMERICAN SYSTEM OF MEASUREMENTS

LENGTH

1 inch (in.)	=	2.54cm
1 foot (ft.)	=	12 in. = 30.48cm = .305m
1 yard (yd.)	=	3 ft. = .915m
1 mile (mi)	=	5,280 ft. = 1.609km

To convert miles to kilometers, multiply the number of miles by 1.61 (example: 50 mi. × 1.61 = 80.5km). Also use to convert speeds from miles per hour (m.p.h.) to kilometers per hour (kmph).

To convert kilometers to miles, multiply the number of kilometers by .62 (example: 25km × .62 = 15.5 mi). Also use to convert kmph to m.p.h.

CAPACITY

1 fluid ounce (fl. oz).	=	.03 liters
1 pint	=	16 fl. oz. = .47 liters
1 quart	=	2 pints = .94 liters
1 gallon (gal.)	=	4 quarts = 3.79 liters
	=	.83 Imperial gal.

To convert U.S. gallons to liters, multiply the number of gallons by 3.79 (example: 12 gal. × 3.79 = 45.48 liters).

To convert liters to U.S. gallons, multiply the number of liters by .26 (example: 50 liters × .26 = 13 U.S. gal.).

To convert U.S. gallons to Imperial gallons, multiply the number of U.S. gallons by .83 (example: 12 U.S. gal. × .83 = 9.95 Imperial gal.).

To convert Imperial gallons to U.S. gallons, multiply the number of Imperial gallons by 1.2 (example: 8 Imperial gal. × 1.2 = 9.6 U.S. gal.).

WEIGHT

1 ounce (oz.)	=	28.35g
1 pound (lb.)	=	16 oz. = 453.6g = .45kg
1 ton	=	2,000 lb. = 907kg = .91 metric tons

To convert pounds to kilograms, multiply the number of pounds by .45 (example: 90 lb. × .45 = 40.5kg).

To convert kilograms to pounds, multiply the number of kilograms by 2.2 (example: 75kg × 2.2 = 165 lb.).

AREA

1 acre	=	.41ha
1 square mile	=	640 acres = 259ha = 2.6km^2

To convert acres to hectares, multiply the number of acres by .41 (example: 40 acres × .41 = 16.4ha).

To convert hectares to acres, multiply the number of hectares by 2.47 (example: 20ha × 2.47 = 49.4 acres).

To convert square miles to square kilometers, multiply the number of square miles by 2.6 (example: 80 square miles × 2.6 = 208km²).

To convert square kilometers to square miles, multiply the number of square kilometers by .39 (example: 150km² × .39 = 58.5 square miles).

TEMPERATURE

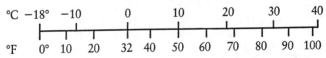

To convert degrees Fahrenheit to degrees Celsius, subtract 32 from °F, multiply by 5, then divide by 9 (example: 85°F − 32 × 5/9 = 29.4°C).

To convert degrees Celsius to degrees Fahrenheit, multiply °C by 9, divide by 5, and add 32 (example: 20°C × 9/5 + 32 = 68°F).

CHAPTER 4

GETTING TO KNOW MIAMI

1. ORIENTATION
2. GETTING AROUND
• FAST FACTS: MIAMI
3. NETWORKS & RESOURCES

Miami is not a complicated city to negotiate, but, like all unfamiliar territories, this metropolis will take a little time to master. In addition to the essentials outlined below, the best up-to-date, specialized information is provided by the Greater Miami Convention and Visitors Bureau. Their address and the addresses of other information sources are listed in "Information" in Chapter 2.

1. ORIENTATION

ARRIVING

One hundred years ago, Miami was a hard place to reach. But no more. Today transportation companies, most notably airlines, fight perpetual price wars to woo tourists to the Sunshine State. In fact, airfares are so competitive that, unless you are visiting from an adjacent state, flying to Miami will almost always be your most economical option. But take a look at your alternatives, too. An overland journey to Florida's Gold Coast is both more scenic and a more flexible way to travel. Greyhound/Trailways offers several types of bus passes, and Amtrak offers a host of rail services to the South.

BY AIR

Originally carved out of scrubland in 1928 by Pan American Airlines, Miami International Airport (MIA) has emerged as one of the busiest airports in the world. Thankfully, it's also one of the most streamlined, making it a wonderful place to land. Since the airport is easy to negotiate, and located only 6 miles west of Downtown, it's likely that domestic passengers can get from the plane to their hotel room in about an hour. International arrivals must pass through Customs and immigration, a process that can double your time in the airport.

The route down to the baggage claim area is clearly marked. You can change money or use your Honor or Plus System ATM card at Barnett Bank of South Florida, located near the exit.

Like most good international airports, MIA has its fair share of boutiques, shops, and eateries. Unless you are starving, or forgot to get a gift for the person picking you up, bypass these overpriced establishments. The airport is literally surrounded by restaurants and shops; if you can wait to get to them, you will save a lot of money.

Note that if you are exiting Miami on an international flight, the excellent duty-free selection in the departure lounge shouldn't be missed.

If you are renting a car at the airport (see "Getting Around," below), you will have to take one of the free shuttles to the rental site. Buses and vans, clearly marked with rental-car logos, circle the airport regularly, and stop at the wave of a hand. Signs at the airport's exit clearly point the way to various parts of the city.

Taxis line up in front of a dispatcher's desk outside the airport's arrivals terminals. Cabs are metered and will cost about $14 to Coral Gables, $16 to Downtown, and $18 to South Miami Beach. Tip 10% to 15%.

Group limousines (multipassenger vans) also circle the arrivals area looking for fares. Destinations are posted on the front of each van, and a flat rate is charged for door-to-door service to the area marked. SuperShuttle (tel. 871-2000) is one of the largest airport operators, charging between $10 and $17 per person for a ride within Dade County. Their vans operate 24 hours a day and accept American Express, MasterCard, and VISA.

Private limousine arrangements can be made in advance through your local travel agent. A one-way meet-and-greet service should cost about $50.

Public transportation is not a recommended way to get from the airport to your hotel, or anywhere, for that matter. Buses heading downtown leave the airport only once per hour (from the arrivals level), and connections are spotty at best.

BY TRAIN

If you are traveling to Miami by train (see "Getting There," in Chapter 2), you will pull into Amtrak's Miami terminal at 8303 NW 37th Avenue (tel. 835-1205). Unfortunately, none of the major car-rental companies have offices at the train station; you'll have to go to the airport (see "Getting Around," below). Hertz (tel. toll free 800/654-3131) will reimburse your cab fare from the train station to the airport provided you rent one of their cars.

IMPRESSIONS

Miami . . . the city of the future.
—JULIA TUTTLE

Miami is a place of the future.
—ISAAC BASHEVIS SINGER

Taxis meeting each Amtrak arrival are plentiful. The fare to downtown will cost about $14; the ride takes less than 20 minutes.

BY CAR

No matter where you start your journey, chances are you'll reach Miami by way of I-95. This north-south interstate is the city's lifeline and an integral part of the region. The highway connects all of Miami's different neighborhoods, the airport, and the beach; and it connects all of South Florida to the rest of America. Every part of Miami is easily reached from I-95, and well-lit road signs clearly point the way. Take time out to study I-95's placement on the map. You will use it as a reference point time and again. For a detailed description of the city's main arteries and streets, see "City Layout," below.

BY BUS

Greyhound/Trailways buses pull into a number of stations around the city including: 99 NE 4th St. (Downtown); 16250 Biscayne Blvd., North Miami Beach; and 7101 Harding Ave., Miami Beach. Consult your local directory for the office nearest you.

CITY LAYOUT

Miami may seem confusing at first, but it quickly becomes easy to negotiate. The small cluster of buildings that make up the Downtown area is at the geographical heart of the city. You can see these sharp stalactites from most anywhere, making them a good reference point. In relation to Miami's Downtown, the airport is west, the beaches are east, Coconut Grove and Coral Gables are south, and the rest of the country is north.

FINDING AN ADDRESS

Miami is divided into dozens of areas with official and unofficial boundaries. To make map-reading easier, all the addresses listed in this book are followed by an area listing, indicating which part of the city it is in.

Street numbering in the **City of Miami** is fairly straightforward, but you must first be familiar with the numbering system. The mainland is divided into four sections, NE, NW, SE, and SW, by the intersection of Flagler Street and Miami Avenue. First Street and First Avenue begin near this corner, and, along with Places, Courts, Terraces, and Lanes, the numbers increase from this point. Hialeah streets are the exception to this pattern; they are listed separately in map indexes.

Establishment addresses are often descriptive; 12301 Biscayne Boulevard is located at 123rd Street. It's also helpful to remember that avenues generally run north-south, while streets go east-west.

Getting around the barrier islands of **Miami Beach** is somewhat easier than moving around the mainland. Street numbering starts with First Street, near Miami Beach's southern tip, and increases to 192nd Street, in the northern part of Sunny Isles. Collins Avenue makes the entire journey from head to toe. As in the City of Miami, some streets in Miami Beach have numbers as well as names. When they are part of listings in this book, both names and numbers are given.

You should know that the numbered streets in Miami Beach are not the geographical equivalents of those on the mainland. The 79th Street Causeway runs into 71st Street on Miami Beach.

NEIGHBORHOODS IN BRIEF

Much of Miami is sprawling suburbia. But every city has its charm, and aside from a fantastic tropical climate, and the vast stretch of beach that lies just across the bay, Miami's unique identity comes from extremely interesting cultural pockets within various residential communities.

Coral Gables Just over 70 years old, Coral Gables is the closest thing to "historical" that Miami has. It's also one of the prettiest parcels in the city. Created by George Merrick in the early 1920s, the Gables was one of Miami's first planned developments. Houses here were built in a "Mediterranean style" along lush tree-lined streets that open onto beautifully carved plazas, many with centerpiece fountains. The best architectural examples of the era have Spanish-style tiled roofs and are built from Miami oolite, a native limestone, commonly called "coral rock." Coral Gables is a stunning example of "boom" architecture on a grand scale—and a great area to explore. Some of the city's best restaurants are located here, as are top hotels and good shopping. See the appropriate chapters for listings and "Driving Tour 2," in Chapter 8, for details.

Coconut Grove There was a time when Coconut Grove was inhabited by artists and intellectuals, hippies and radicals. But times have changed. Gentrification has pushed most alternative types out; leaving in their place a multitude of cafés, boutiques, and nightspots. The intersection of Grand Avenue, Main Highway, and McFarlane Road pierces the area's heart, which sizzles with dozens of interesting shops and eateries. Sidewalks here are often crowded with business-people, college students, and loads of foreign tourists—especially at night, when it becomes the best place to people-watch in all of South Florida.

Coconut Grove's link to the Bahamas dates from before the turn of the century, when islanders came to the area to work in a newly opened hotel called the Peacock Inn. Bahamian-style wooden homes, built by these early settlers, still stand on Charles Street. Goombay, the lively annual Bahamian festival, celebrates the Grove's Caribbean link and has become one of the largest black heritage street festivals in America (see "When to Go" in Chapter 2).

Miami Beach To tourists in the 1950s, Miami Beach *was*

Miami. Its huge self-contained resort hotels were vacations unto themselves, providing a full day's worth of meals, activities, and entertainment.

In the 1960s and '70s people who fell in love with Miami began to buy apartments rather than rent hotel rooms. Tourism declined and many area hotels fell into disrepair.

But since the late 1980s Miami Beach has witnessed a tide of revitalization. Huge beach hotels are finding their niche with new, international tourist markets, and are attracting large convention crowds. New generations of Americans are discovering the special qualities that made Miami Beach so popular to begin with, and are finding out that the beach now comes with a thriving, international, exciting city.

Note: North Miami Beach is a residential area on the mainland near the Dade-Broward county line. It is in no way connected to Miami Beach.

Surfside, Bal Harbour, and Sunny Isles Lying just north of Miami Beach, on barrier islands, Surfside, Bal Harbour, and Sunny Isles are, for the most part, an extension of the beach community below it. Collins Avenue crosses town lines with hardly a sign, while hotels, motels, restaurants, and beaches continue to line the strip.

In exclusive Bal Harbour, fancy homes—tucked away on the bay—hide behind walls, gates, and security cameras. For tourists, it seems that—with some outstanding exceptions—the farther north you go, the cheaper lodging becomes. All told, excellent prices, location, and facilities make Surfside, Bal Harbour, and Sunny Isles attractive places to locate.

South Miami Beach—The Art Deco District Officially part of the City of Miami Beach, the community at the southern tip of the island is treated separately in this book due to its unique architecture, atmosphere, and offerings.

The Miami Beach Architectural District of South Miami Beach contains the largest concentration of art deco architecture in the world. South Beach, or SoBe, as it is more chicly known, is an exciting renaissance community with pensioners, soon-to-be-monied young investors, perpetually poor artists, and the usual Miami smattering of Cubans, African-Americans, and Caribbeans. Everywhere you go there is an air of excitement of being on the cusp of an important revolution. Hip clubs and cafés are filled with working models and their photographers, musicians and writers in addition to in-the-know locals, vacationers, and others. See "A Walking Tour," in Chapter 8, for an in-depth tour of Miami's most fascinating area.

Key Biscayne The first island in the Florida Key chain is Miami's forested and fancy Key Biscayne. Located south of Miami Beach, off the shores of Coconut Grove, Key Biscayne is protected from the troubles of the mainland by the long Rickenbacker Causeway and a $1 toll. Key Biscayne is largely an exclusive residential community with million-dollar homes and sweeping water

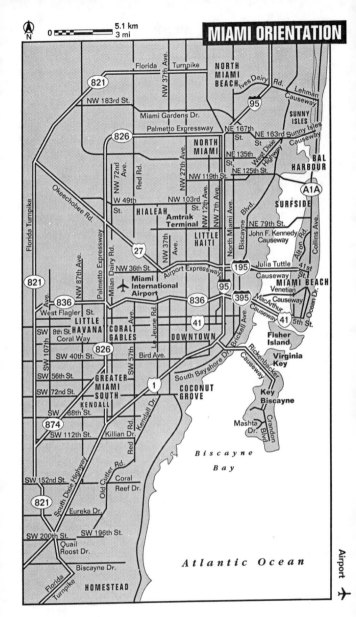

views. For tourists, this key offers great beaches, some top resort hotels, and several good restaurants. Hobie Beach, adjacent to the causeway, is the city's premier spot for sailboarding and jetskiing (see "Sports & Recreation" in Chapter 7). On the island's southern tip is Bill Baggs State Park, offering great beaches, bike paths, and dense forests for picnicking and partying.

Downtown   Miami's Downtown boasts one of the world's most beautiful cityscapes. If you do nothing else in Miami, make sure you take your time studying the area's inspired architectural designs. The streets of Downtown are unusually free of pedestrian traffic even during the height of lunch hour. You'll see plenty of stores and eateries here, but most sell discount goods and quick lunches. Unless you're bargain hunting for necessary items, there's not too much in the way of window shopping. But the Downtown area does have its mall (Bayside Marketplace), its culture (Metro-Dade Cultural Center), and a number of good restaurants (listed in Chapter 6).

Little Haiti   During a brief period in the late 1970s and early 1980s, almost 35,000 Haitians arrived in Miami. Most of the new refugees settled in a decaying 200-square-block area north of Downtown. Extending from 41st to 83rd streets, and bordered by I-95 and Biscayne Boulevard, Little Haiti, as it has become known, is a relatively depressed neighborhood with over 60,000 residents, 65% of whom are of Haitian origin.

Northeast Second Avenue, Little Haiti's main thoroughfare, is highlighted by the colorful new Caribbean Marketplace, located at the corner of 60th Street. Keep an eye out for one of the many Haitian religious shops selling aromatic herbs, roots, incense, and other items related to Santería and other voodoo ceremonies.

Little Havana   Miami's Cuban center is the city's most important ethnic enclave. Referred to locally as "Calle Ocho," SW Eighth Street, located just west of Downtown, is the region's main thoroughfare. Car repair shops, tailors, electronic stores, and inexpensive restaurants all hang signs in Spanish. Salsa rhythms thump from the radios of passersby, while old men in guayaberas chain-smoke cigars over their daily game of dominoes.

Greater Miami South   To locals, South Miami is both a specific area, southwest of Coral Gables, and a general region that encompasses all of southern Dade County and includes Kendall, Perrine, Cutler Ridge, and Homestead. For the purposes of clarity, this book has grouped all these southern suburbs under the rubric "Greater Miami South." Similar attributes unite the communities: They are heavily residential, and all are packed with condominiums and shopping malls as well as acres upon acres of farmland. Tourists don't stay in these parts, as there is no beach and few cultural offerings. But Greater Miami South does contain many of the city's top attractions (see Chapter 7), making it likely that you'll spend some time during the day here.

MAPS

It's easy to get lost in sprawling Miami, so a reliable map is essential. If you are not planning on moving around too much, the tourist board's maps, located inside their free publication *Destination Miami*, may be adequate. But if you really want to get to know the city, it pays to invest in one of the large, accordion-fold maps, available at most gas stations and bookstores. The Trakker Map of Miami ($2.50) is a four-color accordion that encompasses all of Dade County, handy if you are planning on visiting the many attractions in Greater Miami South.

Some maps of Miami list streets according to area, so you'll have to know which part of the city you are looking for before the street can be found. All the listings in this book include area information for just this reason.

2. GETTING AROUND

Officially, Dade County has opted for a "unified, multi-modal transportation network," which basically means that you can get around the city by train, bus, and taxi. Here's how:

BY PUBLIC TRANSPORTATION

BY RAIL

Two rail lines, operated by the Metro-Dade Transit Agency (information tel. 638-6700), run in concert with each other.

Metrorail, the city's modern high-speed commuter train, is a 21-mile elevated line that travels north-south, between Downtown Miami and the southern suburbs. If you are staying in Coral Gables or Coconut Grove you can park your car at a nearby station and ride the rails Downtown. Unfortunately for visitors, the line's usefulness is limited. There are plans to extend the system to service Miami International Airport, but until those tracks are built, these trains don't go most places that tourists go. Metrorail operates daily from 6am to midnight. Fare is $1.25.

Metromover, a 1.9-mile elevated line, connects with Metrorail at the Government Center stop and circles the city's downtown area. Riding on rubber tires, the single-train car winds past 10 stations and through some of the city's most important office locations. Metromover offers a fun, futuristic ride that you might want to take to complement your tour of Downtown (see Chapter 8). System hours are the same as Metrorail. Fare is 25¢.

BY BUS

Miami's suburban layout is not conducive to getting around by bus. Lines operate, and maps can be had, but instead of getting to know the city, you'll find that relying on bus transportation will only acquaint you with how it feels to wait at bus stops. You can get a bus map by mail, either from the Greater Miami Convention and Visitors

Bureau (see "Information" in Chapter 2) or by writing the Metro-Dade Transit System, 3300 NW 32nd Ave., Miami 33142. In Miami call 638-6700 for public transit information. Fare is $1.25.

BY TAXI

If you're not planning on traveling much within the city, an occasional taxi is a good alternative to renting a car. If you plan on spending your holiday within the confines of South Miami Beach's art deco district, you may also wish to avoid the parking hassles that come with renting your own car. The taxi's meter drops at $1.10 for the first ½ mile, and rises 20¢ for each additional ½ mile. An average cross-city ride will cost about $10.

Major cab companies include Metro (tel. 888-8888) and Yellow (tel. 444-4444).

BY CAR

Tales circulate about vacationers who have visited Miami without a car, but they are very few indeed. If you are counting on exploring the city, even to a modest degree, private motor transportation will be essential to your plans. Unless you are going to spend your entire vacation at a resort, or are traveling directly to the Port of Miami for a cruise, a car is a necessity. Miami's restaurants, attractions, and sights are far from one another and any other form of transportation is impractical.

When driving across a causeway, or through Downtown, allow extra time to reach your destination due to frequent drawbridge openings. Bridges open about every half hour, stalling traffic for several minutes. Don't get frustrated by the wait. The bridges keep the city's pace from becoming too fast and frenetic.

RENTALS

It seems as though every car-rental company, big and small, has at least one office in Miami. Consequently, the city is one of the cheapest places in the world to rent a car. Many firms regularly advertise prices in the neighborhood of $89 per week for their bottom-of-the-line tin can—not an unreasonable sum for seven days of sun and fun.

Most rental firms pad their profits by selling an additional Loss/Damage Waiver (LDW), which usually costs an extra $8 to $10 per day. Before agreeing to this, however, check with your insurance carrier and credit-card companies. Many people don't realize that they are already covered by either one or both. If you're not, the LDW is a wise investment.

A minimum age, ranging from 19 to 25, is usually required of renters. Some rental agencies have also set maximum ages. If you are concerned that these limits may affect you, ask about rental requirements at the time of booking to avoid problems later.

National car-rental companies include: Alamo (tel. 800/327-9633), Avis (tel. 800/331-1212), Budget (tel. 800/527-0700), Dollar (tel. 800/822-1181), General (tel. 800/327-7607), Hertz (tel. 800/654-3131), National (tel. 800/328-4567), and Thrifty (tel. 800/367-2277). Literally dozens of other regional companies—some offering lower rates—can be found in the Miami "Yellow Pages" under "Automobile Renting & Leasing."

Finally, think about splurging on a convertible. Few things in life can match the feeling of flying along warm Florida freeways with the sun smiling on your shoulders and the wind whipping through your hair.

PARKING

Always keep plenty of quarters, dimes, and nickels on hand in order to feed hungry meters. Parking is usually plentiful, but when it's not, be careful: Fines for illegal parking can be stiff.

In addition to parking garages, valet services are commonplace and often used. Expect to pay from $3 to $5 for parking in Coconut Grove and on South Miami Beach's Ocean Drive on busy weekend nights.

LOCAL DRIVING RULES

Florida law allows drivers to make a right turn on a red light, unless otherwise indicated. In addition, all passengers are required to wear seat belts, and children under 3 years of age must be securely fastened in government-approved car seats.

BY BICYCLE

Miami's two best bicycling areas are vastly different from each other.

The hard-packed sand that runs the length of **Miami Beach** is one of the best places in the world to ride a bike. An excellent alternative to the slow pace of walking, biking up the beach is great for surf, sun, sand, exercise, and people-watching. You may not want to subject your bicycle to the salt and sand, but there are plenty of oceanfront rental places here. Most of the big beach hotels rent bicycles as does **Beach Skates,** Ocean Drive at the 10th Street Bandshell (tel. 534-2252). Located in South Miami Beach, the shop rents mountain cruisers for $10 per hour. It's open daily from 11am to 8pm.

The beautiful and quiet streets of **Coral Gables and Coconut Grove** beg for the attention of bicyclists. Old trees form canopies over wide, flat roads lined with grand homes and quaint street markers. Several bicycle trails are spread throughout these neighborhoods, including one that begins at the doorstep of **Dade Cycle**, 3216 Grand Avenue, Coconut Grove (tel. 444-5997). It's open Monday through Saturday from 9:30am to 5:30pm, on Sunday from 10:30am to 5:30pm. MasterCard and VISA are accepted.

ON FOOT

With the exception of isolated pockets in Coconut Grove and South Miami Beach, Miami is not a walker's city. Because it is so spread out, most attractions are too far apart to make walking feasible. In fact, most Miamians are so used to driving that they drive even when going just a few blocks. See Chapter 8 for a walking tour through Miami Beach's art deco district.

FAST FACTS MIAMI

Airport   See "Arriving," above, in this chapter.

American Express   For travel arrangements, traveler's checks, currency exchange, and other member services, Miami offices include: 330 Biscayne Blvd., Downtown (tel. 358-7350); 9700 Collins Ave., Bal Harbour (tel. 865-5959); and 32 Miracle Mile, Coral Gables (tel. 446-3381). Offices are open Monday through Friday from 9am to 5pm, and on Saturday from 9am until noon.

To report lost or stolen traveler's checks, call 800/221-7282.

Area Code   The area code for Miami and all of Dade County is 305. All phone numbers in this book assume this prefix unless otherwise noted.

Auto Rentals   See "Getting Around," above, in this chapter.

Babysitters   Hotels can often recommend a babysitter or child-care service. If yours can't, try Central Sitting Agency, 1764 SW 24th St. (tel. 856-0550). Other child-minding agencies are listed in the "Yellow Pages" under "Sitting Services."

Barbers   See "Hairdressers and Barbers" below.

Bookstores   Chain bookstores can be found in almost every shopping center in the city. A top bookseller in the city is Books & Books, 296 Aragon Ave. (tel. 442-4408), in Coral Gables. See Chapter 9 for details.

Buses   See "Getting Around," above, in this chapter.

Business Hours   Banking hours vary, but most banks are open Monday to Friday from 9am to 3pm. Several stay open until 5pm or so at least one day during the week, and many banks feature Automated Teller Machines (ATMs) for 24-hour banking (see "Money," below).

Most stores are open daily from 10am to 6pm; however, there are many exceptions. Shops in the Bayside Marketplace are usually open until 9 or 10pm, as are the boutiques in Coconut Grove. Stores in Bal Harbour and other malls are usually open one extra hour one night during the week (usually Thursday).

As far as business offices are concerned, Miami is generally a 9am-to-5pm town.

Car Rentals   See "Getting Around," above, in this chapter.

Climate   See "When to Go" in Chapter 2.

Currency   See "Fast Facts" in Chapter 3.

Dentists   The East Coast District Dental Society staffs an Emergency Dental Referral Service (tel. 285-5470). Michael H. Schenkman, D.D.S., in the Suniland Shopping Center, 11735 South Dixie Hwy. (tel. 235-0020), features 24-hour emergency service and takes all major credit cards. All Dade Dental Associates, 11400 N. Kendall Dr., Mega Bank Building (tel. 271-7777), also offers round-the-clock care and accepts MasterCard and VISA.

Doctors   In an emergency, call an ambulance by dialing 911 from any phone. No coins are required.

The Dade County Medical Association sponsors a Physician Referral Service (tel. 324-8717) Monday to Friday from 9am to 5pm.

In Miami, doctors still make house calls. Twenty-four hours a day, seven days a week, a doctor will be sent to your hotel within an hour. The basic fee is $60. Call 945-6325.

Doctors' Hospital of Coral Gables, 5000 University Dr., Coral Gables (tel. 666-2111), is a 285-bed nonprofit hospital with a 24-hour physician-staffed emergency department.

Documents   See "Necessary Documents" in Chapter 3.

Driving Rules   See "Getting Around," above, in this chapter.

Drugstores   Walgreens Pharmacies are all over town, including 8550 Coral Way (tel. 221-9271), in Coral Gables; and 6700 Collins Ave. (tel. 861-6742), in Miami Beach. Their branch at 5731 Bird Rd. (tel. 666-0757), is open 24 hours, as is Eckerd Drugs, 1825 Miami Gardens Dr. NE (185th Street), North Miami Beach (tel. 932-5740).

Embassies and Consulates   See "Fast Facts" in Chapter 3.

Emergencies   To reach the police, ambulance, or fire department, dial 911 from any phone. No coins are needed. Emergency hotlines include: Crisis Intervention (tel. 358-4357); Poison Information Center (tel. 800/282-3171); and Rape Hotline (tel. 549-7273).

Eyeglasses   Pearle Vision Center, 326 Miracle Mile (tel. 448-3039), in Coral Gables, can usually fill prescriptions in about an hour.

Film   See "Photographic Needs" below.

Hairdressers and Barbers   The chain Supercuts, 9803 Bird Rd. (tel. 553-4965), offers one of the lowest-priced shears in the city, while the salon at the Grand Bay Hotel, 2669 South Bayshore Dr., Coconut Grove (tel. 858-9600), boasts one of the most costly pamperings around. Many other major hotels also have hair salons and are listed under the appropriate heading in Chapter 5.

Hospitals   See "Doctors," above.

Information   Always check local newspapers for special things to do during your visit. The city's highest-quality daily, the

Miami Herald, is an especially good source for current events listings, particularly the "Weekend" section in Friday's edition. For a complete list of tourist boards and other information sources, see "Information" in Chapter 2.

Laundry and Dry Cleaning   All Laundry Service, 5701 NW 7th St. (west of Downtown; tel. 261-8175), does dry cleaning and offers a wash-and-fold service by the pound in addition to self-service machines. It's open daily from 6am to midnight. Clean Machine Laundry, 226 12th St., South Miami Beach (tel. 534-9429), is convenient to South Beach's art deco hotels. It's open 24 hours. Coral Gables Laundry & Dry Cleaning, 250 Minorca Ave., Coral Gables (tel. 446-6458), has been dry cleaning, altering, and laundering since 1930. They offer a lifesaving same-day service. Open Monday through Friday from 7am to 6:30pm, on Saturday from 8am to 3pm.

Libraries   The Main Library in the Dade County system is located Downtown at 101 West Flagler St. (tel. 375-2665). It's open Monday from 9am to 9pm, Tuesday through Saturday from 9am to 6pm, and Sunday from 1 to 5pm.

Liquor Laws   Only adults 21 years of age or older may legally purchase or consume alcohol in the state of Florida. Minors are usually permitted in bars that serve food. Liquor laws are strictly enforced; if you look young, carry identification. In addition to specialty shops, beer and wine are also sold in most supermarkets and convenience stores. The City of Miami's liquor stores are closed on Sunday. Liquor stores in the City of Miami Beach are open all week.

Lost Property   If you lost it at the airport, call the Airport Lost and Found office (tel. 876-7377). If you lost it on the bus, Metrorail, or Metromover, call Metro-Dade Transit Agency (tel. 638-6700). If you lost it somewhere else, phone the Dade County Police Lost and Found (tel. 375-3366). You may also wish to fill out a police report for insurance purposes.

Luggage Storage and Lockers   In addition to the baggage check at Miami International Airport (see "Arriving," above, in this chapter), most hotels offer luggage storage facilities. If you are taking a cruise from the Port of Miami (see Chapter 11), bags can be stored in your ship's departure terminal.

Mail   Miami's Main Post Office, 2200 Milam Dairy Rd., Miami, FL 33152 (tel. 599-0166), is located west of Miami International Airport. Letters addressed to you and marked "General Delivery" can be picked up here. Conveniently located post offices include 1300 Washington Ave. (tel. 531-7306), in South Miami Beach; and 3191 Grand Ave. (tel. 443-0030), in Coconut Grove. Holders of American Express cards or traveler's checks can receive mail, free, addressed c/o American Express, 330 Biscayne Blvd., Miami, FL 33132.

Maps   See "Orientation," above, in this chapter.

Money   In addition to paying close attention to the details below, foreign visitors should also see "Fast Facts" in Chapter 3 for monetary descriptions and currency exchange information.

U.S. dollar **traveler's checks** are the safest, most negotiable way to carry currency. They are accepted by most restaurants, hotels, and shops, and can be exchanged for cash at banks and check-issuing offices. American Express offices are open weekdays from 9am to 5pm, and on Saturday from 9am until noon. Convenient locations include: 330 Biscayne Blvd., Downtown (tel. 358-7350); 32 Miracle Mile, Coral Gables (tel. 446-3381); and Bal Harbour Shops, 9700 Collins Ave., Bal Harbour (tel. 865-5959).

Most banks offer **Automated Teller Machines (ATMs),** which accept cards connected to a particular network. Citicorp Savings of Florida, 8750 NW 36th St., and at other locations (tel. 599-5555), accepts cards on Cirrus, Honor, and Metroteller networks. Southeast Bank, N.A., 1390 Brickell Ave., and at other locations (tel. 599-2265), is on line with the Plus network. For additional bank locations, dial 800/424-7787 for the Cirrus network, 800/843-7587 for the Plus Network.

Banks making **cash advances** against MasterCard and VISA cards include Barnett Bank (tel. 800/342-8472), Florida National Bank (tel. 593-6200), and NCNB National Bank (tel. 800/524-8114).

Newspapers and Magazines The well-respected *Miami Herald* is the city's best-selling daily. It is especially known for its mammoth Sunday edition, and its excellent Friday "Weekend" entertainment guide. There are literally dozens of specialized Miami magazines geared toward tourists and natives alike. Many are free and can be picked up at hotels, restaurants, and in vending machines all around town. The best entertainment freebie is the weekly tabloid *New Times.* But, keep an eye out for *Welcome, Key, Miami Beach News, Coral Gables News, Florida Sports,* and others. *South Florida* is the area's best glossy for upscale readers.

Photographic Needs Drugstores and supermarkets are probably the cheapest places to purchase film. You'll pay loads more for the same product at specialized kiosks near tourist attractions. One Hour Photo in the Bayside Marketplace (tel. 377-FOTO) charges $16 to develop and print a roll of 36 pictures. Open Monday to Saturday from 10am to 10pm, on Sunday from noon to 8pm. Coconut Grove Camera, 2911 Grand Ave. (tel. 445-0521), features 30-minute color processing and maintains a huge selection of cameras and equipment. They rent, too.

Police For emergencies, dial 911 from any phone. No coins are needed. For other matters, call 595-6263.

Radio and Television About five dozen **radio** stations can be heard in the Greater Miami area. On the AM dial, 610 (WIOD), 790 (WNWS), 1230 (WJNO), and 1340 (WPBR) all specialize in news and talk. WDBF (1420) is a good Big Band station, and WPBG (1290) features golden oldies. The best rock stations on the FM dial include WZTA (94.9), WGTR (97.3), and the progressive rock station WVUM (90.5). WKIS (99.9) is the top country station, and public radio (PBS) can be heard either on WXEL (90.7) or WLRN (91.3). In addition to cable **television** stations, available in most hotels, all the major networks and a couple of independent stations are represented. They include: Channel 4, WTVJ (NBC); Channel 6, WCIX (CBS); Channel 7 WSVN (Fox); Channel 10, WPLG (ABC); Channel 17 WLRN (PBS); Channel 23 WLTV (independent); and Channel 33, WBFS (independent).

Religious Services Miami houses of worship are as varied as the city's population and include: **St. Hugh Catholic Church,** 3460 Royal Rd., at the corner of Main Highway (tel. 444-8363); **Temple Judea,** 5500 Granada Blvd., Coral Gables (tel. 667-5657); **Bryan Memorial United Methodist,** 3713 Main Hwy. (tel. 443-0880); **Christ Episcopal Church,** 3481 Hibiscus St. (tel. 442-8542); **Plymouth Congregational Church,** 3400 Devon Rd., at Main Highway (tel. 444-6521).

Restrooms Stores rarely let customers use the restrooms, and many restaurants offer their facilities for customers only. Most malls have bathrooms, as do many of the ubiquitous fast-food restaurants. Many public beaches and large parks provide toilets; in some places you have to pay, or tip an attendant. Most large hotels have clean restrooms in their lobbies.

Safety Whenever you're traveling in an unfamiliar city or country, stay alert. Be aware of your immediate surroundings. Wear a moneybelt and don't sling your camera or purse over your shoulder; wear the strap diagonally across your body. This will minimize the possibility of your becoming a victim of crime. Every society has its criminals. It's your responsibility to be aware and alert, even in the most heavily touristed areas. For all of Miami's notoriety, it should be noted that innocent tourists are rarely the victims of violent crime. Still, few locals would recommend walking alone in Liberty City or Overtown at night.

Shoe Repair There are dozens of shoe- and leather-repair shops around the city. Check the Miami "Yellow Pages" for the location nearest you, or visit Miller Square Shoe Repair, 13846 SW 56th St. (tel. 387-2875). It's open Monday to Friday from 9am to 7pm, on Saturday until 6pm.

Taxes A 6% state sales tax is added on at the register for all goods and services purchased in Florida. In addition, most municipalities levy special taxes on restaurants and hotels. In Surfside, hotel taxes total 8%; in Bal Harbour, 9%; and in the rest of Dade County, a whopping 11%.

In Miami Beach, Surfside, and Bal Harbour, the resort (hotel) tax also applies to restaurants with liquor licenses.

Taxis See "Getting Around," above, in this chapter.

Telephone, Telex, and Fax Find out how much it costs to use the direct-dial telephone in your hotel room before you pick up the receiver. Hotel surcharges are often astronomical, and even a local call can cost 75¢ or more! You can often save yourself a lot of money by using one of the hotel's public telephones in the lobby.

Most large Miami hotels have telex and fax (facsimile) machines; their numbers are included in this book with the appropriate listings. You should know that many hotels charge several dollars per page even to *receive* fax messages! Beware of the hotel copy service and other high-price fax services.

Time Miami, like New York, is in the eastern standard time zone. Between April and October, eastern daylight saving time is adopted, and clocks are set one hour ahead. America's eastern seaboard is five hours ahead of Greenwich mean time. To find out what time it is, call 324-8811.

Tipping Waiters and bartenders expect a 15% tip, as do taxi drivers and hairdressers. Porters should be tipped 50¢ to $1 per bag, and parking valets should be given $1. It's nice to leave a few dollars on your pillow for the hotel maid, and lavatory attendants will appreciate whatever change you have.

Transit Information For Metrorail or Metromover schedule information, phone 638-6700. See "Getting Around," above, in this chapter for more information.

Weather For an up-to-date recording of current weather conditions and forecast reports, dial 661-5065.

3. NETWORKS & RESOURCES

FOR STUDENTS

Located in south Coral Gables, the large main campus of the **University of Miami** encompasses dozens of classrooms, a huge athletic field, a large lake, a museum, a hospital, and more. For general information, call the university (tel. 372-0120).

The school's main student building is the **Whitten University Center,** 1306 Stanford Drive (tel. 284-2318). Social events are often scheduled here, and important information on area activities is always posted. The building houses a recreation area, a swimming pool, a snack shop, and a Ticketmaster outlet.

The Ring Theatre, on the University of Miami Campus, 1380 Miller Drive (tel. 284-3355), is the main stage for the Department of Theater Arts' advanced student productions. Faculty and guest actors are regularly featured, as are contemporary works by local playwrights. See "The Performing Arts," in Chapter 10 for more information.

The **Gusman Concert Hall,** 1314 Miller Drive (tel. 284-2438 voice, 284-6477 recording), features performances by faculty and students of the university's School of Music, as well as concerts by special guests. The auditorium is also home to the Miami Chamber Symphony. See "Major Multipurpose Performance and Concert Halls" in Chapter 10 for more information, and call for schedules and tickets.

For tickets to Miami Hurricanes basketball, football, and baseball home games, call the **U of M Athletic Department** (tel. 284-3822 or 800/GO-CANES in Florida). See "Sports and Recreation" in Chapter 7 for more information.

The University's **Beaumont Cinema** (tel. 284-2211) features new and classic films. Call for ticket prices and screening schedules.

FOR GAY MEN & LESBIANS

Miami has a significant gay community, supported by a wide range of services.

The **Gay and Lesbian Community Hotline** (tel. 759-3661), an interactive recording that can be reached with a push-button phone, lists 14 categories of information of interest to the gay community. These include: political issues, gay bars, special events, support groups, business serving the gay community, doctors and lawyers, help wanted, and others.

The **Gay Community Bookstore,** 7545 Biscayne Boulevard (tel. 754-6900), features quality literature, newspapers, videos, music, cards, and more. It's open Monday through Saturday, 11am to 9pm, Sunday noon to 6pm.

The *Weekly News* is the best local gay publication. It is available free at bookstores and gay bars throughout South Florida. Other local literature to look for include the magazines *David* and *Hot Shots*.

CHAPTER 5

MIAMI ACCOMMODATIONS

Miami is chock full of hotels. Whether you're looking to locate on a quiet strip of beach or right in the heart of the hustle, accommodation possibilities seem endless. Hotels here offer a huge variety of locations and services, and they appeal to a multiplicity of personalities and pocketbooks.

You may already know that South Florida's tourist season is well defined, beginning in mid-November, and lasting through Easter. From the season's commencement, hotel prices escalate until about February, after which they again begin to decline. During the off-season, hotel rates are typically 30% to 50% lower than their winter highs. Oceanfront rooms are also more accessible between Easter and November, as are shops, roads, and restaurants.

But timing isn't everything. In many cases, rates will also depend on your hotel's proximity to the beach and how much ocean you can see from your window. Small motels, a block or two from the water, can be up to 40% cheaper than similar properties right on the sand. When a hotel *is* right on the beach, it is probable that its oceanfront rooms will be significantly more expensive than similar accommodations in the rear. Still, despite their higher prices, oceanfront rooms can often be hard to get; if you desire one, a reservation is definitely recommended.

There are so many hotels in Miami—in every price range—that few regularly fill to capacity. Even during the height of the tourist season, you can usually drive right into the city and find decent accommodations fairly quickly. But be careful. If you have your sights set on one particular hotel, if you have to have an oceanfront room, or if you want to stay in an area where accommodations are not particularly plentiful, you should reserve your room in advance.

Hotel toll-free telephone numbers will save you time and money when inquiring about rates and availability. Some of the larger hotel reservations chains with properties in the Miami area include: Best Western (tel. 800/528-1234), Days Inn (tel. 800/325-2525), Holiday Inn (tel. 800/465-4329), Howard Johnson (tel. 800/228-9000),

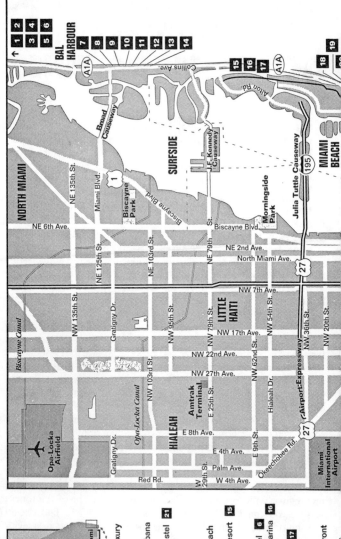

MIAMI AREA ACCOMMODATIONS

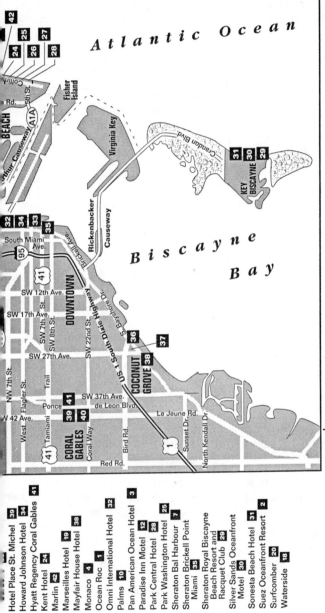

Hotel Place St. Michel **39**
Howard Johnson Hotel **34**
Hyatt Regency Coral Gables **41**
Kent Hotel **24**
Marlin **42**
Marseilles Hotel **19**
Mayfair House Hotel **38**
Monaco **4**
Ocean Roc **1**
Omni International Hotel **32**
Palms **10**
Pan American Ocean Hotel **3**
Paradise Inn Motel **12**
Park Central Hotel **28**
Park Washington Hotel **25**
Sheraton Bal Harbour **7**
Sheraton Brickell Point Miami **35**
Sheraton Royal Biscayne Beach Resort and Racquet Club **29**
Silver Sands Oceanfront Motel **30**
Sonesta Beach Hotel **31**
Suez Oceanfront Resort **2**
Surfcomber **20**
Waterside **18**

Quality Inn (tel. 800/228-5151), Ramada Inn (tel. 800/272-6232), and TraveLodge (tel. 800/255-3050).

If, after inquiring about room availability at the hotels listed in this book, you still come up empty handed (an extremely unlikely prospect), look for an availability along Miami Beach's Collins Avenue. There are dozens of hotels and motels on this strip—in all price categories—so a room is bound to be available.

To help you decide on the accommodations option that's best for you, hotels below are divided first by area, then by price, using the following guide: Expensive (over $130); Moderate ($80 to $130); and Budget (below $80). Prices are for an average double room during the high season. Read carefully. Many hotels also offer rooms at rates above and below the price category they have been assigned. Most hotel rates are significantly lower between Easter and Thanksgiving.

Prices listed below do not include state and city taxes, which, in most parts of Miami, total 11% (see "Fast Facts" in Chapter 4). Be aware that many hotels make additional charges for parking and levy heavy surcharges for telephone use. Some, especially those in South Miami Beach, also tack on an additional service charge. Inquire about these extras before committing. Room rates include breakfast where noted.

1. MIAMI BEACH

You probably have never seen more hotels than the solid wall of high-rises that seems to go on forever along Collins Avenue. The buildings are so effective at blocking the ocean from the view of passersby that you hardly know you're driving along the coast. But reserve a room at one of these behemoths and you'll have some of the world's best beach at your doorstep.

Most of these big beach resorts are so encompassing that it's possible to spend your entire stay on the premises of a single hotel. But when you're ready to explore, Miami Beach is within easy reach of the art deco district and the entire mainland, which is just across the bay.

EXPENSIVE

THE ALEXANDER ALL-SUITE LUXURY HOTEL, 5225 Collins Ave., Miami Beach, FL 33140. Tel. 305/865-6500 or toll free 800/327-6121. Fax 305/864-8525. Telex 808172. 150 suites. A/C MINIBAR TV TEL

$ Rates: Dec 17–Easter, $205–$415 one-bedroom suite, $295–$550 two-bedroom suite; rest of the year $270–$540 one-bedroom suite, $370–$750 two-bedroom suite. Additional person $25. Children under 18 stay free in parents' room. Packages available. AE, CB, DC, MC, V. **Parking:** $8.

One of the nicest offerings on Miami Beach, the Alexander is an all-suite hotel, featuring spacious one- and two-bedroom miniapartments. All suites have a living room, a fully equipped kitchen, two bathrooms, and a balcony. The hotel itself is well decorated with fine sculptures, paintings, antiques, and tapestries, most of which were garnered from the Cornelius Vanderbilt mansion. The pretty hotel's two oceanfront pools are surrounded by lush vegetation; one of the "lagoons" is also fed by a cascading waterfall.

Dining/Entertainment: Dominique's, a gourmet restaurant for a top-drawer dinner, offers French cuisine featuring seafood, rack of lamb, rattlesnake, and Everglades alligator. Piano lounge. Pool bar.

Services: Valet/laundry service, room service, turn-down service, currency exchange.

Facilities: 2 heated freshwater swimming pools, 4 Jacuzzis, Sunfish and catamaran rentals, gift shop.

DORAL OCEAN BEACH RESORT, 4833 Collins Ave., Miami Beach, FL 33140. Tel. 305/532-3600 or toll free 800/223-6725. Fax 305/534-7409. 420 rms, including 127 suites. No-smoking rooms available. A/C MINIBAR TV TEL.

$ Rates: Dec 21–Apr, $180–$285 single/double, from $290 suite; the rest of the year, $120–$200 single/double, from $240 suite. Additional person $20. Weekend and other packages available. AE, CB, DC, DISC, MC, V. **Parking:** $9.

The 18-story Doral Resort stands guard over Collins Avenue with the proud self-confidence of a truly grand hotel. This is one of the beach's famous "big boys," and it's one of the city's luxury leaders. For an oceanfront resort, the hotel is relatively quiet. Its immediate neighbors are private apartment buildings and, except for its 18th-floor restaurant, the Doral offers practically no nightlife.

Still, the hotel features all the activities you'd expect from a top waterfront resort, including sailing, waterskiing, jetskiing, and windsurfing. The Seabreeze Restaurant, specializing in stir-fries, gourmet pizzas, and health-oriented edibles, sits adjacent to an outdoor, Olympic-size pool. The biggest benefit of locating here, however, is that guests are entitled to use the facilities of the Doral's affiliated hotels, which include six golf courses and one of the best health spas in America. A free shuttle bus connects this beach resort with the others.

Dining/Entertainment: 3 restaurants, a nightclub, 2 lounges, and a pool bar.

Services: 24-hour room service, laundry service, car rental, complimentary transportation to other resorts, child care, and complimentary child-activity center.

Facilities: Heated outdoor swimming pool, Jacuzzi, fitness center, 2 lighted tennis courts, and a game room.

EDEN ROC HOTEL AND MARINA, 4525 Collins Ave., Miami Beach, FL 33140. Tel. 305/531-0000 or toll free 800/327-8337. Fax 305/531-6955. Telex 807120. 351 rms, including 45 suites. A/C TV TEL

$ Rates: Dec 22–Apr, $120–$185 single/double, from $195 suite; rest of the year, $99–$160 single/double, from $175 suite.

Additional person $15. Weekend and other packages available. AE, CB, DC, DISC, MC, V. **Parking:** $8.

Another major star of the beach, the Eden Roc is one of those big, beautiful hotels that help give Miami Beach its flamboyant image. Accommodations here are more than a bit gaudy, but compared to other monoliths on the strip, the atmosphere is relatively laid back.

Rooms are unpretentious, unusually spacious, and priced better than other nearby deluxe properties. All are recently renovated and alternately decorated in deep, dark colors, and lighter earth tones. Bathrooms are covered with marble and pretty mirrors.

The Eden Roc is a hotel that wants to show off, and it's best enjoyed when you let yourself "ooh" and "aah." The circular pink pastel lobby is as fanciful as the entrance. But most awesome is the lounge-side swimming pool, adjacent to the Porch Restaurant; its transparent glass sides give drinkers an underwater view of the underwater frolicking.

Dining/Entertainment: 3 lounges, 2 restaurants (one fancy, one casual), 1 coffee shop, and a deli.

Services: Concierge, laundry, room service, and car rental.

Facilities: 2 outdoor swimming pools, one freshwater, one saltwater; water-sports concession; game room; beauty salon; and shopping arcade.

FONTAINEBLEAU HILTON, 4441 Collins Ave., Miami Beach, FL 33140. Tel. 305/538-2000 or toll free 800/HILTONS. Fax 305/534-7821. Telex 519362. 1206 rms, including 63 suites. No-smoking rooms available. A/C TV TEL

$ Rates: Dec 16–Apr, $180–$250 single, $190–$275 double, from $330 suite; the rest of the year, $130–$205 single, $150–$225 double, from $300 suite. Additional person $20. Children stay free in parents' room. Weekend and other packages available. AE, CB, DC, DISC, MC, V. **Parking:** $8.

Far and away the most famous hotel in Miami, the Fontainebleau (pronounced "fountain-blue") has built its reputation on garishness and excess. For most visitors, this spectacle is more tourist attraction than hotel; its massive structure, with an incredible free-form swimming pool and waterfall, really shouldn't be missed.

Since opening its doors in 1954, the hotel has hosted presidents, pageants, and movie productions—including the James Bond thriller *Goldfinger*. The sheer size of the Fontainebleau, with its full complement of restaurants, stores, recreational facilities, and over 1,100 employees, makes this a perfect hotel for conventioneers. Unfortunately, the same recommendation cannot be extended to individual travelers. It's easy to get lost here, both physically and personally. The lobby is terminally crowded, the staff is overworked, and lines are always long. Still, this is the one and only Fontainebleau, and in many ways the quintessential Miami hotel. Facilities are terrific and, for all its shortcomings, this is one place you'll never forget.

Dining/Entertainment: Four large restaurants include the

FROMMER'S SMART TRAVELER: HOTELS

1. Always remember that at any time of year a hotel room is a perishable commodity: If it's not sold, the revenue is lost forever. Therefore, it is a fact that rates are linked to the hotel's occupancy level. If it's 90% occupied the price goes up; if it's 50% occupied the price goes down. So always try negotiating by stating *your* price.
2. In summer, ask about summer discounts. At this time of year, hotels in Miami are very negotiable. Downtown hotels are less elastic.
3. Many hotels offer big discounts or package rates on weekends (Friday to Sunday night). If you're staying on a weekend, always ask about these. Downtown hotels are more elastic.
4. Before selecting a hotel, always ask about parking charges. Charges can be as much as $10—a big difference if you're planning on staying a while.

flagship Dining Galleries, featuring continental cuisine, and Chez Bon Bon, which serves breakfast, lunch, and dinner. There are a half dozen or so other cafés and coffee shops (including two by the pool), as well as a number of cocktail lounges, including the Poodle Lounge, which offers live entertainment and dancing nightly. Club Tropigala (see Chapter 10, "More Entertainment"), just off the lobby, features a "Las Vegas–style" floor show with dozens of performers and not one, but two orchestras.

Services: Room service, house doctor, limousine service, complimentary child care during holidays and summer, laundry service.

Facilities: Shopping arcade with 28 shops, games room, 2 outdoor swimming pools (one fresh-, one saltwater), 3 whirlpool baths, 7 lighted tennis courts, award-winning health spa, special activities for children.

MODERATE

DEZERLAND SURFSIDE BEACH HOTEL, 8701 Collins Ave., Miami Beach, FL 33154. Tel. 305/865-6661 or toll free 800/331-9346 (800/331-9347 in Canada). Fax 305/866-2630. Telex 4973649. 225 rms. No-smoking rooms available. A/C TV TEL

$ Rates: Dec 26–Mar, $85–$125 single/double; rest of the year, $60–$75 single/double. Additional person $8. Children under 19 stay free in parents' room. Special packages and group rates available. No-smoking rooms available. AE, CB, DC, MC, V.
Parking: Free.

Designed by car enthusiast Michael Dezer, Dezerland is a unique place—part hotel and part 1950s automobile wonderland. Visitors are welcomed by a 1959 Cadillac stationed by the front door, and a '55 Thunderbird hardtop sits in the lobby. A dozen other mint-condition classics are scattered about the floors, while walls are decorated with related 1950s and 1960s memorabilia.

Billed as "America's largest '50s extravaganza," this unique Quality Inn member features rooms that are named after some of Detroit's most famous models. Dezerland is located directly on the beach and features a mosaic of a pink Cadillac at the bottom of its surfside swimming pool.

Dining/Entertainment: American Classics restaurant and a lobby lounge with nightly entertainment.

Services: Laundry, babysitting.

Facilities: Adjacent tennis courts, gift shop featuring 1950s memorabilia.

BUDGET

THE GOLDEN SANDS, 6910 Collins Ave., Miami Beach, FL 33141. Tel. 305/866-8734 or toll free 800/932-0333 (800/423-5170 in Canada). Fax 305/866-0187. Telex 6974107. 100 rms, including 20 efficiencies. A/C TV TEL

$ Rates: Dec–Mar, $50–$60 single, $57–$77 double, $80 efficiency; Apr–Nov, $43 single, $47–$57 double, $60 efficiency. Additional person $10. Children stay free in parents' room. AE, MC, V. **Parking:** $5.

Furnishings and decor are a bit dated in this 1950s-era hotel, but excellent rates and good services make the Golden Sands one of the best deals in Miami Beach. Located on the corner of 69th Street, right on the ocean, the hotel sports a large pool, an indoor lounge, and an inexpensive restaurant catering to a primarily German clientele.

PARADISE INN MOTEL, 8520 Harding Ave., Miami Beach, FL 33141. Tel. 305/865-6216. Fax 305/865-9028. 96 rms, including 48 efficiencies. A/C TV TEL

$ Rates: Dec 21–Jan 23 and Mar 6–Apr 15, $40 single, $44 double; Jan 24–Mar 5, $44 single, $48 double; Apr 15–June and Sept–Dec 20, $28 single, $32 double; July 1–Aug, $30 single, $34 double. Extra person, $3 in efficiencies. Children under 13 stay free in parents' room. AE, CB, DC, DISC, MC, V.

It's amazing how inexpensive, simple, clean, and perfectly acceptable accommodations can be just one block from the ocean in Miami Beach. Nothing fancy here, but all rooms in this cedar-roofed motel have color television and air conditioning. The motel features free parking and laundry facilities, and it's a two-minute walk from public tennis courts and the huge beachfront North Shore Park. Harding Avenue runs parallel to Collins Avenue.

THE WATERSIDE, 2360 Collins Ave., Miami Beach, FL

33139. Tel. 305/538-1951. Fax 305/531-3217. 100 rms.
AC TV TEL

$ Rates: Dec 16–Apr, $75–$90 single/double; rest of the year
$40–$60 single/double. Extra person $10. Children free in par-
ents' room. AE, DC, MC, V.

Across Collins Avenue from the beach, The Waterside is a medium-
size bilevel motel popular with European tourists. The new owners,
French-born Gérard and Maryse Meulien, recently sold their hotel in
Marseille to give their full attention to the completely renovated
Waterside. This blue-and-white motel wraps around a large swimming pool and features simple, well-kept rooms with free parking
and excellent rates.

2. SOUTH MIAMI BEACH

In South Miami Beach, hotels are pretty and surrounded by well-
priced restaurants and some of Miami's best nightlife options.

Ocean Drive, an inviting 10-block strip inside Miami's historic art
deco district is, hands down, the beach's best esplanade. Fronting the
Atlantic Ocean, this historic street is lined with squat, ice cream–
colored hotels and coconut palms taller than most of the buildings.

Collins Avenue, just one block back, runs parallel to Ocean Drive.
This pretty stretch of the street is not on the water, but staying here
usually means lower room rates and easier parking.

EXPENSIVE

**THE MARLIN, 1200 Collins Ave., South Miami Beach, FL
33139. Tel. 305/673-8770.** Fax 305/673-9609. 10 rms, 7
suites. A/C TV TEL

$ Rates: Dec–Apr, $170 studio, $185 1-bedroom suite, $205
deluxe 1-bedroom suite, $250 2-bedroom suite; the rest of the
year, $95 studio, $105 1-bedroom suite, $125 deluxe 1-bedroom
suite, $150 2-bedroom suite. AE, CB, DC, DISC, MC, V.

Opened in early 1992 after extensive renovations and a complete
exterior make-over, this hotel is, visually, one of the most outstanding
on the beach. The hotel's proprietor, former Island Records owner
Chris Blackwell, has attracted a rock-and-roll clientele that has made
an instant hit out of the high-profile Marlin. The hotel's beautifully lit
powder-blue exterior gives way to a far less grand interior filled with
gaily painted, but rather small and simple, rooms and suites.

Although the relatively high prices might not be warranted by the
quality of the rooms themselves, contemporary touches and an
in-the-know staff give guests a sense of being someplace special. In
addition to a kitchenette, every Jamaican-style room is outfitted with
a TV, VCR, CD player, and a host of tropical toiletries. Deluxe
1-bedroom suites have two bathrooms. Room service is provided by
Shabeen, the hotel's in-house Caribbean restaurant.

MODERATE

AVALON HOTEL, 700 Ocean Dr., Miami Beach, FL 33139. Tel. 305/538-0133 or toll free 800/933-3306. Fax 305/534-0258. 60 rms. A/C TV TEL

$ Rates (including continental breakfast): Oct 15–May 15, $85–$135 single/double; rest of the year, $55–$110 single/double. Additional person $10. A 10% discount for stays of 7 days or more. Weekly packages available. AE, MC, V. **Parking:** $6.

The Avalon is an excellent example of classic art deco digs right on the beach. Occupying a pretty parcel that wraps around the corner of 7th Street, the hotel is striking both inside and out. Rooms are well decorated in traditional 1930s style, and all are equipped with compact refrigerators, cable televisions, and individually controlled air conditioning. The hotel's modest lobby is occupied by a casual restaurant, best for sandwiches at lunch either inside or on the breezy outdoor patio.

The experienced management, known for their excellent inns in Newport, Rhode Island, run this hotel with an even hand. If the Avalon is full, don't hesitate to accept a room in their other property, the Majestic, located across the street.

Dining/Entertainment: The lobby restaurant is a top pick in the area for an informal lunch or a relaxing snack. By night, the menu gets fancier, prices get higher, and the cozy bar becomes a romantic place to pass the time.

Services: Like other hotels on the strip, reception can arrange car rental, babysitting, hairstyling, and other services.

CAVALIER HOTEL AND CABANA CLUB, 1320 Ocean Dr., Miami Beach, FL 33139. Tel. 305/534-2135 or toll free 800/338-9076. Fax 305/531-5543. Telex 204978. 45 rms, including 2 suites. A/C TV TEL

$ Rates (including continental breakfast): Oct 16–Apr 14, $105–$135 single/double, $175 suite; the rest of the year, $65–$120 single/double, $150 suite. All rates subject to 10% service charge. AE, DC, DISC, MC, V.

This beautiful architectural masterpiece, built in 1936, was one of Ocean Drive's first art deco renovations. It's one of the fanciest, too. Completely restored in 1987, the Cavalier now sports central air conditioning, beautifully restored period furnishings, and an ultra-contemporary atmosphere recalling less-hurried times.

Popular with fashion photography crews, rooms here are luxuriously carpeted, and guests are pampered with fluffy towels, fresh mineral water, and a newspaper every morning. Still, this place is no stuffed shirt. Like other area hotels, there are no parking attendants, no porters, and not a single tie in sight. The Cavalier is on the best strip on the beach, within walking distance to the area's most noted restaurants and clubs. Still, it's easy to get a quiet night's sleep here as the lobby is devoid of bars, bands, or restaurants.

A full continental breakfast buffet, including fresh fruit and croissants, is served in the breakfast room each morning.

Services: Reception can make arrangements for hair cutting, massage, limousine, and laundry services.

ESSEX HOUSE, 1001 Collins Ave., Miami Beach, FL 33139. Tel. 305/534-2700 or toll free 800/55-ESSEX. Fax 305/532-3827. 50 rms, including 12 suites. A/C TV TEL

$ Rates (including continental breakfast): Oct–May 1, $100–$145 single/double, $155–$185 petite suite, $205–$310 grande suite; rest of the year, about 20% lower. A 10% service charge is additional. Minimum on weekends, 2 nights; holidays, 3 nights. AE, MC, V.

This art deco delight is one of South Beach's plushest gems. Now a TraveLodge affiliate, the pretty Essex House is the result of a painstaking restoration and is a textbook example of the famous "Streamline Moderne" style, complete with large porthole windows, original etched glasswork, ziggurat arches, and detailed crown moldings. The solid oak bedroom furnishings are also original and, like many other details in this special hotel, were painstakingly restored.

The homey, personal touches include teddy bears on the beds, "touch-sensitive" lamps, evening turn-down, and an extremely attentive staff. The Essex also features 24-hour reception, a high-tech piano in the lobby/lounge, and a state-of-the-art security system.

Located just one block from the ocean, this hotel is both romantic and spick-and-span clean. Smoking is not permitted in any of the rooms and, according to the hotel staff, children are "inappropriate" here.

Dining/Entertainment: The hotel's lobby/lounge is sort of an all-purpose room serving light lunches, afternoon tea, and evening cocktails. Pianists sometimes entertain.

Services: Limousine and laundry service.

HOTEL LESLIE and **HOTEL CARDOZO, 1244 and 1300 Ocean Dr., Miami Beach, FL 33139. Tel. 305/534-2135** or toll free 800/338-9076. Fax 305/531-5543. Telex 204978. 77 rms total, including 8 suites. A/C TV TEL

$ Rates (including continental breakfast): Oct 16–Apr 15, $105–$135 single/double, $175 suite; the rest of the year, $65–$120 single/double, $150 suite. All rates subject to a 10% service charge. AE, DC, DISC, MC, V.

Operated by Tecton Management, the Leslie and the Cardozo were among the first properties on Ocean Drive to undergo extensive renovation.

Designed by noted architect Albert Anis in 1937, the Leslie is one of the area's smallest and quietest hotels. The light and airy beds and bureaus that dominate the hotel's art nouveau interior are a departure from the building's distinct art deco design. Still, the modern furniture and whimsical wall hangings look right in place.

The 40-room Cardozo is equally cozy but, by contrast, contains original walnut furniture and a new, as yet unnamed, lobby restaurant and bar. It was here that Frank Sinatra filmed the 1950s movie *Hole in the Head;* today the hotel's soft pastels still grace the background of many fashion shoots.

These hotels are among the best in Miami. Guests in each are pampered with free morning newspapers and a hearty continental breakfast buffet.

Services: Reception can make arrangements for hair-cutting, massage, babysitting, limousine, and laundry services.

PARK CENTRAL HOTEL, 640 Ocean Dr., Miami Beach, FL 33139. Tel. 305/538-1611. Fax 305/534-7520. 80 rms. A/C TV TEL

$ Rates (including continental breakfast): Dec–Apr, $75–$135 single/double; rest of the year, $55–$110 single/double. Additional person $10. Senior discounts available. AE, DC, DISC, MC, V.

The Park Central is an architectural masterpiece, and one of the prettiest art deco hotels on the beach. Built in 1937, and reestablished 50 years later by New York developer Tony Goldman, the hotel competently combines the sophisticated style of a bygone era with the excitement and services of a modern-day hotspot. The smallish rooms are comparable, both in size and appointments, to others on the block, all with air conditioning, color television, and direct-dial phones.

Dining/Entertainment: The Borroco restaurant in the lobby's rear, serves competent Italian food at moderate to high prices. Sip a cocktail in the lobby; it's a great place to see and be seen, especially on weekend nights when it's quite crowded.

Services: If you're staying in the hotel, Borroco delivers. Limousine, laundry, and other services can be arranged at reception.

BUDGET

CLAY HOTEL & YOUTH HOSTEL, 1438 Washington Ave., Miami Beach, FL 33139. Tel. 305/534-2988. Fax 305/673-0346. 180 beds in singles, doubles, and multishares.

$ Rates: $21–$23 single, $25–$29 double, $10–$13 multishare. Sheets $2 additional. $3 per night additional for non-IYHF members. Weekly rates available. MC, V.

A member of the International Youth Hostel Federation (IYHF), the Clay occupies a beautiful 1920s-style Spanish Mediterranean building at the corner of historic Espanola Way. Like other IYHF members, this hostel is open to all ages and is a great place to meet like-minded travelers. The usual smattering of Australians, Europeans, and other budget travelers make this place the best clearinghouse of "inside" travel information in Miami. Even if you don't stay here, you might want to check out the ride board and make some friends.

Understandably, rooms here are basic. Reservations are recommended from December through April, and the above rates reflect accommodations with and without air conditioning.

**KENT HOTEL, 1131 Collins Ave., Miami Beach, FL 33139.
Tel. 305/531-6771.** Fax 305/531-0720. 56 rms. A/C TV TEL
$ Rates (including continental breakfast): Dec 15–Easter, $50–
$60 single/double; rest of the year, $40–$50 single/double.
Weekly discounts available. AE, MC, V.

The well-located Kent is an excellent example of the way hotel prices
drop dramatically when you get away from Ocean Drive. Typically
art deco, the squat Kent is not fancy and is elegant only in a historical
kind of way. Still, the hotel is comfortable and full of character.
Breakfast is served both inside and on the porch, and street parking is
always available.

**MARSEILLES HOTEL, 1741 Collins Ave., Miami Beach, FL
33139. Tel. 305/538-5711** or toll free 800/327-4739. Fax
305/673-1006. Telex 441106. 100 rms, including 6 suites. A/C TV
TEL
$ Rates (including continental breakfast): Dec 21–Easter, $65–
$70 single/double, $70 single/double with kitchenette, $75 suite;
rest of the year, $45–$50 single/double, $50 single/double with
kitchenette, $55 suite. Additional person, $5. Children under 8
stay free in parents' room. AE, DC, MC, V. **Parking:** $4.

A skyscraper by area standards, this pretty and basic hotel is not one
of the area's fanciest, but it is well located, well run, and extremely
well priced. The hotel's furnishings are outdated but functional, and
all rooms come equipped with a refrigerator and remote-control
television. The Marseilles's lobby café, a casual eatery with light
American food, is welcoming, but a short walk in almost any
direction will put you right in the middle of some of the area's hottest
nightspots and eateries.

**PARK WASHINGTON HOTEL, 1020 Washington Ave., Mi-
ami Beach, FL 33139. Tel. 305/532-1930.** Fax 305/672-
6706. 50 rms, including 15 suites. A/C TV TEL
$ Rates: Nov–Apr, $49 single, $69 double, $129–$170 suite; the
rest of the year, $39 single, $59 double, $119–$160 suite.
Additional person $10. Children stay free in parents' room. AE,
MC, V.

The Park Washington, a newly refurbished, large hotel offers
some of the best values in South Beach. Located three blocks
from the ocean, this hotel is trying to make a name for itself by
offering good-quality accommodations at incredible prices. It's not
too fancy here. But unlike many other hotels in the area that accept
long-term residents, this hostelry is strictly geared toward tourists.

Originally designed in the 1930s by Henry Hohauser, one of the
beach's most famous architects, the new Park Washington reopened
only in 1989. Most of the rooms do not have original furnishings, but
they do include color television, direct-dial telephone, refrigerator,
and individual air conditioning and heating.

Look out for the opening of the Astor Hotel, across the street, in
early 1993—it's owned by the same folks who own the Park
Washington.

THE SURFCOMBER, 1717 Collins Ave., Miami Beach, FL 33139. Tel. 305/532-7715 or toll free 800/336-4264. Fax 305/532-7280. 194 rms. A/C TV TEL

$ Rates (including continental breakfast): Dec 15–Easter, $60–$80 single/double; Easter–June 19, $50–$70 single/double; rest of the year, $45–$65 single/double. Kitchenettes $5 per day additional. Children under 15 stay free in parents' room. Monthly and seasonal rates, and senior discounts available. AE, CB, DC, DISC, MC, V.

Family-owned since 1949, the Surfcomber has been one of the art deco district's traditional standbys since the beginning. Well located, and fronting 150 feet of beach, the hotel has been undergoing continual renovations for years. Some rooms are definitely more desirable than others, but all feature private bath, television, direct-dial phone, and in-room movies. Refrigerators are available upon request.

Hotel services include a coffee shop, a gift shop, a health-food restaurant, and an outdoor bar alongside an Olympic-size heated swimming pool.

3. SURFSIDE, BAL HARBOUR & SUNNY ISLES

The residents of Surfside, Bal Harbour, and Sunny Isles like to think of their towns as more exclusive and sedate than the overpopulated, frenetic Miami Beach to their south. In reality, though, these towns are so similar to Miami Beach that most of their hotels use Miami Beach in their address.

I have separated the listings in these municipalities from Miami Beach's only on the basis of location: They are significantly farther than Miami Beach from Coconut Grove and Downtown. On the plus side, the beaches here are just as good as Miami Beach's, and the hotel prices are generally some of the lowest in Miami.

EXPENSIVE

PAN AMERICAN OCEAN HOTEL, 17875 Collins Ave., Sunny Isles, FL 33160. Tel. 305/932-1100 or toll free 800/327-5678. Fax 305/935-2769. Telex 6812038. 142 rms, including 4 suites. A/C TV TEL

$ Rates: Dec 24–Apr, $139–$185 single/double, from $185 suite; May–Oct, $85–$125 single/double, from $130 suite; Nov–Dec 23, $99–$145 single/double, from $140 suite. Additional person $15. Children under 17 stay free in parents' room. Weekend and other packages, and senior discounts available. AE, CB, DC, DISC, MC, V. **Parking:** Free.

A Radisson Resort, the Pan American is situated on the waterfront and is a good choice for businesspeople as well as tourists. Located close to the Broward County line, the hotel is minutes from the exclusive Bal Harbour shops, and it's equidistant from Miami and Ft. Lauderdale airports.

Each room offers twice-daily maid service, ceiling fans, a minibar, and complimentary morning newspaper. Most have an ocean view and overlook a lively pool area. The Pan American is not deluxe, but accommodations are high quality and offer all the necessary amenities—and more. The staff is exceedingly friendly, and a full schedule of guest activities is scheduled daily.

Dining/Entertainment: The Ocean Terrace, an attractive dining room and lounge, is complemented by the less formal Terrace Café and (weather permitting) a poolside grill. There are bars inside and out. Entertainment varies seasonally, but there is often a solo pianist in the lounge.

Services: Room service, complimentary afternoon tea, coin-operated laundry machines, scheduled guest activities, daily transportation to local shops and racetrack.

Facilities: Swimming pool, 9-hole putting green, 4 tennis courts, game room, gift shop, hair salon.

SHERATON BAL HARBOUR, 9701 Collins Ave., Bal Harbour, FL 33154. Tel. 305/865-7511 or toll free 800/325-3535. Fax 305/864-2601. Telex 519355. 675 rms, including 50 suites. No-smoking rooms available. A/C MINIBAR TV TEL

$ Rates: Dec 16–Easter, $225–$310 single/double, from $415 suite; the rest of the year, $155–$235 single/double, from $315 suite. Additional person $25. Children under 18 stay free in parents' room. Weekend and other packages, and senior discounts available. AE, CB, DC, DISC, MC, V. **Parking:** $9.

This hotel has the best location in Bal Harbour, on the ocean and just across the street from the swanky Bal Harbour Shops. It's one of the nicest Sheratons I've seen, with large, well-decorated rooms and a two-story glass-enclosed atrium lobby. A spectacular staircase wraps itself around a cascading fountain full of wished-upon pennies.

One side of the hotel caters to corporations, complete with ballrooms and meeting facilities, but the main sections of the hotel are relatively uncongested and removed from the convention crowd. A full complement of aquatic playthings can be rented on the beach, including sailboats and jet skis.

Dining/Entertainment: 7 restaurants and lounges, including a pool bar and grill.

Services: Room service, laundry, currency exchange.

Facilities: 2 swimming pools, 2 tennis courts, water-sports concession, gift shop.

MODERATE

THE PALMS, 9449 Collins Ave., Surfside, FL 33154. Tel. 305/865-3551 or toll free 800/327-6644 (800/843-6974 in

Canada). Fax 305/861-6596. 170 rms, including 50 efficiencies.
A/C TV TEL

$ Rates: Dec 16–Easter, $90–$110 single/double, from $135
suite; rest of the year, $70–$85 single/double, from $90 suite.
Efficiencies $10 additional. Additional person $10. Children stay
free in parents' room. Weekly rates available. AE, MC, V.
Parking: Free.

The Palms is stereotypical Miami Beach. The majority of the guests
here are retired. The lobby activity board advertises times for the
day's shuffleboard tournaments, and nightlife usually centers around
a singer who performs Eddie Fisher standards.

The hotel's management is intent on widening the hotel's popularity, and staying here can be really fun. Rooms are basic but
comfortable, and all are air conditioned. Many also have balconies
overlooking the large pool and adjacent water-side bar. Located in
the Surfside/Bal Harbour area of Miami Beach, the Palms is
recommended for any traveler who wants to stay on the ocean—but
still stay on a budget.

BUDGET

**CORONADO MOTEL, 9501 Collins Ave., Surfside, FL
33154. Tel. 305/866-1625.** 41 rms, no-smoking rooms
available. A/C TV TEL

$ Rates: Dec 15–Jan 15 and Mar 15–Apr $54–$70 single/double,
Jan 16–Mar 14 $64–$80 single/double; May–Dec 14 $39–$59
single/double. Additional person $8 during winter, $5 summer.
Children stay free in parents' room. AE, CB, DC, DISC, MC, V.

Just one block from the Bal Harbour Shops, the Coronado offers
good budget accommodations with an excellent oceanfront location.
The freshwater pool is heated in the winter, and there is a color TV
and refrigerator in every room. The motel is on the corner of 95th
Street.

**DESERT INN, 17201 Collins Ave., Sunny Isles, FL 33160.
Tel. 305/947-0621** or toll free 800/327-6361 (800/223-5836
in Canada). 104 rms, including 50 efficiencies. A/C TV TEL

$ Rates: Dec 19–Jan 5 $51–$75; Jan 6–Jan 31 $41–$65;
Feb–Apr 6 $60–$85; Apr 7–Apr 30 $41–$65; May–Dec 18
$38–$54. Add $10 for efficiency. Additional person $10. Children
under 16 free in parents' room. AE, CB, DC, MC, V.

A member of the Friendship Inn chain, Desert Inn stands out for its
life-size horse-drawn covered wagon sculpture in front and its free
tennis court out back. In between are a king-size swimming pool,
laundry facilities, a dining room, patio bar, and large, clean rooms
and efficiencies. There is also an outdoor beach shower, and a
children's pool.

**DRIFTWOOD RESORT MOTEL, 17121 Collins Ave., Sunny
Isles, FL 33160. Tel. 305/944-5141** or toll free 800/327-
1263. 118 efficiencies. A/C TV TEL

$ Rates: Dec 20–Jan 7 $50–$80 single/double; Jan 8–Feb 4 $43–$70 single/double; Feb 5–Apr 1 $68–$90 single/double; Apr 2–Apr 22 $38–$70 single/double; Apr 23–Dec 19 $32–$62 single/double. Additional person $10. Children under 12 free in parents' room. AE, DC, MC, V.

The Driftwood's dated but clean rooms are all efficiencies, equipped with either stoves or microwaves, and utensils. Plenty of tiki grass hangs over the motel's entranceway and the large poolside bar. The motel's blue-and-white rooms are just steps from two shuffleboard courts, laundry facilities, a restaurant/lounge, and the parking lot. The motel is located smack in the middle of Motel Row; its pool, surrounded by plenty of lounge chairs, directly overlooks the ocean.

HILYARD MANOR OCEANFRONT SUITES, 9541 Collins Ave., Surfside, FL 33154. Tel. 305/866-7351 or toll free 800/327-1413 (800/453-4333 in Canada). Fax 305/864-3045. Telex 808165. 30 rooms, including 28 suites. A/C KITCHEN TV TEL

$ Rates: Dec 18–Jan 18 and Mar 20–Apr 20 $64–$83 single/double; Jan 18–Mar 20 $75–$92 single/double; Apr 20–June 22 and Sept 6–Dec 18 $43–$65 single/double; June 22–Sep 6 $48–$68 single/double. Extra person $8. Children under 13 free in parents' room. AE, CB, DC, DISC, MC, V.

This U-shaped motel, complete with outdated furnishings and decor, is typical of the area in price and architecture. Atypical, however, is the emphasis on well-stocked suites, complete with bedroom, kitchen, living room, and dining area. The units are well equipped with plates, pots, a toaster, and even an ironing board. Oceanfront corner room no. 36 is best. There is a heated swimming pool and laundry facilities.

THE MONACO, 17501 Collins Ave., Sunny Isles, FL 33160. Tel. 305/932-2100 or toll free 800/227-9006. Fax 305/931-5519. Telex 529400. 113 rms, including 39 efficiencies. A/C TV TEL

$ Rates: Dec 18–Jan 5 $65–$75 single/double; Jan 6–Jan 31 $55–$65 single/double; Feb–Apr 14 $70–$80 single/double; Apr 15–Apr 30 $50–$60 single/double; May–Dec 17 $50–$67 single/double. Efficiencies $5–$7 additional. Extra person $7. Children under 16, free. AE, CB, DC, DISC, MC, V.

The Monaco is one of the largest motels on the beach, encompassing a restaurant, oceanfront bar, and dozens of balconied rooms surrounding a large kidney-shape pool. As usual, nothing fancy here, but the motel's yellow-and-white decor is complemented by a large grassy area and a wide swath of beach.

OCEAN ROC, 19505 Collins Ave., Sunny Isles, FL 33160. Tel. 305/931-7600 or toll free 800/327-0553. Fax 305/866-5881. 95 rms, including 25 efficiencies. No-smoking rooms available. A/C TV TEL

$ Rates: Jan 15–Mar 15, $60 single/double; Mar 16–Apr 15 and Dec 15–Jan 14, $42–$56 single/double; rest of the year $32–$40 single/double. Efficiencies $6 additional. Extra person $6 additional. Children stay free in parents' room. Special rates for longer stays. AE, CB, DC, MC, V. **Parking:** Free.

The Ocean Roc is the last motel on Collins Avenue before the Dade County line. Its simple rectangle shape allows for only eight ocean-front rooms, while the others have ocean views and sweeping parking-lot vistas. In the 1960s, the motel's angled exterior lines probably looked futuristic. Today it's a bit outdated, but the prices can hardly be beat. In addition to an obligatory pool (with a shallow children's area), a coffee shop and laundry facilities are on the premises.

SUEZ OCEANFRONT RESORT, 18215 Collins Ave., Sunny Isles, FL 33160. Tel. 305/932-0661 or toll free 800/327-5278. Fax 305/937-0058. Telex 518883. A/C TV TEL

$ Rates: Dec 22–Apr $55–$89 single/double; May–Dec 21 $40–$60 single/double. Add $12 for kitchenettes. Additional person $5. Children under 16 stay free in parents' room. AE, DC, MC, V.

Guarded by an undersized replica of Egypt's famed Sphinx, the campy Suez offers nice rooms and lounges and some of the best motel facilities on the beach, all at highly competitive rates. Following a fairly strict orange-and-yellow motif, the motel is more reminiscent of a fast-food restaurant than ancient Egypt. The grass umbrellas over beach lounges add to the confused decor. The motel also offers three shuffleboard courts, two large swimming pools, one lighted tennis court, and half a basketball court. There is also a kiddy pool and a beachfront children's playground. The motel's large restaurant overlooks the ocean and features a nightly $16 all-you-can-eat buffet.

4. KEY BISCAYNE

This first island in Florida's Key chain is the water-sports capital of Miami. Palms sway over busy beaches while windsurfers, jet-skiers, and sailboats ply the waters just off shore. There are only a handful of hotels here, though several more are planned. All are on the beach, and room rates are uniformly high. There are no budget listings here, but if you can afford it, Key Biscayne is a great place to stay. The island is far enough from the mainland to make it feel like a secluded tropical paradise, yet close enough to Downtown to take advantage of everything Miami has to offer.

EXPENSIVE

SHERATON ROYAL BISCAYNE BEACH RESORT & RAC-QUET CLUB, 555 Ocean Dr., Key Biscayne, FL 33149.

Tel. 305/361-5775 or toll free 800/325-3535. Fax 305/361-0360. Telex 518802. 192 rms, including 21 suites. No-smoking rooms available. A/C TV TEL

$ Rates: Dec 17–Easter, $160–$240 single/double, from $270 suite; the rest of the year, $95–$155 single/double, from $225 suite. Additional person $20. Weekend and other packages, and senior discounts available. AE, CB, DC, MC, V. **Parking:** Free.

This squat, three-story beachfront hotel is loaded with Caribbean character and Miami delights. Tropical birdcalls combine with wicker furniture to create an atmosphere worthy of any one of the islands it imitates. Although this older hotel is lacking in contemporary design, the Royal Biscayne boasts one of the best spots in Miami. Room windows are well placed and large enough to let in large gulps of the city's freshest air.

Dining/Entertainment: The hotel's 2 restaurants, 2 pool bars, and 1 lounge offer top-quality dining and low-key entertainment.

Services: Room service, laundry service, car rental.

Facilities: Water-sports concession, 2 outdoor heated swimming pools, 10 tennis courts (4 lighted), bicycle rentals, hair salon, gift shop, guest laundry room.

SILVER SANDS OCEANFRONT MOTEL, 301 Ocean Dr., Key Biscayne, FL 33149. Tel. 305/361-5441. 50 efficiency apartments, 4 cottages. A/C TV TEL

$ Rates: Oct 22–Dec 17, $79–$149 standard apartment; Dec 18–Apr 22, $115–$139 standard apartment; Apr 23–Sept 3, $79–$89 standard apartment; Sept 4–Oct 21, $72–$89 standard apartment; year round, oceanfront apartment $149–$215. Extra person $10. AE, MC, V. **Parking:** Free.

The modest Silver Sands motel seems quite out of place on its million-dollar parcel, sandwiched between two luxury high-rises. The owners know this is a special place, so room rates are not particularly low. Still, they are priced well below the name-brand accommodations next door.

Accommodations here are basic; they probably haven't changed much since the 1960s. The standard efficiency apartments have small kitchenettes, and visitors may decide between a room facing the courtyard or one overlooking the parking lot (there's no view from either). The oceanfront apartments are some of the most sought after rooms in Miami, popular with those in the know. Although they are not particularly cheap, they are as close to the ocean as you can get without getting wet, and the whispering surf assures a good night's sleep. The motel's cottages are duplexes, offering more room and larger kitchens. They are a nice alternative to regular hotel rooms, but pale next to the oceanfront accommodations.

Dining/Entertainment: The Sandbar Restaurant, with a deck right on the beach, is one of Miami's most attractive hidden treasures.

Facilities: Olympic-size heated swimming pool.

SONESTA BEACH HOTEL, 350 Ocean Dr., Key Biscayne, FL 33149. Tel. 305/361-2021 or toll free 800/SONESTA.

Fax 305/361-3096. Telex 519303. 300 rms, including 16 suites and 15 villas. A/C MINIBAR TV TEL

$ Rates: Dec 18–Apr, $245–$285 single/double, from $550 suite; June 1–Sept, $155–$225 single/double, from $465 suite; the rest of the year, $205–$260 single/double, from $505 suite. Year round, $395–$900 villa (5-night minimum). Additional person $35. Children stay free in parents' room. Packages available. AE, CB, DC, DISC, MC, V. **Parking:** $4.50

The Sonesta's dominating modern oceanfront pyramid is the sort of structure most communities tend to protest against when the building plans are put forward, since it permanently changes the nature of the town. But now that it's done, enjoy! This place is definitely deluxe, and its balconied beachfront rooms are some of the best in Miami. Accommodations are excellent, but it's the hotel's spectacular location that justifies its high prices.

Services aside, the nicest thing about the Sonesta is its lack of pretension. No one ever forgets this is a beach resort, lending these lodgings a sort of casual luxuriousness.

The hotel's luxurious villas come with a full kitchen (complete with beverages and breakfast foods), laundry facilities, daily chamber service, and a large, private heated pool. Parents with kids will appreciate the hotel's "Just Us Kids" program, a free, supervised play group for children aged 5 to 13. Experienced counselors lead morning field trips as well as daily beach games and evening activities.

Dining/Entertainment: 4 restaurants include The Rib Room, and Two Dragons, with Japanese and Chinese cuisine. Snack-shop/deli. Desires nightclub features daily happy hours and dancing at night.

Services: Room service, laundry service, currency exchange, car rental, complimentary children's programs.

Facilities: Olympic-size heated swimming pool, 10 tennis courts (3 lighted), water-sports concession, bicycle rentals, beauty salon, 3 gift shops, travel agency, health club with Jacuzzi, sauna, and steam rooms.

5. COCONUT GROVE

This intimate enclave hugs the shores of Biscayne Bay just south of U.S. 1. The Grove is a great place to stay, offering ample nightlife, excellent restaurants, and beautiful surroundings. Unfortunately, all of the hotels are expensive. But, even if you don't stay here, you will surely want to spend a night or two exploring the area.

EXPENSIVE

DOUBLETREE HOTEL AT COCONUT GROVE, 2649 S. Bayshore Dr., Coconut Grove, FL 33133. Tel. 305/858-

2500 or toll free 800/528-0444. Fax 305/858-5776. 190 rms, including 18 suites. A/C TV TEL

$ Rates: Jan–Mar, $120 single, $130 double, from $170 suite; rest of the year, $100 single, $120 double, from $150 suite. Additional person $10. AARP and AAA discounts, weekend and other packages available. No-smoking rooms available. AE, CB, DC, DISC, MC, V. **Parking:** $7.

Doubletree hotels are known as business hotels. And although this property is a good choice for working travelers, its superior location and relatively reasonable rates make it an excellent choice for vacationers as well.

Standard rooms are not particularly fancy, but they are more than adequate. Suites are large and pretty and feature floor-to-ceiling windows. On higher floors, guests are treated to sweeping views of Biscayne Bay and Coconut Grove.

Dining/Entertainment: Café Brasserie, just off the lobby, offers an excellent breakfast buffet and relaxed all-day dining. Bars both inside and poolside.

Services: Laundry service, complimentary welcoming chocolate-chip cookies, and complimentary van service to local shops.

Facilities: Outdoor heated swimming pool, 2 lighted tennis courts. Sailing, fishing, and boat docks just across the street.

GRAND BAY HOTEL, 2669 S. Bayshore Dr., Coconut Grove, FL 33133. Tel. 305/858-9600 or toll free 800/327-2788. Fax 305/858-1532. Telex 441370. 181 rms, including 49 suites. No-smoking rooms available. A/C MINIBAR TV TEL

$ Rates: Oct–May, $220–$275 single/double, from $300 suite; rest of the year, $175–$245 single/double, from $300 suite. Additional person $15. Packages available. AE, CB, DC, MC, V. **Parking:** $8.

The Grand Bay opened in 1983 and immediately won praise as one of the fanciest hotels in the world. Designed by The Nichols Partnership, a local architectural firm, and outfitted with the highest-quality interiors, this stunning pyramid-shaped hotel is a masterpiece both inside and out.

Rooms are luxurious, featuring high-quality linens; comfortable, overstuffed love seats and chairs; a large writing desk; and all the amenities you would expect in deluxe accommodations. Bathrooms have hairdryers, robes, telephones, and more towels than you know what to do with. Original art and armfuls of fresh flowers are generously displayed throughout.

There is no check-in counter here; guests are escorted to a goldleaf-trimmed antique desk and encouraged to relax with a glass of champagne while they fill out the forms. The Grand Bay consistently attracts wealthy high-profile people, and it basks in its image as a rendezvous for royalty, socialites, and superstars. Indeed, the list of rich and famous who regularly walk through the lobby is endless. Guests come here to be pampered, to see and be seen.

**FROMMER'S COOL FOR KIDS:
HOTELS**

Doral Ocean Beach Resort (see page 55) provides child care and a complimentary children's activity center.

Fontainebleau Hilton Hotel (see page 56) offers play groups and child care during holiday periods. The hotel's waterfall swimming pool is a child's dream come true.

Sonesta Beach Hotel (see page 69) offers a "Just Us Kids" program and a free, supervised play group for children ages 5 to 13. Experienced counselors lead morning field trips as well as daily beach games and evening activities.

Dining/Entertainment: The hotel's Grand Café is one of the top-rated restaurants in Miami. Drinks are served in the Ciga Bar and the Lobby Lounge, where a traditional afternoon tea is served from 3 to 6pm. Regine's, the top-floor dance club, offers cocktails and dancing Thursday through Saturday from 10pm to 5am.

Services: 24-hour room service, 24-hour concierge, complimentary welcoming champagne, limousine service, same-day laundry and dry cleaning.

Facilities: Outdoor freshwater pool, health club, beauty salon, gift shop.

MAYFAIR HOUSE HOTEL, 3000 Florida Ave., Coconut Grove, FL 33133. Tel. 305/441-0000 or toll free 800/433-4555. 182 suites. No-smoking rooms available. A/C MINIBAR TV TEL

$ Rates: Dec 16–May, $230–$525 single/double, penthouse from $600; rest of the year, $180–$445 single/double, penthouse from $600. Additional person $35. Packages available. AE, DC, DISC, MC, V. **Parking:** $9.50.

Situated inside Coconut Grove's posh Mayfair Shops complex, the all-suite Mayfair House is about as centrally located as you can get. Each guest room has been individually designed, and no two are identical. All are extremely comfortable, and some suites are even opulent. Most of the more expensive accommodations include a private, outdoor, Japanese-style hot tub. Top-floor terraces offer good views, and all are hidden from the street by leaves and latticework.

The hotel contains several no-smoking suites and about 50 rooms with antique pianos. Since the lobby is in a shopping mall, recreation is confined to the roof, where a small swimming pool, sauna and snack bar is located.

Dining/Entertainment: There is a relaxed café in the lobby. The Mayfair Grill is more formal. Rooftop snack bar.

Services: 24-hour room service, twice-daily maid service, complimentary glass of champagne upon arrival, discount shopping card for stores below, laundry service, child care.

Facilities: Rooftop pool and Jacuzzi, beauty salon, travel agency, shopping arcade.

6. CORAL GABLES

Coconut Grove eases into Coral Gables, which extends north toward Miami International Airport. The Gables, as it's affectionately known, was one of Miami's original planned communities, and it's still one of the city's prettiest. Staying here enables you to experience Miami as many monied locals do. It means being close to the shops along Miracle Mile as well as to some of Miami's nicest homes. Land in Coral Gables goes for top dollar, and houses in the area reflect this value. Like other wealthy communities, Coral Gables doesn't offer much in the way of budget accommodations, but if you can afford it, hotels here are great places to stay.

EXPENSIVE

COLONNADE HOTEL, 180 Aragon Ave., Coral Gables, FL 33134. Tel. 305/441-2600 or toll free 800/533-1337. Fax 305/445-3929. 157 rms, including 17 bilevel suites. No-smoking rooms available. A/C MINIBAR TV TEL

$ Rates: Apr 16–Sept. $170–$209 single/double, from $280 suite; the rest of the year $215–$255 single/double, from $295 suite. Packages available. AE, CB, DC, DISC, MC, V. **Parking:** $8.50.

The Colonnade occupies part of a large, historic building, originally built by Coral Gables' inventor, George Merrick. Faithful to its original style, the hotel is a successful amalgam of new and old, with emphasis on the former. An escalator brings guests from street level to the hotel's grand rotunda entrance. The lobby is just down the hall, but pause for a moment and admire the pink-and-black marble floor, domed roof, and stylish column supports. This is the most eye-catching feature of Mr. Merrick's original building.

Guest rooms are outfitted with historic photographs, marble counters, gold-finished faucets, and understated furnishings worthy of the hotel's rates. Champagne upon arrival and morning coffee or tea are complimentary.

Dining/Entertainment: Aragon Café is one of the area's most celebrated restaurants, while the hotel's Doc Dammers Saloon is probably the best happy-hour haunt for the 30-something crowd. There is frequent live entertainment.

Services: 24-hour room service, child care, car rental, complimentary shoe shine, same-day dry cleaning and laundry service, and evening turn-down service.

Facilities: Heated outdoor swimming pool, Jacuzzi, hot tub, and rooftop fitness center.

HYATT REGENCY CORAL GABLES, 50 Alhambra Plaza, Coral Gables, FL 33134. Tel. 305/441-1234 or toll free 800/233-1234. Fax 305/443-7702. Telex 529706. 242 rms, including 50 suites. No-smoking rooms available. A/C MINIBAR TV TEL

$ Rates (including breakfast buffet): $175–$225 single; $195–$245 double; from $200 suite. Additional person $25. Packages and senior discounts available. AE, CB, DC, DISC, MC, V. **Parking:** $8.50.

High on style, comfort, and price, this Hyatt is part of Coral Gables' Alhambra, an office-hotel complex with a Mediterranean motif. The building itself is gorgeous, designed with pink stone, arched entrances, grand courtyards, and tile roofs. Inside you'll find overstuffed chairs on marble floors, surrounded by opulent antiques and chandeliers. The hotel opened in 1987 but, like many historical buildings in the neighborhood, the Alhambra attempts to mimic something much older, and much farther away.

Rooms are a good size and are well appointed, outfitted with everything you'd expect from a top hotel—terry robes and all. Most furnishings are antique.

Dining/Entertainment: A restaurant serving decent, high-priced food is augmented by a good lounge and nightclub.

Services: 24-hour room service, laundry service, babysitting on request.

Facilities: Health club with Nautilus equipment, heated outdoor swimming pool, Jacuzzi, 2 saunas, gift shop.

MODERATE

HOTEL PLACE ST. MICHEL, 162 Alcazar Ave., Coral Gables, FL 33134. Tel. 305/444-1666 or toll free 800/247-8526. Fax 305/539-0074. Telex 4951356. 27 rms, including 3 suites. A/C TV TEL

$ Rates (including continental breakfast): Nov 16–Easter, $100 single, $115 double, $150 suite; the rest of the year $85 single, $95 double, $110 suite. Children under 12 free. Extra person $10. Senior discounts available. AE, CB, DC, MC, V. **Parking:** $3.

It's always a pleasure to stay in this unusual cultured gem in the heart of Coral Gables. The accommodations and hospitality are straight out of old-world Europe, complete with dark wood-paneled walls, cozy beds, beautiful antiques, and a quiet elegance that seems startlingly out of place in hip, future-oriented Miami. Everything here is charming, from the parquet floors to the paddle fans; one-of-a-kind furnishings make each room special. Guests are treated to fresh fruit baskets upon arrival, evening turn-down service, and complimentary continental breakfast each morning.

Hotel Place St. Michel is small, but in no way is it insignificant.

Popular with visiting literati and cognoscenti, the hotel may well be the most romantic spot in the region. The ground-floor restaurant has an equally committed clientele and is widely regarded as one of Miami's finest French restaurants.

7. DOWNTOWN

Understandably, most Downtown hotels cater primarily to business travelers. But this hardly means tourists should overlook these well-located, good-quality accommodations. Miami's Downtown is small, so getting around is relatively easy. Locating here means staying between the beaches and the Grove, and being within minutes of the Bayside Marketplace and the Port of Miami.

Although business hotel prices are often high, and less prone to seasonal markdowns, quality and service are also of a high standard. Look for weekend discounts, when offices are closed and rooms often go empty.

EXPENSIVE

HOTEL INTER-CONTINENTAL MIAMI, 100 Chopin Plaza, Miami, FL 33131. Tel. 305/577-1000 or toll free 800/332-4246. Fax 305/577-0384. Telex 153127. 646 rms, including 34 suites. No-smoking rooms available. A/C MINIBAR TV TEL

$ Rates: Jan 16–Apr 20, $180–$240 single; $200–$260 double; Apr 21–Sept, $150–$210 single; $170–$230 double; Oct–Jan 15, $160–$220 single; $180–$240 double; year round, from $450 suite. Additional person $20. Weekend and other packages available. AE, CB, DC, MC, V. **Parking:** $10.

Hotel Inter-Continental Miami is both an architectural masterpiece and, arguably, the financial district's swankiest hotel. Both inside and out, the hotel boasts more marble than a mausoleum. But the hard stone is often warmed by colorful, homey touches. The five-story lobby features a marble centerpiece sculpture by Henry Moore and is topped by a pleasing skylight. Plenty of plants, palm trees, and brightly colored wicker chairs also add charm and enliven the otherwise stark space. Brilliant building and bay views add luster to already posh rooms that are outfitted with every convenience known to hoteldom.

Dining/Entertainment: 3 restaurants cover all price ranges and are complemented by 2 full-service lounges.

Services: 24-hour room service, laundry service, currency exchange, mobile phone, and car rental.

Facilities: Heated outdoor swimming pool, access to off-premises health spa, jogging track, gift shop, travel agency, and guest laundry room.

OMNI INTERNATIONAL HOTEL, 1601 Biscayne Blvd.,

Miami FL 33132. Tel. 305/374-0000 or toll free 800/THE-OMNI. Fax 305/374-0020. Telex 515005. 535 rms, including 50 suites. No-smoking rooms available. A/C MINIBAR TV TEL

$ Rates: Jan–Apr 15, $130–$150 single, $145–$165 double, from $185 suite; rest of the year, $120–$140 single, $135–$155 double, from $175 suite. Extra person $20. Senior discounts, weekend and other packages available. AE, CB, DC, DISC, MC, V. **Parking:** $8.50.

One of Downtown's best-known megahotels, this glass-and-chrome structure offers contemporary accommodations overlooking the Venetian Causeway and Biscayne Bay. Built in 1977 atop a large multistory shopping mall, the hotel has undergone several renovations and is still one of the luxury leaders in Miami's ever-growing hotel marketplace.

Rooms are traditionally decorated with modest but comfortable furnishings and deluxe fittings like bathroom telephones. But the Omni's most important asset is the 150-plus shopping complex below, a convenience that includes a popular multiplex cinema.

Dining/Entertainment: The Fish Market, the hotel's flagship lobby-level restaurant, is an excellent, elegant place for seafood. A coffee shop offers simpler meals and snacks. Lobby and poolside lounges.

Services: 24-hour room service, child care, currency exchange, car rental, laundry, free beach shuttle, and turn-down service.

Facilities: Fifth-floor heated outdoor pool, beauty salon, gift shop, shopping mall below.

SHERATON BRICKELL POINT MIAMI, 495 Brickell Ave., Miami, FL 33131. Tel. 305/373-6000 or toll free 800/325-3535. Fax 305/374-2279. Telex 6811701. 598 rms, including 14 suites. No-smoking rooms available. A/C TV TEL

$ Rates: Jan–Apr 14, $135–$155 single, $155–$175 double, from $295 suite; rest of the year, $119–$129 single, $129–$149 double, from $275 suite. Additional person $20. Children under 18 stay free in parents' room. Senior discounts, weekend and other packages available. AE, CB, DC, DISC, MC, V. **Parking:** $7.50.

This Downtown hotel's waterfront location is its greatest asset. Nestled between Brickell Park and Biscayne Bay, the Sheraton is set back from the main road and surrounded by a pleasant bayfront walkway.

Just as clean and reliable as other hotels in the Sheraton chain, Brickell Point has a pretty location and good water views from most of the rooms, as well as all the amenities you'd expect from a hostelry in this class. Its identical rooms are well furnished and comfortable.

Dining/Entertainment: Ashley's serves continental and American cuisine overlooking Biscayne Bay. The Coco Loco Club is an indoor/outdoor bar with a good happy-hour buffet and comedy nights.

Services: Room service, car rental, weekday laundry service.

Facilities: Outdoor heated swimming pool, gift shop.

MODERATE

HOWARD JOHNSON HOTEL, 200 SE 2nd Ave., Miami, FL 33131. Tel. 305/374-3000 or toll free 800/654-2000. Fax 305/374-3000 ext. 1504. 256 rms, including 2 suites. No-smoking rooms available. A/C TV TEL

$ Rates: Dec–Feb and July–Sept $80 single, $90 double; the rest of the year $90 single, $100 double. Suites $175–$250 year round. Additional person $10. Children under 18 free in parents' room. AE, CB, DC, DISC, MC, V. **Parking:** $5 per day.

One of the best-priced Downtown hotels is this excellently located property, right in the heart of the city. Guest rooms feature modern decor and are sparkling clean, but they are a far cry from luxurious. Facilities include a games room, seventh-floor pool and sun deck, and the American Café, a moderately priced restaurant.

8. CAMPING

LARRY AND PENNY THOMPSON PARK, 12451 SW 184th St., Miami, FL 33177. Tel. 305/232-1049.
$ Rates: $14 per site (up to 4 people). Open year round.

This inland park encompasses over 270 acres and includes a large freshwater lake for swimming, fishing, and boating. Laundry facilities and a convenience store are also on the premises.

The tent area is huge, and not separated into tiny sites. From Downtown, take U.S. 1 south to SW 184th Street. Turn right and follow signs for about 4 miles. The park entrance is at 125th Avenue.

9. LONG-TERM STAYS

If you plan on visiting Miami for a month, a season, or more, think about renting a room in a long-term hotel in South Miami Beach, or a condominium apartment in Miami Beach, Surfside, Bal Harbour, or Sunny Isles. Rents can be extremely reasonable, especially during the off-season. And there's no comparison to a tourist hotel in terms of the amount of space you get for the same buck. A short note to the chamber of commerce in the area in which you are looking will be answered with a list of availabilities (see "Information," in Chapter 2).

Many area real estate agents also handle short-term (minimum 1 month) rentals. These include: Century 21 Realty, 3100 NW 77th Ct., Miami, FL 33122; and Keys Company Realtors, 100 N. Biscayne Blvd., Miami, FL 33152 (tel. 305/371-3592).

MIAMI DINING

One of the best things about traveling is finding new restaurants and sampling new foods. Packed with an enormous array of foreign and inventive restaurants, Miami will not disappoint. Dozens of different specialty kitchens represent a world of cuisines, and all are available in a variety of price ranges. In addition to Chinese, French, Thai, and Italian eateries, there are, not surprisingly, many area dining rooms specializing in Cuban, Caribbean, and Latin American food. In fact, Miami boasts some of the best cooking those regions have to offer; high demand and good prices attract some of the world's best chefs and most discriminating gourmands.

Be sure to sample Miami's own regional American fare. Based on the California model, these inventive dishes rely heavily on seafood and citrus and are exemplified by creative recipes and fresh, local ingredients.

In addition to the indigenous foods mentioned under "Food and Drink," in Chapter 1, keep an eye out for flavorful tropical fruits like mangoes, papayas, and Surinam cherries. Shellfish, including rock shrimp, clams, oysters, and bay and deep-sea scallops (the former are smaller and sweeter) are also regular menu items.

Most hotels in Miami do not include breakfast in their room rates, but many in South Miami Beach do. These are usually good-sized buffets with fresh fruit, cold cuts, rolls, croissants, coffee, and fresh-squeezed orange juice. At lunch, many business-oriented restaurants offer entrées priced well below those served at dinner. Restaurants often serve dinner until midnight or later.

To help you choose where to eat, restaurants below are divided first by area, then by price, using the following guide: Very Expensive (over $40 per person); Expensive ($30 to $40 per person); Moderate ($20 to $30 per person); Inexpensive ($10 to $20 per person); and Budget (under $10 per person).

These categories reflect the price of the majority of dinner menu items and include an appetizer, main course, coffee, dessert, tax, and tip. Wine is not included. Whenever a special lunch menu is available—typically half the price of a full-course dinner—I have noted it in the heading of each listing.

1. MIAMI BEACH

EXPENSIVE

THE DINING GALLERIES, in the Fontainebleau Hilton Hotel, 4441 Collins Ave. Tel. 538-2000.
   Cuisine: CONTINENTAL. **Reservations:** Recommended.
$ Prices: Appetizers $8–$12, main courses $19–$27. AE, CB, DC, DISC, MC, V.
   Open: Dinner Tues–Sat 6pm–midnight; **Closed:** Sunday and Monday.

Ensconced deep inside Miami Beach's most showy hotel, the Dining Galleries' overindulgence seems somehow appropriate. This restaurant is a pleasant and surprising treat, featuring fine food and tasteful, if overdone, decor. There are plenty of statuary and antique objets d'art and a soothing piano/violin duo.

Nothing here is basic. Soups include pheasant consommé and fresh lobster bisque, and the appetizer list includes shrimp, salmon, and Beluga caviar. The disciplined kitchen regularly turns out beautifully arranged main dishes that look like still lifes, such as tender steak sautéed in herbed butter with medallions of lobster, quail egg, and brandied lobster bisque. It's really quite a mouthful. The menu is heavy on meat and fish—all dressed to the nines—and features the restaurant's flagship crown roast of lamb with fried pears and a homemade Florida citrus chutney.

 FROMMER'S SMART TRAVELER: RESTAURANTS

1. Go ethnic—the city has some great inexpensive ethnic dining.
2. Eat your main meal at lunch when prices are lower—and you can taste the cuisine at the gourmet hot spots for a fraction of the dinner prices.
3. Watch the booze—it can add greatly to the cost of any meal.
4. Look for early-bird specials, which are commonplace in and around the city.
5. Keep an eye out for fixed-price menus, two-for-one specials, and other money-saving deals.

DOMINIQUE'S, in the Alexander All-Suite Luxury Hotel, 5225 Collins Ave. Tel. 865-6500.
   Cuisine: FRENCH/CONTINENTAL. **Reservations:** Recommended, especially at dinner. Jackets requested.

0 ⌂⌂⌂⌂⌂ 2 mi

BAL HARBOUR
Collins Ave.
A1A
Broad Causeway
NORTH MIAMI
NE 135th St.
Miami Blvd.
NE 6th Ave.
Biscayne Park
Biscayne Blvd.
SURFSIDE
J.F. Kennedy Causeway
Morningside Park
Julia Tuttle Causeway
MIAMI BEACH
A1A
Alton Rd.
195
NE 79th St.
Biscayne Blvd.
NE 2nd Ave.
North Miami Ave.
27
NW 7th Ave.
NE 125th St.
NW 135th St.
Gratigny Dr.
NW 103rd St.
LITTLE HAITI
NW 17th Ave.
NW 22nd Ave.
NW 27th Ave.
NW 62nd St.
NW 54th St.
NW 95th St.
Biscayne Canal
Opa-Locka Canal
HIALEAH
Amtrak Terminal
E 25th St.
Hialeah Dr.
NW 36th St.
NW 20th St.
Gratigny Dr.
E 8th Ave.
E 4th Ave.
Palm Ave.
E 9th St.
Opa-Locka Airfield
W 29th St.
W 4th Ave.
Red Rd.
Okeechobee Rd.
Airport Expressway
27
Miami International Airport

American Classics 44
Aragon Cafe 24
Au Natural "Gourmet Pizza" 56
Bayside Seafood Restaurant 39
Biscayne Miracle Mile Cafeteria 28
The Bistro 8
Booking Table Café 61
Café Sci Sci 47
Cafe des Arts (Ocean Drive) 51
Café 94 41
Caffè Baci 30
Caffè Milano 46
Caribbean Room 71
Casa Juancho 22
Casona de Carlitos 53
Charade 29
Chef Allen's 1
Christy's 37
Crawdaddy's 40
Curry's 75
Dining Galleries 50
Dominique's 43
East Coast Fisheries 12
El Corral 25
El Torito 75
Estate Wines and Gourmet Foods 48
Fairmont Gardens Restaurant 64
A Fish Called Avalon 45
Fish Market 9
Fish Peddler 58
The Forge Restaurant 51
Hooters 10
House of India 32
Hy Vong Vietnamese Cuisine 23
I Tre Merli 49
Joe's Stone Crab Restaurant 66

Mark's Place ③
Melting Pot ②
Mezzanotte ⑤⑥
Miami Beach Pizza ㊼
Mike Gordon's ⑤
Monty's Bayshore Restaurant ⑭
Mr. Pizza ㊵
News Café ㊽
Pavillon Grill ㊱
Pineapples ㊸
Pita and Eats ㊹
Place for Steak ㊸
Restaurant St. Michel ㉚
Ristorante Tanino ㉟
Rusty Pelican ㊻
Sandbar ㉒
Señor Frog's ㊺
Strand ㊶
Sundays on the Bay ㊲
Thai Toni ㊳
Tijuana Joe's ㉟
Toni's New Tokyo Cuisine and Sushi Bar ㊳
Versailles ㊶
Wolfie Cohen's Rascal House ㊶
Wolfie's ㊻
Yo-Si Peking ㊽
YUCA ㊴
Zum Alten Fritz ⑦

$ Prices: Hors d'oeuvres $8–$11, main courses $20–$30. AE, CB, DC, MC, V.

Open: Dinner Sun–Thurs 5:30–11pm, Fri–Sat 5:30–midnight; lunch Mon–Sat 11:30am–3pm; breakfast Mon–Sat 7–11:30am; brunch Sun 11:30am–3:30pm during winter only.

Dominique's is one of Miami Beach's best restaurants. Exorbitant and elegant, the dining room is dressed with heavy antique furniture and Oriental rugs, and it boasts a good view of the Atlantic.

The menu spotlights a variety of wild game appetizers that are not just novel, but tasty, too. They include such unusual dishes as buffalo sausage, tender alligator scaloppine, and fresh diamondback rattlesnake salad. Still, it's the more traditional dishes like marinated rack of lamb chops and prime steak that keeps the regulars returning. Service is good, and the heavy French food, the menu's main feature, is consistently excellent.

THE FORGE RESTAURANT, 432 Arthur Godfrey Rd. (41st St.). Tel. 538-8533.

Cuisine: AMERICAN. **Reservations:** Required.

$ Prices: Appetizers $6–$9, main courses $18–$25. AE, DC, MC, V.

Open: Dinner Sun–Thurs 5–11:30pm, Fri–Sat 5pm–1am.

English oak paneling and Tiffany glass suggest high prices and haute cuisine, and that is exactly what you can expect from the remodeled Forge. Each elegant dining room possesses its own character, and features high ceilings, ornate chandeliers, and high-quality, conservative European artwork.

The Forge's huge American menu has a northern Italian bias, evidenced by a long list of creamy pasta appetizers. Equal attention is given to fish, veal, poultry, and beef dishes, many of which are prepared on the kitchen's all-important oak grill. Look for appetizers like oak-grilled tomatoes with mozzarella, or a simple oak-grilled main course of meat or fish. Finally, it is important to note that the Forge has one of Miami's best wine lists, encompassing about 280 pages selected from the on-premises wine cellar.

MODERATE

AMERICAN CLASSICS, in the Dezerland Surfside Beach Hotel, 8701 Collins Ave. Tel. 305/865-6661.

Cuisine: AMERICAN. **Reservations:** Accepted.

$ Prices: Main courses $11–$20; lunch about ⅓ less. AE, MC, V.

Open: Daily 7am–11pm.

Like the hotel where it's located, American Classics is a theme restaurant, planned around vintage cars and '50s memorabilia. Overlooking the hotel's pool, and the ocean beyond, diners sit at tables and booths made of dismantled Fords and Buicks, and order from a high-priced, like-minded menu. Simple seafood specials are given fancy names like shrimp scampi "Duesenberg," and "American

Graffiti" surf and turf. Chicken and steak round off the main dishes, which can then be followed by assorted desserts, or "tailgaters," as they are called. Meals here are competently prepared and presented but, like the hotel, American Classics appeals primarily to enthusiasts.

PLACE FOR STEAK, 1335 79th Street Causeway. Tel. 758-5581.

Cuisine: AMERICAN. **Reservations:** Accepted.

$ Prices: Appetizers $6–$8, main courses $17–$25. AE, CB, DC, MC, V.

Open: Dinner Mon–Thurs, 5pm–11pm, Fri–Sat 5pm–midnight, Sun 5pm–11pm. **Closed:** Jul–Aug.

Place for Steak is known for *huge* portions of prime aged New York sirloin steak, and other heavy foods served in a dark, richly decorated dining room. Appetizers include shrimp cocktail, clams casino, and a platter containing whitefish salad, chopped herring, nova and cream cheese, gefilte fish, and chopped chicken liver. Best perhaps, is the restaurant's nightly 58-foot hot-and-cold buffet—available from 5 to 10pm—that includes roast beef, rotisserie chicken, shrimp, fish, soups, salads, and dozens of other items. The spread is hard to beat at any price. The restaurant is located in North Bay Village, on the 79th Street Causeway between Miami Beach and the mainland.

YO-SI PEKING, in the Eden Roc Hotel, 4525 Collins Ave. Tel. 532-9060.

Cuisine: KOSHER CHINESE/THAI. **Reservations:** Accepted; required for Friday dinner. Jackets recommended.

$ Prices: Appetizers $4–$12, main courses $11–$25. AE, MC, V.

Open: Lunch Sat–Thurs noon–2:30pm, Fri noon–3pm; dinner Sun–Thurs 4–10:30pm. **Closed:** Fri.

⭐ Only in Miami. Well, maybe Miami, New York, and Israel. Yo-Si Peking is a *glatt kosher* (very kosher), Thai-influenced, gourmet Chinese restaurant. It is both expensive and elegant, featuring black lacquer tables with mother-of-pearl inlays, and custom-made silk-covered chairs imported from Hong Kong.

The cooking here is of the highest quality. Needless to say there are no pork dishes on the menu, a category that is substituted by creative veal selections. Unusual Thai twists include a boneless sautéed chicken curry, marinated and grilled beef satay, and a cold shredded chicken salad appetizer, fried in a spicy garlic sauce. Most of the other meals are traditional Chinese favorites, and all the dishes are untraditionally oil free. The Eden Roc Hotel is on the ocean at 45th Street.

INEXPENSIVE

PINEAPPLES, 530 Arthur Godfrey Rd. Tel. 532-9731.

Cuisine: AMERICAN. **Reservations:** Not accepted.

$ Prices: Salads and sandwiches $5–$6, main courses $8–$10. AE, MC, V.

Open: Daily 11am–10pm.

⭐ Half health-food store, half restaurant, Pineapples serves fresh juices, sandwiches, and a variety of menu items, either to take out or eat in. In the busy dining section, an over-worked staff distributes huge menus to patrons sitting at half dozen or so plain wooden tables set atop a clean red-tile floor. Both appetizers and main courses include a unique combination of American and Japanese-style foods, like buffalo chicken wings, miso soup, and California sushi rolls. Steamed vegetables and stir-fries are especially emphasized, as are meal-sized salads including vegetable, chicken, pasta, pineapple, and more. The restaurant is located in the middle of a row of boutiques on the south side of bustling Arthur Godfrey Road.

BUDGET

CURRY'S, 7433 Collins Ave. Tel. 866-1571.
   Cuisine: AMERICAN.
$ Prices: $8–$11, including appetizer, main course, dessert, and coffee. AE, MC, V.
   Open: Mon–Sat 4:30–9:30pm, Sun 4–9:30pm.
Established in 1937, this large dining room on the ocean side of Collins Avenue is one of Miami Beach's oldest restaurants. Neither the restaurant's name, nor the Polynesian wall decorations are indicative of the menu's offerings, which are straightforwardly American and reminiscent of the area's heyday. Broiled and fried fish dishes are available, but the best selections, including steak, chicken, and ribs, come off the open charcoal grill perched by the front window.

Prices are incredibly reasonable here, and all include an appetizer, soup, or salad, as well as a potato or vegetable, dessert, coffee or tea.

MIAMI BEACH PIZZA, 6954 Collins Ave. Tel. 866-8661.
   Cuisine: ITALIAN.
$ Prices: Large cheese pizza $9.50; pasta $5–$6. MC, V.
   Open: Mon–Thurs 11am–midnight, Fri–Sat 11am–1am, Sun noon–midnight.
New York–style pizza is delivered free to most Miami Beach hotels. The cheesy pies are inexpensive and good. Other menu items include veal parmigiana, chicken cacciatore, meatball sandwiches, beer, and soda.

2. SOUTH MIAMI BEACH — THE ART DECO DISTRICT

EXPENSIVE

CAFE DES ARTS, in the Locust Hotel, 918 Ocean Dr. Tel. 534-6267.

Cuisine: MEDITERRANEAN. **Reservations:** Recommended.
$ Prices: Appetizers $6–$7; main courses $14–$24. AE, DC, MC, V.
Open: Dinner Mon–Thurs, Sun 6–11:30pm; Fri–Sat 6pm–midnight. **Closed:** Two weeks in Aug.

Nestled among two of Ocean Drive's best examples of the art deco period, and in one of the oldest Mediterranean buildings in the district, Cafe des Arts has the distinction of being one of the first restaurants to open in this newly revitalized area.

The lighthearted art gallery/restaurant offers contemporary renditions of old favorites, like crabmeat ravioli and baked salmon with pink grapefruit, delivered to your table by artsy waiters. The Mediterranean menu is well planned, apropos of the Venetian Gothic architecture, and features creative selections of fish, pastas, and meats. Especially good is the chef's suggestion, "Ravioli Véronique," a crabmeat-stuffed ravioli bathed in a tangy, smooth seafood grape sauce. Other dishes make liberal use of porcini (mushrooms), sun-dried tomatoes, cilantro, Dijon mustard, and other tasty and trendy ingredients.

CAFFE MILANO, 850 Ocean Dr., South Miami Beach. Tel. 532-0707.

Cuisine: ITALIAN. **Reservations:** Recommended.
$ Prices: Appetizers $8–$15, pasta $10–$15, carpacci $11–$14, meat and fish $12–$23. Lunch about 30% less. AE, MC, V.
Open: Wed–Mon lunch 11am–5pm, dinner 7pm–midnight. **Closed:** Tues.

In South Beach, Italian restaurants seem to change as fast as the seasons, but hopefully Caffè Milano is here to stay. Even on a nice night the restaurant's requisite sidewalk seating might be passed-up for a table in the bustling dining room where hardwood floors and original abstract art can make you feel like you're eating in a SoHo gallery.

The eccentric young proprietors own two restaurants in Milan, and staff this kitchen with trained Italian chefs. Prosciutto, bresaola (air-dried beef), and other meat antipasti precede a good pasta menu (tortelli are recommended), and an unusual selection of carpacci (thinly sliced raw or warmed meats). Fish, chicken, and veal entrées are conservatively prepared according to traditional Italian recipes.

The pretty marble bar that lines an entire wall of the restaurant stocks a full line of beverages, including 15 grappas.

CRAWDADDY'S, 1 Washington Ave. Tel. 673-1708.

Cuisine: SEAFOOD. **Reservations:** Recommended.
$ Prices: Appetizers $5–$9, main courses $14–$20; lunch about half-price. AE, CB, DC, MC, V.
Open: Lunch Mon–Fri 11am–3pm; dinner Mon–Thurs 5–11pm, Fri–Sat 5pm–midnight, Sun 5–10pm; brunch Sun 11am–3:30pm.

The best thing about this restaurant is its location in South Pointe Park, at the southernmost tip of South Miami Beach. Here you can sit in front of Government Cut and watch the cruise and cargo ships slowly ease their way in and out of the Port of Miami.

Crawdaddy's is casual, with several small dining rooms and lots of window seats. Appetizers include Florida alligator (which is not an endangered species) and bacon-wrapped shrimp, as well as raw-bar selections. Fish, in various guises, is the house specialty, but the kitchen gets marks for its tender steak and veal, too.

I TRE MERLI, 1437 Washington Ave., South Miami Beach. Tel. 672-6702.
   Cuisine: ITALIAN. **Reservations:** Recommended.
$ **Prices:** Appetizers $7–$9, pasta $10–$12, meat and fish $16–$20. AE, CB, DC, MC, V.
   Open: Daily 6pm–1am.

Immediately trendy upon opening in 1982, SoBe's I Tre Merli is the spitting image of its popular sister restaurant in New York's SoHo district. Under an unusually high ceiling are exposed red brick walls lined with thousands of bottles of house-labeled wine. A second-floor loft overlooks the main dining room, where about 20 of the most coveted, and congested, tables are located.

The rather mainstream, strictly Italian menu augments all the traditional highlights like gnocchi (potato dumplings), spaghetti vongole (with clams), and veal scaloppine, with a few off-beat offerings like penne with artichokes, and shrimp and salmon with caviar sauce. While the food is not outstanding, it's good. And despite the restaurant's popularity, service is unhurried, as the staff knows that the ability to linger is what ultimately lures the patrons.

√**JOE'S STONE CRAB RESTAURANT,** 227 Biscayne St. Tel. 673-0365.
   Cuisine: SEAFOOD. **Reservations:** Not accepted. No shorts allowed.
$ **Prices:** $31.95 for jumbo crab claws; $23.95 for large claws. AE, CB, DC, MC, V.
   Open: Lunch Tues–Sat 11:30am–2pm; dinner nightly 5–10pm (until 11pm on Miami Heat home-game nights). **Closed:** Late May–early Oct.

⭐ Open since 1913 and steeped in tradition, this restaurant may be the most famous in Florida, as evidenced by ubiquitous long lines to get in. Other menu items are available, but to go to Joe's and not order stone crab is unthinkable. In fact, the restaurant is so identified with this single crustacean that it closes for the six months that the crabs are out of season. Stone crabs are available at other restaurants around Miami, but they just don't seem to taste as good as they do at the place where they were invented. If jumbo claws are available, splurge. *Be warned:* The wait can be long, and many readers have complained that the host gives preference to those who "tip" in advance. Lines are shortest Monday through Wednesday. The restaurant is at the corner of Biscayne Street and Washington Avenue.

MEZZANOTTE, 1200 Washington Ave. Tel. 673-4343.

Cuisine: ITALIAN. **Reservations:** Recommended.

$ Prices: Appetizers $7; main courses $12–$14 for pasta, $15–$25 for meat and fish. AE, CB, DC, MC, V.

Open: Dinner Sun–Thurs 6pm–midnight, Fri–Sat 6pm–2am.

Papparazzo charm is in full swing at this trendy-to-the-max corner bistro. Who cares if better food can be had at any number of places up the street? This is the place where the fashionable new wave can see and be seen. The food is decent enough; traditional antipasti are followed by good veal chops, competent pastas, and simple meat dishes.

The large room is undivided for the best sightlines and easy table hopping. An entire wall is mirrored so that no one's back is to the crowd, and a whip of neon around the ceiling keeps everyone bright enough to be seen. You might pass on dessert, but order a cappuccino; it's a small price to pay to linger.

MODERATE

CASONA DE CARLITOS, 2232 Collins Ave., South Miami Beach. Tel. 534-7013.

Cuisine: ARGENTINEAN. **Reservations:** Accepted.

$ Prices: Appetizers $7–$9; main courses $8–$10 for pasta, $9–$16 for meat and fish; lunch about half-price. AE, CB, DC, DISC, MC, V.

Open: Sun–Thurs noon–midnight, Fri–Sat noon–1am.

Except for its unusually large size, the outside of this corner storefront is rather unassuming. The dining room inside is not very fancy either, opting instead for a casual atmosphere that complements the unpretentious, traditional kitchen. Menus are available in English, Spanish, German, French, and Portuguese, and they contain dozens upon dozens of traditional dishes.

Shrimp ceviche and a delicately marinated eggplant are two of the more unusual appetizers. These can be followed by baked fish smothered in a blue cheese sauce, chicken oreganato in wine sauce, or any one of a number of grilled meats and homemade pastas. The restaurant is located on the corner of 23rd Street, across from the Holiday Inn.

FAIRMONT GARDENS RESTAURANT, in the Fairmont Hotel, 1000 Collins Ave. Tel. 531-0050.

Cuisine: ITALIAN/CONTINENTAL. **Reservations:** Recommended, especially on weekends.

$ Prices: Appetizers $4–$6; main courses $10–$12 for pasta, $14–$16 for meat and fish; brunch buffet $13. AE, CB, DC, MC, V.

Open: Dinner nightly 6pm–midnight; brunch Sun 11am–2:30pm; happy hour Mon–Fri 4–7pm.

The Fairmont's fancy, tropical outdoor courtyard is adjacent to a far less extravagant hotel, one block from the ocean in the art deco district. Brightly colored angled canvas canopies provide a light and airy roof, over a multilevel, pastel-colored dining area. Indoor tables are also available, but are far less desirable on warm nights.

Traditional hot and cold appetizers are bolstered by island-inspired selections like their hearts of palm salad, and a house lobster ravioli. Main dishes are equally adventurous, highlighted by boneless chicken served with sweet red pimientos and flamed in cognac and cream, conservatively prepared steaks, and a variety of fresh fish and pasta dishes. The Fairmont features live music (often calypso) nightly.

A FISH CALLED AVALON, in the Avalon Hotel, 700 Ocean Dr., South Miami Beach. Tel. 532-1727.

Cuisine: MIAMI REGIONAL. **Reservations:** Recommended.

$ Prices: Appetizers $6–$10, main courses $14–$22. AE, MC, V.

Open: Sun–Thurs 6–11pm, Fri–Sat 6pm–1am.

There is something about this well-placed Ocean Drive restaurant that's almost surreal; dramatic paintings are softened by intimate specular light, and mellow pastels counterpoint huge, imposing windows. White linen cloths and matching chair covers highlight each table's centerpiece: a single tropical Siamese fighting fish swimming around in a small glass bowl.

Chef Gillian Lowe changes the menu nightly, but the emphasis is always on fresh local fish, grilled or roasted, served with creative seasonal sauces. Steak and chicken are always on the menu, as are a variety of soups like chilled mango-peach and cream of carrot.

The Avalon's bar, a dramatically beautiful, intimately low-key lounge gets marks as one of the best little places to drink on the strip.

THE STRAND, 671 Washington Ave. Tel. 532-2340.

Cuisine: AMERICAN. **Reservations:** Accepted; recommended on winter weekends.

$ Prices: Appetizers $4–$7; main courses $5–$9 for burgers and sandwiches, $9–$18 for meat and fish; 3-course pretheater menu from 6–7pm $10. MC, V.

Open: Dinner Sun–Thurs 6pm–midnight, Fri–Sat 6pm–2am.

Not just another hot spot for trendies and young professionals, The Strand actually has culinary integrity, offering a well-planned menu punctuated by high-quality and fresh ingredients. Candlelit tables and a large, open-room layout are conducive to both intimate dining and table hopping. And, happily, this old standby is still a good place to see and be seen. The menu changes nightly, but both food and service are extremely consistent, and a number of well-priced and light items are always on offer and excellent homemade mousses and cakes are always freshly prepared. The house wine list contains some good vintages including several selections below $15.

THAI TONI, 890 Washington Ave. Tel. 538-8424.

Cuisine: THAI. **Reservations:** Accepted; recommended on weekends.

$ Prices: Appetizers $6–$7, main courses $7–$13 ($15–$18 for fish). AE, MC, V.

Open: Dinner Sun–Thurs 5:30–11pm, Fri–Sat 5:30pm–midnight.

✪ One of the best restaurants in Miami, Thai Toni sparkles with ultra-contemporary decor, traditional service, and really top-notch food. The most spectacular item on the menu, to both eye and palate, is the hot-and-spicy fish, a whole snapper fileted tableside and fried with a bold, spicy red sauce. Other top picks have tropical twists, like beef curry with coconut milk and avocado, and a tender, boneless crispy duck served with mushrooms, baby corn, water chestnuts, cashews, and a light wine sauce.

The casual atmosphere is complemented by taped jazz and the option of floor-cushion seating at traditional low tables.

TONI'S NEW TOKYO CUISINE AND SUSHI BAR, 1208 Washington Ave. Tel. 673-9368.
Cuisine: JAPANESE. **Reservations:** Accepted.

$ Prices: Appetizers $4–$6, main courses $8–$14, deluxe sushi combination $12. AE, MC, V.

Open: Dinner Sun–Thurs 6–11pm, Fri–Sat 6pm–midnight.

The same owners of Thai Toni, four blocks away, have created a modern restaurant that has become Miami's latest "in" spot for sushi. In addition to partaking of the usual Japanese staples, SoBe models, millionaires, and wanna-bes can also enjoy New Tokyo Cuisine, a combined Japanese and European cooking, exemplified at Toni's by such appetizers as sushi pizza, and main dishes like pasta with stir-fried shrimp and vegetables.

The single most important thing about sushi is freshness, and although cuts here are not unusually generous, high turnover assures top quality. The sushi bar, which is backed by a colorful, contemporary three-dimensional mosaic, features Miami specials like conch and crab nigiri and a "bagel roll" made of smoked salmon, cream cheese, and scallions.

INEXPENSIVE

BOOKING TABLE CAFE, 728 Ocean Dr., South Miami Beach. Tel. 672-3476.
Cuisine: INTERNATIONAL. **Reservations:** Not accepted.

$ Prices: Breakfasts $3–$6, salads and sandwiches $5–$7, meat and fish $9–$11. AE, MC, V.

Open: Daily 8am–2am.

Unlike many Ocean Drive restaurants that seem to put more emphasis on style than substance, this indoor/outdoor café next to the Colony Hotel boasts some of the best food on the strip. Despite the glass brick and European-style marble tables, its decor is considerably more low-key than that of its neighbors.

The colorful menu has everything from soups, sandwiches, and salads to lobsters and steaks. Breakfasts are popular, and include anything from a simple croissant to eggs, waffles, and quiches. The fish is particularly recommended during lunch and dinner, and like most of the other offerings, it's extremely well-priced. Cappuccino drinks and a small, well-chosen list of wines are also available.

TIJUANA JOE'S, 1201 Lincoln Rd. Tel. 674-1051.

Cuisine: MEXICAN. **Reservations:** Not accepted.

$ Prices: $5–$14. AE, MC, V.

Open: Sun–Thurs noon–11pm, Fri–Sat noon–midnight.

⭐ South Beach's best Mexican restaurant is not a phony American margarita chain; it's this simple corner Tex-Mex cantina. There is no separate bar here, just a dozen or so plastic tablecloth-topped tables, with white wooden chairs and a traditional menu. It's often crowded, as the place has caught on. Fajitas are the house specialty, and there is live Mexican music Tuesday through Saturday.

WOLFIE'S, 2038 Collins Ave. Tel. 538-6626.

Cuisine: JEWISH DELICATESSEN.

$ Prices: Omelets and sandwiches $4–$6, other dishes $5–$12. MC, V.

Open: 24 hours.

Wolfie's originally opened in 1947 and quickly became a popular spot. The decor is simple—two wood-paneled rooms, lined on one side by a glass-enclosed display case—and the food is New York traditional. The bowl of pickles and basket of assorted rolls and miniature danishes on each table tells you this is the real thing. Meals include cold smoked-fish platters, overstuffed sandwiches, stuffed cabbage, chicken-in-a-pot, and other favorites. Wolfie's is a relic of the past, but like other South Beach monuments, it has recently received a lease on life from the area's fashionable late-night crowd.

BUDGET

AU NATURAL "GOURMET" PIZZA, 1427 Alton Rd. Tel. 531-0666.

Cuisine: PIZZA.

$ Prices: Large pizza $9–$19. Cash only.

Open: Sun–Thurs 11am–midnight, Fri–Sat 11am–1am.

California-style pizza has reached the glitterati of SoBe, with concoctions like pesto-and-ricotta, or smoked-salmon and cream cheese. Other designer pies include the Mediterranean, with sautéed eggplant, artichoke hearts, and prosciutto, and barbecued chicken with marinated mesquite-smoked poultry. Au Natural also delivers pints of Brices Yogurt and Ben & Jerry's ice cream.

✓ NEWS CAFE, 800 Ocean Dr. Tel. 538-NEWS.

Cuisine: AMERICAN.

$ Prices: Continental breakfast $2.75, salads $4–$8, sandwiches $5–$7. AE, MC, V.

Open: 24 hours.

⭐ Of all the chic spots around trendy South Beach, News Café is tops. Excellent and inexpensive breakfasts and café fare are served at about 20 perpetually congested tables. Most of the seating is outdoors, and terrace tables are the most coveted. This is the regular meeting place for Ocean Drive's multitude of fashion photography crews and their models—who, incidently also occupy most of the area's hotel rooms. Delicious, and often health-oriented dishes include yogurt with fruit salad, various green salads, imported cheese and meat sandwiches, and a choice of quiches. Coffee (including espresso) and a variety of black and herbal teas are also available.

3. SURFSIDE, BAL HARBOUR & SUNNY ISLES

INEXPENSIVE

WOLFIE COHEN'S RASCAL HOUSE, 17190 Collins Ave. Tel. 947-4581.
Cuisine: JEWISH/DELICATESSEN.
$ Prices: Omelets and sandwiches $4–$6, other dishes $5–$10.
Open: Daily 7am–1:45am.

Thirty-eight years young and still going strong, this historical, nostalgic culinary extravaganza is one of Miami Beach's greatest traditions. Simple tables and booths as well as plenty of patrons, fill the airy, 425-seat dining room. The menu is as huge as the portions, which include corned beef, schmaltz herring, brisket, kreplach, chicken soup, and other authentic Jewish staples. Take-out service is available.

BUDGET

MR. PIZZA, 18120 Collins Ave., Sunny Isles. Tel. 932-6915.
Cuisine: ITALIAN
$ Prices: $3.50–$4.50 for sandwiches, $4–$6 for pastas, $8 for a large pizza. AE, CB, MC, V.
Open: Daily 11:30am–2am.

Darkwood walls and red-and-white-checked tablecloths surround the restaurant's open kitchen. Mr. Pizza specializes in New York–style Sicilian and Neapolitan pies. Good pastas, subs, and calzones are also available. Best of all, they deliver—from 71st Street to the Dade County line—for $1.

4. KEY BISCAYNE

EXPENSIVE

RUSTY PELICAN, 3201 Rickenbacker Causeway. Tel. 361-3818.
Cuisine: CONTINENTAL. **Reservations:** Recommended.

$ Prices: Appetizers $4–$8, main courses $16–$20; lunch about half-price. AE, CB, DC, MC, V.

⭐ The Pelican's private tropical walkway leads over a lush waterfall into one of the most romantic dining rooms in the city, located right on beautiful blue-green Biscayne Bay. The restaurant's windows look out over the water onto the sparkling stalactites of Miami's magnificent Downtown. Inside, quiet wicker paddle fans whirl overhead and saltwater fish swim in pretty tableside aquariums.

The restaurant's surf-and-turf menu features conservatively prepared prime steaks, veal, shrimp, and lobster. The food is good, but the atmosphere is even better, especially at sunset when the western view is especially awesome.

SUNDAYS ON THE BAY, 5420 Crandon Blvd. Tel. 361-6777.

Cuisine: AMERICAN. **Reservations:** Accepted; recommended for Sunday brunch.

$ Prices: Appetizers $6–$7, main courses $15–$24; lunch about half-price; Sunday brunch $15.95. AE, CB, DC, MC, V.

Open: Lunch Mon–Sat 11:30am–5pm; dinner Mon–Wed, and Sun 5pm–2am, Thurs–Sat 5pm–2:30am; brunch Sun from 10:30am.

Steak, chicken, pasta, veal . . . it's all on the menu here. But fish is the specialty, and all the local favorites—grouper, tuna, snapper, and so on—are broiled, boiled, or fried to your specifications. Competent renditions of classic shellfish dishes such as oysters Rockefeller, shrimp scampi, and lobster fra diablo are also recommendable. Sundays is a fantastically fun tropical bar, with an upbeat, informal atmosphere. Sunday brunches are particularly popular, when a buffet the size of Bimini attracts the city's late-rising in-crowd.

The lively bar stays open all week until 2:30am, and live reggae music is featured Thursday through Saturday from 9pm and all day Sunday. For more information, see Chapter 10, "Miami Nights."

MODERATE

THE CARIBBEAN ROOM, in the Sheraton Royal Biscayne Hotel, 555 Ocean Dr. Tel. 361-5775.

Cuisine: SEAFOOD/TROPICAL. **Reservations:** Accepted; recommended for Friday dinner.

$ Prices: Appetizers $3–$7, main courses $13–$16, Friday night all-you-can-eat $25. AE, MC, V.

Open: Nightly 6–11pm.

A good pick any night of the week, The Caribbean Room becomes the find of the city every Friday, when it features a truly fantastic seafood extravaganza. On this night the restaurant features an all-you-can-eat fin-and-claw buffet, complete with mussels, clams, oysters, lobsters, shrimp, and other seafood delights. A roast is also on the table for landlubbers, as is a good selection of vegetables and homemade breads. The all-inclusive price includes dessert.

INEXPENSIVE

BAYSIDE SEAFOOD RESTAURANT AND HIDDEN COVE BAR, 3501 Rickenbacker Causeway. Tel. 361-0808.

Cuisine: SEAFOOD.

$ Prices: Raw clams or oysters $7 per dozen; appetizers, salads, and sandwiches $4.50–$6; platters $7–$13. AE, MC, V.

Open: Sun–Thurs noon–11pm, Fri–Sat noon–midnight.

Known by locals as "The Hut," this ramshackle restaurant and bar is a laid-back eating and drinking place with an especially pleasant outdoor tiki hut and terrace. Good soups and salads make heavy use of local fish, conch, clams, and other seafood. Chicken wings, hamburgers, and sandwiches are also available, as is a long list of finger foods to complement the drinks and the view. On weekends, the Hut features their house band playing live reggae and calypso.

THE SANDBAR, in the Silver Sands Motel, 301 Ocean Dr. Tel. 361-5441.

Cuisine: AMERICAN.

$ Prices: Main courses $7–$11; lunch about half-price. AE, MC, V.

Open: Breakfast Sat–Sun 8–11am; lunch daily 11:30am–3:30pm; dinner nightly 5–10pm.

The Sandbar is a Miami institution, boasting Key Biscayne's best beach location at any price. Situated oceanfront, in a motel that would hardly get a second look if it were anywhere else, the restaurant features fish, burgers, and salads, and a deck right on the beach. Extremely informal, patrons regularly dine barefoot, having just come off the beach. Eggs and omelets are served for breakfast on the weekends; otherwise, grouper sandwich, the house specialty, should be ordered.

5. DOWNTOWN

VERY EXPENSIVE

PAVILLON GRILL, in the Inter-Continental Hotel, 100 Chopin Plaza. Tel. 577-1000.

Cuisine: MIAMI REGIONAL. **Reservations:** Recommended.

$ Prices: Appetizers $7–$12, main courses $18–$24. AE, CB, DC, MC, V.

Open: Dinner Mon–Sat 6–11pm.

Private club by day, deluxe restaurant by night, the Pavillon Grill maintains its air of exclusivity, with leather sofas and an expensive salon setting. Dark green marble columns divide the spacious dining room, while well-spaced booths and tables provide comfortable seating and a sense of privacy. The menu features both heavy club-room fare and lighter dishes prepared with a masterful Miami Regional hand. Prices here are rounded off to the highest dollar and spelled out in lieu of numerals—a practice that seems a touch pretentious, until your food arrives.

Standouts include the chilled trout appetizer, stuffed with seafood and basil, and an unusual grilled shrimp cocktail with pineapple relish and a citrus-flavored lobster mayonnaise. Skillfully prepared, adventurous dishes include boneless quail Louisiana, stuffed with oysters and andouille sausage. Meat, fish, and chicken dishes are abundant, as are a host of creative pastas, including an artichoke, garlic, truffles, and a cheese-stuffed ravioli that redefines the limits of these Italian tiny turnovers. The Hotel Inter-Continental is located adjacent to the Bayside Marketplace.

EXPENSIVE

THE FISH MARKET, in the Omni International Hotel, 1601 Biscayne Blvd. Tel. 374-0000.
Cuisine: SEAFOOD. **Reservations:** Recommended.
$ Prices: Appetizers $6–$8; main courses $17–$22; AE, CB, DC, MC, V.
Open: Lunch Mon–Fri 11:30am–2:30pm; dinner Mon–Sat 6:30–11pm.

One of the city's most celebrated seafood restaurants is this under-stated, elegant dining room right in the heart of the city. Located in an unassuming corner, just off the Omni International Hotel's fourth-floor lobby, the restaurant is both spacious and comfortable, featuring high ceilings, reasonable prices and a sumptuous dessert table centerpiece.

Don't overlook the appetizers here, which include a meaty Mediterranean-style seafood soup and a delicate yellowfin tuna carpaccio. Local fish prepared and presented simply is always the menu's main feature; sautéed or grilled, it's this guide's recommendation. The Omni International Hotel is just north of Downtown at the corner of 16th Street.

MODERATE

EAST COAST FISHERIES, 360 W. Flagler St. Tel. 373-5516.
Cuisine: SEAFOOD. **Reservations:** Recommended.
$ Prices: Appetizers and grazing $4–$8, main courses $9–$15, most under $14; Lunch from $7. AE, DISC, MC, V.
Open: Daily 10am–10pm.

East Coast Fisheries is a no-nonsense retail market and restaurant, offering a terrific variety of the freshest fish available. The dozen or so plain wood tables are surrounded by refrigerated glass cases filled with snapper, salmon, mahi-mahi, trout, tuna, crabs, oysters, lobsters and the like. The menu is absolutely huge, and features every fish imaginable, cooked the way you want it—grilled, fried, stuffed, Cajun-style, Florentine, hollandaise, blackened. It's a pleasure to walk around and ask questions about the many local fishes before choosing. Service is fast. But good prices and an excellent product still mean long lines on weekends. Highly recommended. The restaurant is located on the Miami River, at the edge of West Flagler Street.

LAS TAPAS, in the Bayside Marketplace, 401 Biscayne Blvd. Tel. 372-2737.

Cuisine: SPANISH. **Reservations:** Accepted.

$ Prices: Tapas $4–$7, main courses $12–$19; lunch about half-price. AE, CB, DC, DISC, MC, V.

Open: Sun–Thurs 11:30am–midnight, Fri–Sat 11:30am–1am.

Occupying a large corner of Downtown's Bayside Marketplace, glass-wrapped Las Tapas is a pretty and fun place to dine in a laid-back, easy atmosphere.

Tapas, small dishes of Spanish delicacies, are the featured fare here. Good chicken, veal, and seafood main dishes are on the menu, but it's more fun to taste a variety of the restaurant's tapas. The best include: shrimp in garlic, smoked pork shank with Spanish sausage, baby eel in garlic and oil, and chicken sauté with garlic and mushroom.

An open kitchen in front of the entrance greets diners with succulent smells. The long dining room is outlined in red Spanish stone and decorated with hundreds of hanging hams. Bayside Marketplace is on Biscayne Bay in the middle of Downtown.

ZUM ALTEN FRITZ, 1840 NE 4th Ave. Tel. 530-8640.

Cuisine: GERMAN. **Reservations:** Accepted.

$ Prices: Appetizers $3–$8, main courses $8–$17, half-liter of beer $5. CB, DC, MC, V.

Open: Lunch Mon–Fri 11am–3pm, dinner Mon–Sat 5pm–11pm.

Offering a veritable survey of authentic German cooking, this excellent "essenhaus" is known for its homemade wursts and its on-site brewery, which operates during winter months. The wieners, flavored with veal, paprika, or garlic, are all served with homemade sauerkraut, mashed potatoes, and a hearty German mustard. A number of schnitzels are also available, including an unusual vegetarian cheese variety.

Live oom-pah music is performed every Wednesday, Friday, and Saturday night. See Chapter 10, "Miami Nights," for more information. The restaurant is located one block east of Biscayne Boulevard, 3 blocks north of the Omni International Hotel.

BUDGET

HOOTERS, in the Bayside Marketplace, 401 Biscayne Blvd. Tel. 371-3004.

Cuisine: AMERICAN.

$ Prices: $5–$12. AE, MC, V.
   Open: Mon–Thurs 11am–midnight, Fri–Sat 11am–1am, Sun 11am–10pm.

Hooters' hiring policy seems to mean buxom waitresses in midriff tops, giving it a reputation as one of the most sexist restaurants in Florida. Despite this (or because of it, depending on your perspective), the casual second-floor restaurant does offer good, inexpensive meals, and a great terrace overlooking Bayside Marketplace and Biscayne Bay. Large chicken, fish, and meat burgers are served with massive quantities of beer. Local fraternity brothers are a common sight here, huddled around mountains of chicken wings and full pitchers. Hooters is on the second floor of the Marketplace's north pavilion. There is a second location in Coconut Grove's Cocowalk, 3015 Grand Ave. (tel. 442-6004).

6. LITTLE HAVANA

Southwest 8th Street, also known as Calle Ocho, is the center of Little Havana, home to a large number of Cuban immigrants. In addition to shops and markets, this area contains some of the world's best Cuban and Latin American restaurants, treasures that help make the city a unique and wonderful place to visit.

Most restaurants list menu items in English for the benefit of "norteamericano" diners. Here's a sample of what you can expect:

Arroz con pollo   Roast chicken served with pimento-seasoned yellow rice.
Picadillo   A rich stir-fry of ground meat, brown gravy, peas, pimentos, raisins, and olives.
Platanos   A deep-fried, soft, mildly sweet banana.
Pan cubano   This is the famous long, white crusty Cuban bread that should be ordered with every meal.
Ropa vieja   Literally meaning "old clothes," this is a delicious stringy beef stew.
Café cubano   Very strong black coffee, served in thimble-size cups with lots of sugar. A real eye-opener.
Palomilla   Similar to American minute steak, thinly sliced beef usually served with onions, parsley, and a mountain of french fries.
Camarones   Shrimp.
Paella   A Spanish dish of chicken, sausage, seafood, and pork mixed with saffron rice and peas. Very good.
Fabada asturiana   A hearty black bean and sausage soup.
Tapas   A general name for Spanish-style hors d'oeuvres; served in grazing-size portions.

MODERATE

CASA JUANCHO, 2436 SW 8th St. Tel. 642-2452.

Cuisine: SPANISH/CUBAN. **Reservations:** Recommended; not accepted Fri–Sat after 8pm.

$ Prices: Tapas $6–$8, main courses $11–$20; lunch about half price. AE, CB, DC, MC, V.

Open: Mon–Fri noon–midnight, Sat–Sun noon–1am.

Perhaps one of Miami's finest Hispanic restaurants, Casa Juancho offers an ambitious menu of excellently prepared main dishes and tapas. Except for a few outstanding entrées like roast suckling pig, baby eels in garlic and olive oil, and Iberian-style snapper, diners would be wise to stick exclusively to tapas, smaller dishes of Spanish "finger food." Some of the best include mixed seafood vinaigrette, fresh shrimp in hot garlic sauce, and fried calamari rings.

The several dining rooms are decorated with traditional Spanish furnishings and are enlivened nightly by strolling Spanish musicians.

INEXPENSIVE

HY VONG VIETNAMESE CUISINE, 3458 SW 8th St. Tel. 446-3674.

Cuisine: VIETNAMESE. **Reservations:** Accepted.

$ Prices: Appetizers $2–$3.50, main courses $8–$12. Cash only.

Open: Tues–Sun 5:30–10:30pm. **Closed:** 2 weeks in Aug.

Similar in style, if not taste, to Thai food, Vietnamese cuisine combines the best of Asian and French cooking with spectacular results. Food at Hy Vong is terrific. Appetizers include small, tightly packed Vietnamese spring rolls, and kimchee, a spicy, fermented cabbage. Star entrées include pastry-enclosed chicken with a watercress cream-cheese sauce, and fish in a tangy mango sauce.

The dining room itself is just a small, sparsely decorated, wood-paneled room. Located in the heart of Little Havana, it attracts an interesting and mixed crowd.

BUDGET

VERSAILLES, 3555 SW 8th St. Tel. 444-0240.

Cuisine: CUBAN.

$ Prices: Soup and salad $2–$5, main courses $5–$8. DC, MC, V.

Open: Mon–Thurs 8am–2am, Fri 8am–3:30am, Sat 8am–4:30am, Sun 9am–2am.

Versailles is the area's most celebrated diner especially after 10pm. The restaurant sparkles with glass, chandeliers, and mirrors, and moves at a quick pace to please patrons at tables and counters and in take-out lines. If you're looking for inexpensive, authentic Cuban cuisine, look no further. Nothing fancy here, just straightforward food from the home country. The menu is a veritable survey of Cuban cooking and includes specialties like Moors and Christians (flavorful black beans with white rice), ropa vieja, and fried whole fish.

7. NORTH DADE

VERY EXPENSIVE

CHEF ALLEN'S, 19088 NE 29th Ave., North Miami Beach. Tel. 935-2900.
  Cuisine: MIAMI REGIONAL. **Reservations:** Accepted.
$ Prices: Appetizers $7–$10, main courses $20–$27. AE, MC, V.
  Open: Sun–Thurs 6–10:30pm, Fri–Sat 6–11pm.

If one needs any evidence that Miami Regional cuisine is strongly influenced by California cooking, look no further than Chef Allen's. Owner/chef Allen Susser, of New York's Le Cirque fame, has built a classy but relaxed restaurant with art deco furnishings, a glass-enclosed kitchen, and a hot-pink swirl of neon surrounding the dining room's ceiling.

The delicious homemade breadsticks are enough to hold you, but don't let them tempt you away from an appetizer that may include lobster-and-crab cakes served with strawberry ginger chutney, or baked Brie with spinach, sun-dried tomatoes, and pine nuts. Served by an energetic, young staff, favorite main dishes include crisp roast duck with cranberry sauce, and mesquite-grilled Norwegian salmon with champagne grapes, green onions, and basil spaetzle. Local fish dishes, in various delectable guises, and homemade pastas are always on the menu. An extensive wine list is well chosen and features several good buys. The restaurant is on the mainland at 190th Street, near the Dade County Line.

EXPENSIVE

MARK'S PLACE, 2286 NE 123rd St., North Miami. Tel. 893-6888.
  Cuisine: MIAMI REGIONAL. **Reservations:** Recommended.
$ Prices: Appetizers $6–$9, main courses $10–$15 for pasta and pizza, $16–$20 for meat and fish; lunch about half-price. AE, MC, V.
  Open: Lunch Mon–Fri noon–2:30pm; dinner Mon–Thurs 6–10:30pm, Fri–Sat 6–11pm, Sun 6–10pm.

Attracting an upscale but leisurely crowd, this restaurant's claim to fame is its owner/chef, Mark Militello, an extraordinarily gifted artist who works primarily with fresh, natural, local ingredients. A smart, modern bistro, Mark's Place shines with off-white walls, an aquamarine ceiling, contemporary glass sculptures, and a friendly, open kitchen. Each table has its own pepper mill, and fresh, home-baked bread.

Mark's food is extremely inspired, often unusual, and rarely misses the mark. Appetizers include oak-grilled mozzarella and prosciutto, curry-breaded fried oysters, and an unusual petite pizza topped with smoked chicken and Monterey Jack cheese. The best main dishes are braised black grouper, Florida conch stew, or flank steak in a sesame marinade. Try one of Mark's suggestions. Desserts like Icky Sticky Coconut Pudding are equally unusual, and baked with the same originality as the rest of the menu.

MODERATE

THE FISH PEDDLER, 8699 Biscayne Blvd. Tel. 757-0648.
   Cuisine: SEAFOOD. **Reservations:** Accepted.
$ Prices: Appetizers $2–$4, main courses $9–$15.
   Open: Tues–Sun 5–10pm.

If it were owned and managed by anyone else, this modest restaurant would hardly deserve a second look. But seafood-king Mike Gordon has made the Fish Peddler his latest hobby, and it's one of the tastiest restaurants around. There is no view and little atmosphere, but knowledgeable locals still pack the place nightly. Dinners are prepared in an open, diner-style kitchen, and served by friendly, similarly styled waitresses. Appetizers include some excellent chowders (black grouper included) and fresh clam dishes. Whole fish are regularly available, and everything is fresh and cooked to order right before your eyes. Say "hi" to Mike, he's the oldest and most energetic man in the place, and always on the premises.

MIKE GORDON'S, 1201 NE 79th St. Tel. 751-4429.
   Cuisine: SEAFOOD. **Reservations:** Not accepted.
$ Prices: Appetizers $3–$6, main courses $13–$17; lunch about half-price. AE, CB, DC, MC, V.
   Open: Daily noon–10pm.

Over 40 years have passed and this Miami institution is now managed by Mike Gordon's sons, but it still offers seafood as fresh as the fish market next door. This is a traditional pier restaurant in a Cape Cod kind of way, with dark wood beams, ceiling fans, and pelicans playing on the docks outside. The huge menu features lobsters, crabs, and the usual array of meaty local fish, traditionally prepared and served with drawn butter and french fries. The best part of this dining experience is the restaurant's interesting location, directly on the Intercoastal Waterway. No matter what time you come, you'll likely have to wait for a table. But the bar is long, and there are few better places in Miami to pass the time. The restaurant is located at the foot of the mainland side of the 79th Street Causeway.

A second restaurant has opened in the Four Ambassadors building, 801 South Bayshore Drive, Coconut Grove (tel. 577-4202).

INEXPENSIVE

THE MELTING POT, in Sunny Isles Plaza shopping center, 3143 NE 163rd St., North Miami Beach. Tel. 947-2228.
   Cuisine: FONDUE. **Reservations:** Accepted.
$ Prices: Main courses $9–$10 for cheese fondue, $11–$16 for meat and fish fondues. AE, MC, V.

Open: Dinner Sun–Thurs 5:30–11pm, Fri–Sat 5:30pm–midnight.

Dipping your own chunks of bread into pots of sizzling cheese is certainly a different dining experience. This traditional dish is supplemented by combination meat-and-fish dinners, which are served with one of almost a dozen different sauces. The Melting Pot's variation on Swiss fondue is a good, alternative dinner decision. But best, perhaps, is dessert: chunks of pineapple, bananas, apples, and cherries that you dip into a creamy chocolate fondue. No liquor is served here, but the wine list is extensive, and beer is available. The restaurant is located on the north side of 163rd Street, between U.S. 1 and Collins Avenue.

A second Melting Pot is located at 9835 SW 72nd Street (Sunset Drive), Kendall (tel. 279-8816).

8. CORAL GABLES & ENVIRONS

VERY EXPENSIVE

CHRISTY'S, 3101 Ponce de Leon Blvd. Tel. 446-1400.
　　Cuisine: AMERICAN. **Reservations:** Essential.
$ Prices: Appetizers $4–$7, main courses $17–$25; lunch about half-price. AE, CB, DC, MC, V.
　　Open: Lunch Mon–Fri 11:30am–4pm; dinner Sun–Fri 4–10:45pm, Sat 5–11:45pm.

Decorated in an elegant, Victorian style, Christy's is one of Coral Gables' most expensive trendy establishments. Frequented by a power-tie crowd, this New American eatery is known primarily for its generous cuts of thick, juicy steaks and ribs. "Big" appears to be the chef's chief instruction; the prime rib is so thick even a small cut weighs about a pound. New York strip, filet mignon, Chateaubriand . . . it's all on the menu here, and all steaks are fully aged without chemicals or freezing. Entrées are served with a jumbo Caesar salad and a baked potato. Seafood, veal, and chicken dishes are also available.

EXPENSIVE

ARAGON CAFE, in the Colonnade Hotel, 180 Aragon Ave. Tel. 448-9966.
　　Cuisine: MIAMI REGIONAL. **Reservations:** Recommended. Jackets required.
$ Prices: Appetizers $6–$8, main courses, $15–$22; lunch about half-price. AE, DC, MC, V.
　　Open: Breakfast daily 6:30–10am; lunch Mon–Fri 11:30am–3pm; dinner Mon–Sat 6–11pm.

Like the hotel itself, the handcrafted mahogany and marble Aragon

Café exudes a quiet elegance with an international flair. The 85-seat restaurant features period furniture and a formal atmosphere that's as elegant as the cuisine.

Appetizers include such delicacies as blue-crab cakes with fried and shredded leeks and radicchio-wrapped lobster. Seafood is the house specialty, and salmon is the fish of choice; several gutsy preparations each claim completely individual flavors. Other main choices include Muscovy duck with duck sausage and various veal selections. For dessert, a lemon torte with raspberry sauce literally takes the cake. Aragon Café is not cheap, but it's highly recommended as one of the best restaurants of its kind in Miami.

THE BISTRO, 2611 Ponce de Leon Blvd. Tel. 442-9671.

Cuisine: FRENCH. **Reservations:** Accepted.

$ Prices: Appetizers $5–$10, lunch $4–$14, main courses $16–$26. AE, CB, DC, MC, V.

Open: Lunch Tues–Fri 11:30am–2pm, dinner Tues–Thurs 6–10:30pm, Fri–Sat 6–11pm. **Closed:** Monday.

The Bistro's intimate atmosphere is heightened by soft lighting, 19th-century European antiques and prints, and an abundance of flowers atop crisp white tablecloths.

Co-owners Ulrich Sigrist and André Barnier keep a watchful eye over their experienced kitchen staff, which regularly dishes out artful French dishes with an international accent. Look for the terrine maison, a country-style veal-and-pork appetizer that is the house specialty. Common French bistro fare like escargots au Pernod and coquilles St-Jacques are prepared with uncommon spices and accoutrements, livening a rather typical continental menu. Especially recommended is the roasted duck with honey mustard sauce and the chicken breasts in a mild curry sauce, each served with fried bananas and pineapple.

CAFFE BACI, 2522 Ponce de Leon Blvd. Tel. 442-0600.

Cuisine: ITALIAN. **Reservations:** Recommended for dinner.

$ Prices: Appetizers $6–$7; main courses $12–$13 for pasta, $14–$19 for meat and fish; lunch about half-price. AE, CB, DC, DISC, MC, V.

Open: Lunch Mon–Fri 10:30am–2:30pm; dinner Sun–Thurs 6–11pm, Fri–Sat 6–11:30pm.

The most stylish bistro in Miami comes in the form of this tiny, classy restaurant with great food at reasonable prices. Soft pink pastel walls, covered with Roman architectural prints, reflect off a pretty, tin can-shaped gold-metal ceiling. A typical meal, served by courteous, professional waiters, might start with fresh tuna carpaccio, or a marinated medley of artichoke hearts, mushrooms, tomatoes, and zucchini. Main courses include homemade pastas with sweet Italian sausages, porcini (mushrooms), basil and tomato sauces, as well as a number of succulent, marinated meats and fish topped with tomato and cream sauces and any number of aromatic herbs.

If you have difficulty choosing from the terrific menu—and you will—trust suggestions made by the boisterous proprietor, Domenico Diana.

CHARADE, 2900 Ponce de Leon Blvd. Tel. 448-6077.

Cuisine: FRENCH/SWISS. **Reservations:** Recommended.

$ Prices: Appetizers $5–$7, main courses $15–$20; lunch about half-price. AE, CB, DC, MC, V.

Open: Lunch Mon–Fri 11:30am–3pm; dinner Sun–Thurs 6–11pm. Fri–Sat 6pm–midnight.

A historic Coral Gables low-rise is the setting for this restaurant with soft piano music, a romantic courtyard, and excellent French/Swiss cuisine. More formal than Kaleidoscope, its cousin in Coconut Grove (see below), Charade has a gentleman's club feel with wooden ceilings and furniture and old-world portraits on the walls.

Like many imaginative continental restaurants, eating here is a real culinary experience. Masterful entrées include shrimp and chicken jambalaya, duckling with orange, kiwi, ginger, and Grand Marnier, and Chateaubriand.

LE FESTIVAL, 2120 Salzedo St. Tel. 442-8545.

Cuisine: FRENCH. **Reservations:** Required for dinner.

$ Prices: Appetizers $5–$8, main courses $16–$20; about half-price for lunch. AE, CB, DC, MC, V.

Open: Lunch Mon–Fri 11:45am–2:30pm; dinner Mon–Thurs 6–10:30pm, Fri–Sat 6–11pm. **Closed:** Sun and Sept–Oct.

Le Festival's contemporary, sharp pink awning hangs over one of Miami's most traditional Spanish-style buildings; hinting at the unusual combination of cuisine and decor that awaits inside. In fact, the snazzy, modern dining rooms, which are enlivened with New French features and furnishings, belie the traditional features that are the highlights of a well-planned menu.

Shrimp and crab cocktails, fresh pâtés, and an unusual cheese soufflé are star starters. Both meat and fish are either simply seared with herbs and spices, or doused in the wine and cream sauces that have made the French famous. Dessert can be a delight with a modest amount of foresight. Grand Marnier and chocolate soufflés are individually prepared, and must be ordered at the same time as the entrées. A wide selection of other homemade sweets should also entice you to leave room for dessert.

Le Festival is located 5 blocks north of Miracle Mile, in an area slightly removed from other Coral Gables restaurants.

RESTAURANT ST. MICHEL, in the Hotel Place St. Michel, 162 Alcazar Ave. Tel. 444-1666.

Cuisine: FRENCH/MEDITERRANEAN. **Reservations:** Recommended.

$ Prices: Appetizers $6–$8; main courses $14–$16 for pasta, $18–$22 for meat and fish. AE, CB, MC, V.

Open: Lunch Mon–Sat 11am–4pm; dinner Sun–Thurs 6–10:30pm, Fri–Sat 5–11:30pm; brunch Sun 11am–2:30pm.

⭐ One of the most subtly sensuous restaurants in Miami is, quite appropriately, located in the city's most romantic hotel. Art deco chandeliers, hardwood floors, delicate antiques, and armfuls of flowers re-create the feeling of a quaint 1930s Parisian café.

The creative menu complements the artful decor with its metropolitan French coast cuisine. Scallop ceviche and grilled, marinated lamb highlight the hors d'oeuvres, while prosciutto-stuffed veal chops, and an excellent couscous lead the winning entrées. Goose, rabbit, venison, and other unusual meats often grace the tables, topped with tangy fruit sauces and spicy wine creations. A special six-course dinner is prepared and priced nightly.

YUCA, 148 Giralda. Tel. 444-4448.

Cuisine: CUBAN/AMERICAN. **Reservations:** Recommended.

$ Prices: Appetizers $5–$7, main courses $15–$20. AE, CB, DC, DISC, MC, V.

Open: Lunch Mon–Fri noon–2:30pm; dinner nightly 6–11pm.

⭐ One of Miami's most celebrated ethnic eateries, Yuca features an exciting menu that bridges traditional Cuban ingredients with the latest international influences. Fun is always the dish of the day, and not just due to the restaurant's catchy name, an anagram for Young Upscale Cuban-American. The kitchen is strictly gourmet, but one can't help but think that the colorful menu and decor were created with tongue firmly in cheek. Star entrées include barbecue ribs with a tangy guava sauce, and grilled kosher chicken with garlic, lime, and thyme. A rear-wall mural of smartly dressed young professionals looks down at diners, who sit in a small, busy room at simple round tables atop clean tile floors.

MODERATE

EL CORRAL, 3545 Coral Way. Tel. 444-8272.

Cuisine: NICARAGUAN. **Reservations:** Accepted.

$ Prices: Appetizers $3–$5; main courses $9–$15, served 2-for-1 Mon–Thurs 5–7pm. AE, MC, V.

Open: Mon–Thurs 11:30am–11pm, Fri 11:30am–midnight, Sat noon–midnight, Sun noon–11pm.

This untraditional Nicaraguan steak house serves punchy marinated beef filets, along with plantains, rice, and beans from the barrio. Antojitos, Nicaragua's answer to appetizers, include homemade sausages with salad and plantains, fried pork with creole sauce, and a wonderful deep-fried cheese. Aside from a couple of obligatory fish and chicken listings, the long entrée menu focuses strictly on beef in various guises. Tender filet tips are served under a sauce of butter, brandy, cream, and Roquefort cheese. And a center cut tenderloin is matched with pickled onions and marinara sauce.

Most Nicaraguans don't even think of eating dinner before 9 or 10pm, so El Corral entices hungry others with a great 2-for-1 entrée "early-bird" special, Monday to Thursday from 5 to 7pm. It's a good deal for vacationing carnivores on a budget.

RISTORANTE TANINO, 2312 Ponce de Leon. Tel. 446-1666.

Cuisine: ITALIAN. **Reservations:** Accepted.

$ Prices: Lunch main courses $5–$8; dinner main courses $7–$8 for pasta, $9–$16 for meat, fish, and poultry.

Open: Lunch Mon–Fri 11:30am–3pm; dinner nightly 6–11pm.

Restaurants in the Gables come and go. But hopefully, Ristorante Tanino is here to stay. The beautiful, petite exterior houses an equally intimate dining room, where great Italian cuisine is remarkably underpriced. Lunch offers the best deals, with daily $6 specials that include a saucy manicotti, a robust lasagne, and a particularly well-done penne with eggplant and tomato sauce. All are served with soup or salad. Specials would easily sell for twice the price in New York. Dinner is à la carte, and the well-chosen menu is also kindly priced. Pastas, like fettuccine Alfredo with smoked salmon, are as good or better than similar dishes served elsewhere at twice the cost. Most of the other meals are more traditionally prepared, like chicken parmigiana, veal marsala, and saltimbocca, representing both good cooking and good value.

INEXPENSIVE

HOUSE OF INDIA, 22 Merrick Way. Tel. 444-2348.

Cuisine: INDIAN. **Reservations:** Accepted.

$ Prices: Appetizers $1–$5, main courses $7–$10, lunch buffet, served Mon–Fri 11:30am–3pm and Sat noon–3pm $6.95. AE, MC, V.

Open: Mon–Thurs 10:30am–10pm, Fri–Sat 11:30am–11pm, Sun 5–10pm.

House of India's curries, kormas, and kebabs are some of the city's best, but the restaurant's well-priced all-you-can-eat lunch buffet is unsurpassed. All the favorites are on display including tandoori chicken, naan bread, various meat and vegetarian curries, as well as rice and dal (lentils). If you've never had Indian food before, this is an excellent place to experiment, since you can see the food before you choose it. Veterans will know this is high-quality cooking from the subcontinent.

The restaurant is not fancy, but nicely decorated, with hanging printed cloths, and traditional music. It is located one block north of Miracle Mile.

BUDGET

BISCAYNE MIRACLE MILE CAFETERIA, 147 Miracle Mile, Coral Gables. Tel. 444-9005.

Cuisine: SOUTHERN AMERICAN.

$ Prices: Main courses $3–$4. Cash only.
    Open: Lunch Mon–Sat 11am–2:15pm; dinner 4–8pm; Sun 11am–8pm.

No bar, no music, and no flowers on the tables; just great Southern-style cooking at unbelievably low prices. The menu changes, but roast beef, baked fish, and barbecue ribs are typical entrées, few of which exceed $4.

    Like the name says, food is picked up cafeteria-style, and brought to one of the many unadorned Formica tables. The restaurant is always busy.

CAFE 94, 94 Miracle Mile. Tel. 444-7933.
    Cuisine: CUBAN.
$ Prices: $2–$5 breakfast and lunch. Cash only.
    Open: Mon–Sat 7am–4pm. **Closed:** Sun.

This Cuban coffee shop is a great place to try the island's specialties. Daily lunch specials cost less than $5 and usually include grilled chicken or steak, rice, black beans, and plantains. Cuban-style sandwiches are also available, as are hearty American-style breakfasts. Café 94 occupies a narrow storefront in the heart of the Gables' main shopping thoroughfare.

THE ESTATE WINES & GOURMET FOODS, 92 Miracle Mile. Tel. 442-9915.
    Cuisine: POLISH/AMERICAN.
$ Prices: $4–$6. Cash only.
    Open: Mon–Fri 10am–8pm, Sat 10am–6pm. **Closed:** Sun.

This storefront, in the heart of Coral Gables main shopping strip, is primarily a wine shop. But, Magdalena A. von Freytag, one of the friendliest storekeepers in Miami, also serves gourmet meals to a handful of lucky lunchers. Deliciously thick soups are served with pâtés, salads, and sandwiches around an overturned barrel that can only accommodate a handful of diners. I hesitate to write about this find for fear of spoiling it. Magdalena's only advertisement is word of mouth, and knowledgeable locals are her dedicated regulars.

9. COCONUT GROVE

EXPENSIVE

CAFE SCI SCI, 3043 Grand Ave. Tel. 446-5104.
    Cuisine: ITALIAN. **Reservations:** Accepted.
$ Prices: Appetizers $7–$9; main courses $11–$13 for pasta, $16–$23 for meat and fish; lunch about half-price. AE, MC, V.
    Open: Lunch Tues–Sun noon–4pm; dinner Sun–Thurs 5:30pm–12:30am, Fri–Sat 5:30pm–1am.

The original Sci Sci café (pronounced "shi shi") was a turn-of-the-century Naples eatery and a meeting place for international artists and intellectuals. That restaurant also claims it was the site where gelato—the silky smooth Italian ice cream—was perfected. Like its namesake, Café Sci Sci in the Grove is also an inviting place to lounge and linger. Their solid marble floors and columns combine with ornate decor and furnishings to create one of the area's most stunning European-style cafés. Visually and gastronomically this restaurant is a pleasing combination of old and new.

The large menu offers both hot and cold antipasti, including carpaccio, sautéed mussels, ham and melon, and fried mozzarella with marinara sauce. Pasta entrées feature such winning combinations as homemade black fettuccine with vodka, tomato, cream, and black pepper; tortellini filled with smoked cheese in Gorgonzola sauce; and Parpadella Rustiche—wide noodles with shrimp, saffron, peas, and cream.

Meat, fish, and chicken dishes also combine traditional and contemporary styles. The pace here is relaxed, as every order is freshly prepared. The restaurant is at the Groves' primary intersection, at the top of Main Highway.

KALEIDOSCOPE, 3112 Commodore Plaza. Tel. 446-5010.
  Cuisine: CONTINENTAL. **Reservations:** Recommended.
$ Prices: Appetizers $6–$9; main courses $12–$15 for pasta, $14–$18 for meat and fish; lunch about half-price. AE, CB, DC, DISC, MC, V.
  Open: Lunch Mon–Fri 11:30am–3pm; dinner 6–11pm Mon–Sat, 5:30–10:30pm Sun.

Kaleidoscope is one of the few restaurants in the heart of Coconut Grove that would still be recommended if it were located somewhere less exciting. The atmosphere is elegantly relaxed, with attentive, low-key service, comfortable seating, and a well-designed terrace overlooking the busy sidewalks below. Dishes are extremely well prepared and pastas, topped with meaty sauces like seafood and fresh basil, or pesto with grilled yellowfin tuna, are especially tasty. The linguini with salmon and fresh dill is prepared to perfection. The appetizers are tempting, but even hearty eaters should be warned that entrées are large, and all are preceded by a house salad.

MODERATE

MONTY'S BAYSHORE RESTAURANT, 2560 S. Bayshore Dr. Tel. 858-1431.
  Cuisine: SEAFOOD. **Reservations:** Accepted.
$ Prices: Chowder $3, appetizers and sandwiches $6–$8, platters $7–$12, main courses $15–$20. AE, CB, DC, MC, V.
  Open: Daily 11am–3am.

Monty's comes in three parts: a lounge, a raw bar, and a restaurant. Between them, they serve everything from steak and seafood to munchies like nachos, potato skins, and buffalo chicken wings. This is a fun kind of place, usually with more revelers and drinkers than diners. Sitting at the outdoor, dockside bar can be a pleasant way to spend an evening. There is live music nightly, as well as all day on the weekends (see "The Bar Scene," in Chapter 10).

SEÑOR FROG'S, 3008 Grand Ave. Tel. 448-0999.

Cuisine: MEXICAN. **Reservations:** Accepted, recommended on weekends.

$ Prices: Main courses $9–$12. AE, CB, DC, MC, V.

Open: Mon–Thurs 5pm–1am, Fri 5pm–2am, Sat 2pm–2am, Sun 2pm–1am.

You know you're getting close to Señor Frog's when you hear laughing and singing spilling out of the restaurant's courtyard. Filled with the college-student crowd, this restaurant is known for a raucous good time, its mariachi band, and powerful margaritas. The food at this rocking cantina is as good as its atmosphere, featuring excellent renditions of traditional Mexican/American favorites. The mole enchiladas, with 14 different kinds of mild chilies mixed with chocolate, is as flavorful as any I've tasted. Almost everything is served with rice and beans and, like all good Mexican places, portions are so large, few diners are able to finish.

PITA AND EATS, 3138 Commodore Plaza. Tel. 448-8226.

Cuisine: MIDDLE EASTERN.

$ Prices: Pita sandwiches $4–$5, platters $5–$11.

Open: Mon–Sat 10am–7pm, Sun 10am–5pm.

This contemporary, bright, second-floor diner has an excellent location and a Middle Eastern flavor. From tofu and vegetables to avocados and felafel, most everything is served in pita bread. Greek salads, gyros, and hamburgers are also available, as are a host of breakfast items, served until 11:30am. The restaurant is three blocks from Cocowalk, toward the heart of Coconut Grove.

10. SOUTH MIAMI

INEXPENSIVE

EL TORITO, in The Falls shopping center, 8888 Howard Dr. Tel. 255-6506.

Cuisine: MEXICAN. **Reservations:** Accepted.

$ Prices: Appetizers $4–$5.50, main courses $6–$9. AE, MC, V.

Open: Daily 11am–11pm.

Red clay tile, Mexican artifacts, and three-dimensional murals create an authentic south-of-the-border atmosphere only found in American restaurant chains. It's nice though. And seeing how it is pretty difficult to mess up Mexican "cuisine," especially when it is prepared by authentic Latinos, the food is pretty good too. All the hits are here, including enchiladas, tacos, chimichangas, and tostadas. It's pretty cheap, and very unlikely that you'll leave hungry.

A second El Torito is located in the Miami International Mall, 10633 NW 12th Street (tel. 591-0671).

BUDGET

LB'S EATERY, 5813 Ponce de Leon Blvd. Tel. 661-8879.
   Cuisine: AMERICAN.
$ Prices: Salads and sandwiches $3–$4.50, main courses $5–$8.
   DISC, MC, V.
   Open: Mon–Thurs 11am–10pm, Fri–Sat 11am–11:30pm.
   Closed: Sun.

High-quality, low-priced meals are served cafeteria-style in this popular, no-nonsense eatery. A good selection of salads include chicken, tuna-apple, and a variety of green combinations. Sandwiches are built on breads or croissants, and include almost every known variation. For an entrée, look for lasagne, chicken, roast beef, and vegetarian selections like ratatouille. Five nightly dinner specials include entrée, salad, and garlic bread, and start under $5. There are no waiters here. Order at the counter, and wait to be called. Despite its listing in this category, LB's is technically in Coral Gables, a half block from the University of Miami stadium, across from the Metrorail tracks.

11. SPECIALTY DINING

Use these supplemental listings to help you find an eatery that's perfect for your mood and desire.

HOTEL DINING

ARAGON CAFE, in the Colonnade Hotel, 180 Aragon Ave., Coral Gables. Tel. 448-9966.
   Cuisine: MIAMI REGIONAL. **Reservations:** Recommended. Jackets required.
$ Prices: Appetizers $6–$8, main courses $15–$22; lunch about half-price. AE, DC, MC, V.
   Open: Breakfast daily 6:30–10am; lunch Mon–Fri 11:30am–3pm; dinner Mon–Sat 6–11pm.

The atmosphere is as elegant as the cuisine. Look forward to masterfully prepared delicacies like blue-crab cakes and radicchio-wrapped lobster. Seafood is the house specialty, and salmon is the fish of choice. Aragon Café is not cheap, but it comes highly recommended as one of the best restaurants of its kind in Miami.

THE DINING GALLERIES, in the Fontainebleau Hilton Hotel, 4441 Collins Ave., Miami Beach. Tel. 538-2000.
   Cuisine: CONTINENTAL. **Reservations:** Recommended.

$ Prices: Appetizers $8–$12, main courses $19–$27. AE, CB, DC, DISC, MC, V.

Open: Nightly 6pm–11pm, Sun brunch 10am–3pm.

The Dining Galleries is filled with statuary, antique objets d'art, and pleasantly overdone decor.

The menu is heavy on meat and fish with such specialties as pheasant consommé, medallions of lobster, quail egg, and brandied lobster bisque. The Galleries are especially known for their crown roast of lamb with fried pears and a homemade Florida citrus chutney.

DOMINIQUE'S, in the Alexander All-Suite Luxury Hotel, 5225 Collins Ave., Miami Beach. Tel. 865-6500.

Cuisine: FRENCH/CONTINENTAL. **Reservations:** Recommended, especially at dinner. Jackets required.

$ Prices: Hors d'Oeuvres $8–$11, main courses $20–$30. AE, CB, DC, MC, V.

Open: Dinner Sun–Thurs 5:30pm–11pm, Fri–Sat 5:30pm–midnight; lunch Mon–Sat 11:30am–3pm; breakfast Mon–Sat 7–11:30am; brunch Sun 11am–3pm during winter months only.

Widely hailed as one of Miami Beach's best restaurants, Dominique's is both elegant and opulent. The menu is equally as rich and spotlights a variety of wild game appetizers like alligator scaloppini, and fresh Diamondback rattlesnake salad. But it's the tender traditional entrées like marinated rack of lamb chops and prime steak that keeps the regulars coming back.

THE FISH MARKET, in the Omni International Hotel, 1601 Biscayne Blvd. (Downtown) Tel. 374-0000.

Cuisine: SEAFOOD. **Reservations:** Recommended.

$ Prices: Appetizers $6–$8; main courses $17–$22; AE, CB, DC, MC, V.

Open: Lunch Mon–Fri 11:30am–2:30pm; dinner Mon–Sat 6:30–11pm. **Closed:** Sun.

Located just off the Omni International Hotel's fourth floor lobby, the comfortable Fish Market features high ceilings, reasonable prices and one of the best seafood menus in town. Simply prepared and presented local fish is always the menu's main feature, and sautéed or grilled, it's this guide's recommendation.

PAVILLON GRILL, in the Inter-Continental Hotel, 100 Chopin Plaza (Downtown). Tel. 577-1000.

Cuisine: MIAMI REGIONAL. **Reservations:** Recommended.

$ Prices: Appetizers $7–$12, main courses $18–$24. AE, CB, DC, MC, V.

Open: Dinner Mon–Sat 6–11pm. **Closed:** Sun.

One of the city's most deluxe restaurants the Pavillon Grill has a beautifully spacious dining room with an intimate club room feel. Some of the more adventurous main courses include boneless quail Louisiana, stuffed with oysters and andouille sausage, and a host of creatively stuffed pastas.

RESTAURANT ST. MICHEL, in the Hotel Place St. Michel, 162 Alcazar Ave., Coral Gables. Tel. 444-1666.
Cuisine: FRENCH/MEDITERRANEAN. **Reservations:** Recommended.

$ Prices: Appetizers $6–$8, lunch $4–$14, main courses $14–$16 for pasta, $18–$22 for meat and fish. AE, CB, MC, V.
Open: Lunch Mon–Sat 11am–4pm; dinner Sun–Thurs 6–10:30pm, Fri–Sat 5–11:30pm; brunch Sun 11am–2:30pm.

More laid-back than other hotel choices, the Restaurant St. Michel is one of the most subtly sensuous restaurants in Miami. The creative menu, featuring a flavorful metropolitan French coast cuisine, complements an artful deco decor. A special six-course dinner is prepared and priced nightly. Highly recommended.

DINING WITH A VIEW

CRAWDADDY'S, 1 Washington Ave., South Miami Beach. Tel. 673-1708.
Cuisine: SEAFOOD. **Reservations:** Recommended.

$ Prices: Appetizers $5–$7, main courses $14–$19; lunch about half-price. AE, CB, DC, MC, V.
Open: Lunch Mon–Fri 11am–4pm; dinner Mon–Thurs 5–11pm, Fri–Sat 5pm–midnight, Sun 4:30–11pm; brunch Sun 11am–3:30pm.

Crawdaddy's offers a large menu with competently prepared foods. The best thing about this restaurant, though, is its location—on the water in South Pointe Park, at the southernmost tip of South Miami Beach. Plenty of window seats give you the chance to watch the cruise and cargo ships slowly ease their way in and out of the Port of Miami.

MONTY'S BAYSHORE RESTAURANT, 2560 South Bayshore Dr., Coconut Grove. Tel. 858-1431.
Cuisine: SEAFOOD. **Reservations:** Accepted.

$ Prices: Chowder $3, appetizers and sandwiches $6–$8, platters $7–$12, main courses $15–$20. AE, CB, DC, MC, V.
Open: Daily 11am–3am.

There are few better places in Miami to spend an afternoon or evening with some friends than at this dockside restaurant and bar. Usually catering to more revelers and drinkers than diners, Monty's is known for fresh fish and top-notch appetizers like nachos, potato skins, and Buffalo chicken wings.

NEWS CAFE, 800 Ocean Dr., South Miami Beach. Tel. 538-NEWS.
Cuisine: AMERICAN.

$ Prices: Continental breakfast $2.75, salads $4–$8, sandwiches $5–$7. AE, DC, MC, V.
Open: 24 hours.

Nowhere in trendy South Beach is the people-watching better than at the News Café. This small eatery is the unofficial meeting place for the area's multitudes of models and artsy types. Excellent and inexpensive breakfasts and café fare are served at about 20 perennially congested tables.

THE SANDBAR, in the Silver Sands Motel, 301 Ocean Dr., Key Biscayne. Tel. 361-5441.

    Cuisine: AMERICAN.

$ Prices: Main courses $7–$11; about half-price at lunch. AE, MC, V.

    Open: Breakfast Sat–Sun 8–11am, lunch daily 11:30am–3:30pm, dinner nightly 5–10pm.

The Sandbar, a Miami institution, is an inexpensive restaurant boasting Key Biscayne's best beach location at any price. The informal oceanfront eatery features fish, burgers, and salads, served on a deck that's right on the beach.

SUNDAYS ON THE BAY, 5420 Crandon Blvd., Key Biscayne. Tel. 361-6777.

    Cuisine: AMERICAN. **Reservations:** Accepted; recommended for Sunday brunch.

$ Prices: Appetizers $6–$7, main courses $15–$24; lunch about half-price; Sunday brunch $15.95. AE, CB, DC, MC, V.

    Open: Lunch Mon–Sat 11:30am–5pm; dinner Mon–Wed and Sun 5pm–2am; Thurs–Sat 5pm–2:30am; brunch Sun from 10:30am.

Located on the water in Key Biscayne, Sundays is one of the best places in the city for good food and terrific views. Live rock and reggae often complement the hearty portions of steak, chicken, pasta, veal, and fish.

LIGHT & CASUAL

HOOTERS, in the Bayside Marketplace, 401 Biscayne Blvd. (Downtown). Tel. 371-3004.

    Cuisine: AMERICAN.

$ Prices: $5–$12. AE, MC, V.

    Open: Mon–Thurs 11am–midnight, Fri–Sat 11am–1am, Sun 11am–10pm.

Hooters' has a reputation as the most sexist restaurant in Florida with buxom waitresses wearing midriff tops. The casual second-floor restaurant offers good, inexpensive meals, and a great terrace overlooking Bayside Marketplace and Biscayne Bay. Large chicken, fish, and meat burgers, are served with massive quantities of beer. Hooters is on the second floor of the Marketplace's north pavilion. There is a second location in Coconut Grove's Cocowalk, 3015 Brand Ave. (tel. 442-6004).

PINEAPPLES, 530 Arthur Godfrey Rd., Miami Beach. Tel. 532-9731.

    Cuisine: AMERICAN. **Reservations:** Not accepted.

$ Prices: Salads and sandwiches $5–$6, main courses $8–$10. AE, MC, V.

Open: Daily 11am–10pm.

Half health food store, half restaurant, Pineapples serves fresh juices, sandwiches, and a variety of menu items, either to go, or to eat in. Both appetizers and entrées include a unique combination of American and Japanese-style foods like Buffalo chicken wings, miso soup, and California sushi rolls. Steamed vegetables and stir-fry are especially emphasized, as are meal-sized salads including vegetable, chicken, pasta, pineapple, and more. The busy restaurant is located in the middle of a row of boutiques on the south side of bustling Arthur Godfrey Road.

BREAKFAST/BRUNCH

THE DINING GALLERIES, in the Fontainebleau Hilton Hotel, 4441 Collins Ave., Miami Beach. Tel. 538-2000.
　Cuisine: CONTINENTAL. **Reservations:** Recommended.
$ Prices: Appetizers $8–$12, main courses $19–$27. AE, CB, DC, DISC, MC, V.
　Open: brunch Sun 10am–3pm.

The Sunday brunch at the Fontainebleau's unique Dining Galleries is one of Miami's most unique experiences. Eggs cooked to order, carved meats, and fresh-baked breads are served buffet style, ensuring that no one leaves hungry. The Dining Galleries are a good bet any night of the week (see above), but breakfasts are special in this wonderfully overdone restaurant. See also page 79.

FAIRMONT GARDENS RESTAURANT, in the Fairmont Hotel, 1000 Collins Ave., South Miami Beach. Tel. 531-0050.
　Cuisine: ITALIAN/CONTINENTAL. **Reservations:** Recommended, especially on weekends.
$ Prices: Appetizers $4–$10; main courses $10–$12 for pasta, $14–$22 for meat and fish. AE, CB, DC, MC, V.
　Open: Tues–Sun 6pm–midnight; happy hour Mon–Fri 4–7pm.

The Fairmont's fancy, brunch buffet features traditional dishes like eggs Benedict and florentine, served with fruit-flavored buns and well-prepared potatoes. The tropical outdoor courtyard is a pleasant place to dine, right in the heart of South Miami Beach's art deco district.

NEWS CAFE, 800 Ocean Dr., South Miami Beach. Tel. 538-NEWS.
　Cuisine: AMERICAN.
$ Prices: Continental breakfast $2.75, salads $4–$8, sandwiches $5–$7. AE, DC, MC, V.
　Open: 24 hours.

Excellent and inexpensive breakfasts are served all day at about 20 perennially congested tables. Delicious, and often health-oriented dishes include yogurt with fruit salad, a choice of quiches, and a full egg menu. Coffee (including espresso), and a variety of black and herbal teas are also available.

SUNDAYS ON THE BAY, 5420 Crandon Blvd., Key Biscayne. Tel. 361-6777.

Cuisine: AMERICAN. **Reservations:** Accepted; recommended for Sunday brunch.

$ Prices: Appetizers $6–$7, main courses $15–$24; lunch about half-price; Sunday brunch $15.95. AE, CB, DC, MC, V.

Open: Lunch Mon–Sat 11:30am–5pm; dinner Mon–Wed, and Sun 5pm–2am, Thurs–Sat 5pm–2:30am; brunch Sun from 10:30am.

Sundays is a fun, tropical eatery with an upbeat, informal atmosphere. The restaurant's Sunday brunches may be the most popular in Miami, and feature a buffet the size of Bimini. Reservations are recommended, but still expect a wait.

LATE NIGHT

Most (but not all) 7-Eleven food stores are open around the clock, including: Downtown at 2 SE 7th St. (tel. 358-5409); 1447 Alton Rd., South Miami Beach (tel. 672-1520); and 51 Harbor Dr., Key Biscayne (tel. 361-6857).

NEWS CAFE, 800 Ocean Dr., South Miami Beach. Tel. 538-NEWS.

Cuisine: AMERICAN.

$ Prices: Continental breakfast $2.75, salads $4–$8, sandwiches $5–$7. AE, DC, MC, V.

Open: 24 hours.

This regular meeting place for Ocean Drive's multitude of fashion photography crews and their models serves great food at terrific prices until the wee hours. See listings above for more information.

VERSAILLES, 3555 S.W. 8th St. (Little Havana). Tel. 444-0240.

Cuisine: CUBAN.

$ Prices: Soup and salad $2–$5, main courses $5–$8. DC, MC, V.

Open: Mon–Thurs 8am–2am, Fri 8am–3:30am, Sat 8am–4:30am, Sun 9am–2am.

Little Havana's most celebrated diner is both busy and brusk, especially after 10pm. The menu is a veritable survey of Cuban cooking, and includes specialties like Moors and Christians (flavorful black beans with white rice), ropa vieja, and fried whole fish.

WOLFIE'S, 2038 Collins Ave. (South Miami Beach). Tel. 538-6626.

Cuisine: JEWISH DELICATESSEN.

$ Prices: Omelets and sandwiches $4–$6, other main courses $5–$12. MC, V.

Open: 24 hours.

This simple, traditional New York–style eatery is one of the city's only all-night eateries. Bowls of assorted pickles and rolls decorate each table and are a mark of the restaurant's authenticity. Meals

Ⓕ FROMMER'S COOL FOR KIDS: RESTAURANTS

American Classics (see page 82) is a theme restaurant, planned around vintage cars and '50s memorabilia. If you think your child would like to eat dinner inside a 1950s automobile, this is the place to go. The "surf and turf" menu is rounded off by a good assortment of desserts, or "tailgaters."

The Melting Pot (see page 99) is a fondue joint where diners dip chunks of bread into pots of sizzling cheese. It's definitely a fun way to eat, for kids as well as adults. But save room for dessert—chunks of pineapple, bananas, apples, and cherries are served with a creamy chocolate fondue for dipping.

Señor Frog's (see page 107) is both fun and filling, featuring a house mariachi band and excellent food. The restaurant is right in the heart of Coconut Grove, so you can walk around and see the sights before or after dinner.

include cold smoked fish platters, overstuffed sandwiches, stuffed cabbage, chicken-in-a-pot, and other traditional favorites.

DINING COMPLEXES

The **Bayside Marketplace Food Court,** 401 Biscayne Boulevard (tel. 577-3344), is not a single eatery. It is a restaurant shopping mall with over 30 stalls and stands to choose from, representing a myriad of international cuisine. Choices range from bagel sandwiches and burgers, to grilled chicken, Chinese stir-fry, creole conchs, and Middle-Eastern kebabs. Few dishes top $7. Plenty of public tables means your entire party can be satisfied by different delights, and still eat together.

Many of the counters here specialize in dessert, including Bimini Bay Brownies, The Cookie Bar, Everything Yogurt, and The Fudgery, making the Food Court an excellent stop, even if it's not mealtime. For more information on stores in the Bayside Marketplace, see Chapter 9, "Miami Shopping." The Food Court is located on the entire second level of the Marketplace's main pavilion. It's open Monday to Saturday 10am to 10pm, Sunday noon to 8pm. Some eateries open later.

PICNIC FARE

Publix is one of Miami's largest supermarket chains, with locations that include 18330 Collins Avenue, (Sunny Isles; tel. 931-9615); 2551

LeJeune Road (Coral Gables; tel. 445-2641); and 4870 Biscayne Boulevard (Greater Miami North; tel. 576-4318). Small groceries can be very convenient, and are literally located all over Miami. Ask at your hotel for the closest.

Because of the "immigrant" nature of the city, Caribbean staples can be found in even the most conservative supermarkets. Look for unusual sauces and dressings, as well as tropical fruits like guava and papaya. **One Man and His Dog,** 834 NE 183rd Street (tel. 770-1558), is a grocery in the heart of Miami's Jamaican community. Here you can pick up Rasta staples like jerk sauce, lime pepper, yam flour, extra-hot meat patties, and Red Stripe beer. A real find.

CHAPTER 7

WHAT TO SEE & DO IN MIAMI

1. THE TOP ATTRACTIONS
- **FROMMER'S FAVORITE MIAMI EXPERIENCES**

2. MORE ATTRACTIONS

3. COOL FOR KIDS

4. ORGANIZED TOURS

5. SPORTS & RECREATION

Many of Miami's attractions were built in the 1940s and '50s, designed to cash in on the growing tourist-oriented economy. Like the Fontainebleau hotel along Collins Avenue, the city's still-extant showplaces are time capsules—relics of an earlier age.

Miami has always been a city of dreams; a place for tourists to relax and recuperate. Apart from the fact that most of Miami's attractions are located outdoors, its single most common attribute is its ability to entertain. The city's top tourist destinations highlight curiosities in architecture, plants, animals, and human beings. And leaping lizards! They are extremely entertaining.

SUGGESTED ITINERARIES

IF YOU HAVE 1 DAY

In the morning, drive to Miami Beach's art deco district, and take an informal tour of the area (see "A Walking Tour," in Chapter 8). Spend some time on the beach along Ocean Drive, and eat lunch in a nearby café. In the afternoon, head to Miami's Seaquarium, on Key Biscayne, then drive through the sparkling city at sunset.

IF YOU HAVE 2 DAYS

Day 1 Spend the first day as outlined above.

Day 2 On your second day, drive down to Greater Miami South to visit one or more of the attractions listed below, such as Monkey Jungle or Coral Castle. Alternatively, visit the Miami Metrozoo, or go Downtown to shop and stroll in Bayside Marketplace.

IF YOU HAVE 3 DAYS

Days 1–2 Spend days 1 and 2 as outlined above.

Day 3 On your third day visit historical Miami. Start with a tour of Villa Vizcaya, one of the city's first estates. Visit the Barnacle in Coconut Grove, then drive through Coral Gables (see "Driving Tour

2," in Chapter 8), and stroll around the grounds of the grand Biltmore Hotel and the Venetian Pool. If there's time, head north to the Spanish Monastery Cloisters, America's oldest standing structure.

IF YOU HAVE 5 OR MORE DAYS

Days 1–3 Spend days 1 to 3 as outlined above.

Days 4–5 Take time out from sight-seeing and head for the beach. Play golf or tennis, fish, sail, water-ski, or even place a bet at the horse or dog races. Relax at a sidewalk café in Coconut Grove, spend an evening dining in an elegant restaurant or dancing into the wee hours. With an extra day, you can drive up to Fort Lauderdale, down to the Everglades (see Chapter 11), visit Key West, or even hop on a one-day cruise to Freeport or Nassau in the Bahamas (see Chapter 11).

1. THE TOP ATTRACTIONS

THE ART DECO DISTRICT

Miami's best sight is not a museum or an amusement park, but a part of the city itself. Located at the southern end of Miami Beach, the art deco district is a whole community made up of outrageous, fanciful 1920s and '30s architecture that shouldn't be missed. (See "A Walking Tour," in Chapter 8.)

MIAMI METROZOO, SW 152nd St. and SW 124th Ave., (south of Coral Gables). Tel. 251-0400.

Rarely does a zoo warrant mention as a city's "Top Attraction," but Miami's Metrozoo is different. This huge 290-acre complex is completely cageless; animals are kept at bay by cleverly designed moats. Star attractions include two rare white Bengal tigers, a 1.5-acre free-flight tropical aviary, a monorail "safari," and one of the few koala bear exhibits in America. Especially appealing for both adults and children is PAWS, a newly designed petting zoo. The elephant ride is particularly fun.

Admission: $8.25 adults, $4.25 children 3–12, under 3 free. Reduced rates for Florida residents.

Open: Daily 9:30am–5:30pm. Ticket booth closes 4pm. **Directions:** From U.S. 1, take SW 152nd St. exit west 3 blocks to the Metrozoo entrance.

MIAMI SEAQUARIUM, 4400 Rickenbacker Causeway (south side), Key Biscayne. Tel. 361-5705.

Visitors walk around the 35-acre oceanarium, admiring the various mammals' beauty, creativity, and intelligence. One entertain-

FLORIDA

Miami

Art Deco District ⑦
Barnacle ㉘
Bass Museum of Art ⑥
Bayfront Park ⑩
Biltmore Hotel ㉑
Calle Ocho ⑫
Caribbean Marketplace ③
Coconut Grove Exhibition Center ㉕
Coconut Grove ㉙
Coconut Grove Playhouse ㉗
Coral Castle ㊶
Crandon Park ⑳
Cuban Museum of Arts and Culture ⑭
Dinner Key Marina ㉔
Fairchild Tropical Garden ㉝
Fruit and Spice Park ㊵
Gulfstream Park

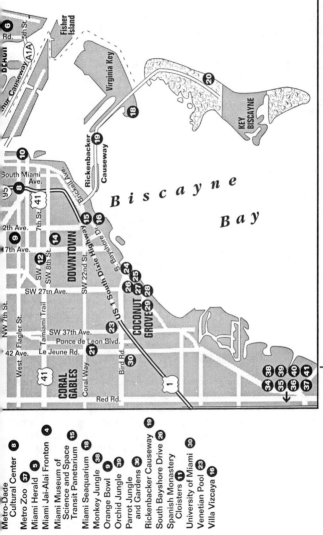

Atlantic Ocean

Fisher Island

Virginia Key

KEY BISCAYNE

Biscayne

Bay

Rickenbacker Causeway

South Miami Ave.

DOWNTOWN

COCONUT GROVE

CORAL GABLES

Airport

Metro-Dade
Cultural Center ⑧

Metro Zoo ㊲

Miami Herald ⑤

Miami Jai-Alai Fronton ④

Miami Museum of
Science and Space
Transit Panetarium ⑮

Miami Seaquarium ⑱

Monkey Jungle ⑨

Orange Bowl ⑨

Orchid Jungle ㊴

Parrot Jungle
and Gardens ㉟

Rickenbacker Causeway ⑲

South Bayshore Drive ㉖

Spanish Monastery
Cloisters ⑪

University of Miami ㉚

Venetian Pool ㉓

Villa Vizcaya ⑯

ing exhibit stars Flipper, the original dolphin from the television series. Other performances are highlighted by the antics of a trained killer whale.

Miami Seaquarium is a profit-making enterprise and admission is steep. Still, their shows are entertaining, and they help visitors gain insight into these interesting marine mammals.

Admission: $16.95 adults, $13.95 seniors over 65, $11.95 children under 13.

Open: Daily 9:30am–6pm. Ticket booth closes at 4:30pm. **Directions:** From Downtown Miami, take I-95 South to the Rickenbacker Causeway.

VILLA VIZCAYA, 3251 South Miami Ave., just south of Rickenbacker Causeway (north Coconut Grove). Tel. 579-2708.

You already know that South Florida is wacky, and this place proves it. Sometimes referred to as the "Hearst Castle of the East," this magnificent villa was built in 1916 as a winter retreat for James Deering, former vice-president of International Harvester. The industrialist was fascinated by 16th-century art and architecture, and his ornate mansion—which took 1,000 artisans five years to build—became a celebration of these designs.

Pink marble columns, topped with intricately designed capitals, reach up toward hand-carved European-style ceilings. Antiques decorate 34 of the 70 rooms, which are filled with baroque furniture and Renaissance paintings and tapestries. The spectacularly opulent villa wraps itself around a central courtyard. Outside, lush formal gardens, accented with statuary, balustrades, and decorative urns, front an enormous swath of Biscayne Bay.

Admission: $8 adults, $4 children 6–12, under 6 free.

Open: Daily 9:30am–5pm; gardens open until 5:30. Ticket booth closes 4:30pm. **Closed:** Christmas Day. **Directions:** Take I-95 South to Exit 1 and follow signs to Vizcaya.

GREATER MIAMI SOUTH

Many of Miami's tourist attractions are located in Howard, Perrine, Homestead, and other communities south of Downtown. The best way to visit these attractions is via U.S. 1, a major highway that extends all the way down into the Keys. You can't get lost; blaring billboards point the way to all the attractions listed in this book. Think about combining several of the following sights, put your car's top down, turn the music up, and prepare yourself for wacky times!

CORAL CASTLE, 28655 S. Dixie Hwy. (Homestead). Tel. 248-6344.

There's plenty of competition, but Coral Castle is probably the zaniest attraction in Florida. In 1917, the story goes, a crazed Latvian, suffering from unrequited love, emigrated to South Florida and spent the next 25 years of his life carving massive amounts of stone into a roofless, prehistoric-looking "castle." It was a monumental task that may remind you, in a light-hearted way, of the Great Pyramids or Stonehenge. If you're in the area, especially with kids in tow, take an hour to visit this monument of one man's madness.

Admission: $7.75 adults, $4.50 children 6–12, under 6 free.

Open: Daily 9am–6pm, except Thanksgiving when they close at 5pm. **Directions:** Take U.S. 1 South to SW 286th St. in Homestead.

MONKEY JUNGLE, 14805 SW 216th St. (Greater Miami South). Tel. 235-1611.

See rare Brazilian Golden Lion Tamarins! Watch the "skin diving" Asian Macaques! Yes, folks, it's primate paradise! Visitors are protected, but there are no cages to restrain the antics of monkeys, gorillas, and chimpanzees as they swing, chatter, and play their way into your heart! Where else but in Florida would an attraction like this still be popular after 50 years? Screened-in trails wind through acres of "jungle," and daily shows feature the talents of the park's most progressive pupils. Their newest exhibit is an Enchanted Topiary Garden.

Admission: $10.50 adults, $9.50 seniors, $5.35 children 4–12. Children under 4 free.

Open: Daily 9:30am–6pm. Tickets sold until 5pm. **Directions:** South on U.S. 1 to 216th St.; about 20 minutes from Downtown.

ORCHID JUNGLE, 26715 SW 157th Ave. (Homestead), at 272nd St., just off U.S. 1. Tel. 247-4824.

Bathed in rich colors and heavenly scents, visitors wind their way on a self-guided tour through what may be the world's largest outdoor orchid garden. The "jungle," and adjacent glass-enclosed cloning and growth laboratory are on the premises of Fennell Orchid Company. And all of the dozens of gorgeous varieties, which cling to huge old oak trees, are for sale.

Admission: $5 adults, $4 students 13–17 and seniors, $1.50 children 6–12, under 6 free.

Open: Daily 8:30am–5:30pm. **Directions:** From Downtown, follow U.S. 1 South about 25 miles. Turn right on 272nd St. (Epmore Dr.). Orchid Jungle is ½ mile on right.

PARROT JUNGLE AND GARDENS, 11000 SW 57th Ave. (Greater Miami South). Tel. 666-7834.

Not just parrots, but hundreds of magnificent macaws, prancing peacocks, cute cockatoos, and fabulous flamingos fly in this 50-year-old park. Alligators, tortoises, and iguanas are also on exhibit. But it's the parrots you came for, and it's parrots you get! With brilliant splashes of color, these birds appear in every shape and size. Continuous shows in the Parrot Bowl Theater star roller-skating cockatoos, card-playing macaws, and more stunt-happy parrots than you ever thought possible! New attractions include a wildlife show called "Primate Experience," a children's playground, and a petting zoo.

Admission: $10.50 adults, $6 children 3–12; children under 3 free.

FROMMER'S FAVORITE
MIAMI EXPERIENCES

Airboat Through the Everglades You've seen these wide, flat boats driven by huge fans in the rear. Airboat rides, offered by the Miccosukee Indian Village (see "Everglades National Park" in Chapter 11) and other organizations, are fantastic half-hour, high-speed tours through some of America's most pristine lands. Birds scatter as the boats approach, and when you slow down, alligators and other animals appear.

Bayside Marketplace Miami's best shopping mall is this outdoor Rouse Company development, located on the water in the heart of the city's Downtown. About 100 shops and carts sell everything from plastic fruit to high-tech electronics (see Chapter 9, "Shopping A to Z"). Upstairs, a mammoth fast-food eating arcade is a great place for a meal or snack. (See Chapter 6, "Miami Dining.")

Coconut Grove at Night The intersection of Grand Avenue, Main Highway, and McFarlane Road, creates the heart of Coconut Grove, a sedate village by day, and busy meeting place by night. Sizzling with dozens of interesting cafés, boutiques, and nightspots, the Grove's sidewalks are crowded with business people, students, and tourists.

Little Havana Miami's Cuban center is the city's most important ethnic enclave. Located just west of Downtown, Little Havana is centered around "Calle Ocho," SW 8th Street. This busy street is exciting and warrants exploration. Car-repair shops, tailors, electronic stores, and restaurants all hang signs in Spanish; salsa rhythms thump from the radios of passersby; and old men in guayaberas chain-smoke cigars over their daily game of dominoes.

Ocean Drive The beauty of the celebrated art deco district in South Miami Beach culminates on the 15-block beachfront strip known as Ocean Drive. Most of the buildings on this stretch are hotels that were built in the late 1930s and early 1940s. Even if you are not staying here, take a stroll along this colorful street. (See "A Walking Tour," in Chapter 8.)

View from the Rickenbacker Causeway Almost every building in Miami's sleek, 21st-century skyline is a gem. The best view of this spectacular cluster is from the causeway that connects mainland Miami with Key Biscayne. You'll have to pay a toll of $1 for the privilege of such a view, but it's worth it.

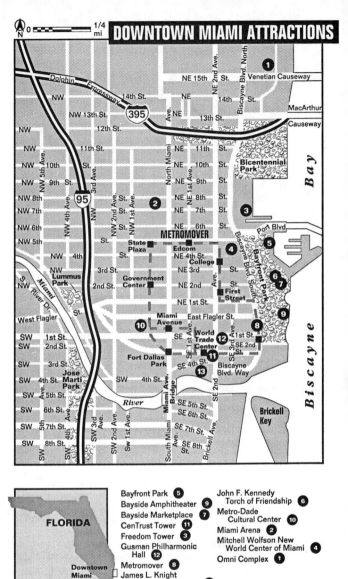

DOWNTOWN MIAMI ATTRACTIONS

Bayfront Park **5**
Bayside Amphitheater **9**
Bayside Marketplace **7**
CenTrust Tower **11**
Freedom Tower **3**
Gusman Philharmonic Hall **12**
Metromover **8**
James L. Knight International Center **13**

John F. Kennedy Torch of Friendship **6**
Metro-Dade Cultural Center **10**
Miami Arena **2**
Mitchell Wolfson New World Center of Miami **4**
Omni Complex **1**

Open: Daily 9:30am–6pm. **Directions:** Take U.S. 1 South, turn left at SW 57th Ave., and continue straight for 2½ miles.

PRESTON B. BIRD AND MARY HEINLEIN FRUIT AND SPICE PARK, 24801 SW 187th Ave. (Homestead). Tel. 247-5727.

Miami's early settlers were terrific horticulturalists. It was the weather that originally brought them here, and plant lovers experimented with unusual tropical breeds that couldn't thrive elsewhere in America. This 20-acre living plant museum is an example of these early experiments. You'll be amazed by the unusual varieties of fruit growing on dozens of strange-looking trees with unpronounceable names.

You are free to sample anything that falls to the ground on any day you visit, but you would be wise to wait until Saturday or Sunday, when an excellent and informative tour guide can tell you what it is before you put it in your mouth.

Admission: $1 adults, 50¢ children.

Open: Daily 10am–5pm. Tours: Sat and Sun 1 and 3pm, for an additional cost of $1.50 adults, $1 children. **Directions:** Take U.S. 1 South, turn right on SW 248th St., and go straight for 5 miles to SW 187th Ave.

2. MORE ATTRACTIONS

THE BARNACLE, 3485 Main Hwy., Coconut Grove. Tel. 448-9445.

The former home of naval architect and early settler Ralph Middleton Munroe, is now a museum in the heart of Coconut Grove, 2 blocks south of Commodore Plaza. The house's quiet surroundings, wide porches, and period furnishings are a good illustration of the way Miami's privileged class lived in the days before skyscrapers and luxury hotels. Enthusiastic and knowledgeable state park employees and innumerable period objects offer a wealth of historical information.

Admission: $2.

Tours: Thurs–Mon 10am, 11:30am, 1pm, and 2:30pm. **Directions:** From Downtown Miami, take U.S. 1 South to So. Bayshore Dr. Continue to the end, turn right onto McFarlane Ave. and left at the traffic light on to Main Hwy. The museum is 5 blocks on the left.

THE BASS MUSEUM OF ART, 2121 Park Ave., at the corner of 21st St., South Miami Beach. Tel. 673-7530.

The Bass is the most important visual arts museum in Miami Beach. European paintings, sculptures, and tapestries from the Renaissance, baroque, rococo, and modern periods make up the bulk of the small permanent collection. Temporary exhibitions alternate between traveling shows and rotations of the Bass's stock, with themes ranging widely, from 17th-century Dutch art, to contemporary architecture.

Built from coral rock in 1930, the Bass sits in the middle of six landscaped, tree-topped acres. Be sure to visit the funky outdoor fountain made up of bath tubs, sinks, and shower bases donated by the Formica Corporation, one of the museum's latest acquisitions.

Admission: $2 adults, $1 students, children under 16 free. Tuesday admission is by donation.

Open: Tues–Sat 10am–5pm, Sun 1–5pm. **Closed:** Mon and holidays.

THE BILTMORE HOTEL, 1200 Anastasia Ave., Coral Gables.

See "Driving Tour 2," in Chapter 8.

THE CRIMINAL JUSTICE BUILDING, Civic Center, 1351 NW 12th St., at the corner of NW 13th Ave. (Downtown). Tel. 547-4888.

Okay, you've seen it in the newspaper, you've seen it on TV, but so far the infamous Miami crime scene has eluded you. If you really want to see the city's judicial system in process, stop into the city's main courthouse, right behind the Miami city jail, for some real-life drama.

You are free to come and go as you wish, so check out a few courtrooms before settling on a case.

Admission: Free.

Open: Mon–Fri 9am–4:30pm.

CUBAN MUSEUM OF ARTS AND CULTURE, 1300 SW 12th Ave. at the corner of SW 13th St. (Little Havana). Tel. 858-8006.

This unique museum displays significant works of art and memorabilia important for the promotion and preservation of the Cuban culture. The collection of paintings and drawings only adds up to about 200, but they are well selected, and representative of a wide range of styles. The museum has also been designated as the official repository for the mementos of Agustino Acosta, the famous Cuban poet.

Admission: $2 adults, $1 students and seniors.

Open: Wed–Sun 1–5pm. **Directions:** From Downtown, head west on SW 7th St. Turn left on 12th Ave. The museum is 6 blocks ahead on the right.

FAIRCHILD TROPICAL GARDENS, 10901 Old Cutler Rd. (Coral Gables). Tel. 667-1651.

These large botanical gardens feature a veritable rain forest of both rare and exotic plants. Palmettos, vine pergola, palm glades, and other unique species create a scenic, lush environment. It costs an extra dollar, but it's well worth taking the hourly tram tour, where you can learn what you always wanted to know about the various flowers and trees.

Admission: $5 adults, children under 13 free.

Open: Daily 9:30am–4:30pm. **Directions:** From U.S. 1 South, turn left on LeJeune Rd. Follow straight to traffic circle, and take Cutler Rd. 2½ miles to the park.

METRO-DADE CULTURAL CENTER, 101 W. Flagler St. (Downtown).

In addition to the Dade County Public Library, the Metro-Dade Cultural Center houses the Historical Museum of Southern Florida (tel. 375-1492) and the Center for Fine Arts (tel. 375-1700).

The Historical Museum's primary exhibit is "Tropical Dreams," a state-of-the-art, chronological history of the last 10,000 years in South Florida. The hands-on displays, audiovisual presentations, and hundreds of artifacts are really quite interesting.

The Center for Fine Arts features an eclectic mix of modern and contemporary works by such artists as Eric Fischl, Max Beckman, Jim Dine, and Stuart Davis.

Admission to both museums: $5 adults, $2.50 seniors 65 and over, $2 children 6–12, under 6 free.

Open: Tues–Sat 10am–5pm (Thurs to 9pm), Sun noon–5pm. **Closed:** Monday. **Directions:** From I-95 North, take NW 2nd St. exit and turn right; continue east to NW 2nd Ave.; turn right and park at the Metro-Dade Garage. From I-95 South, exit at Orange Bowl–NW 8th St. exit and continue south to NW 2nd St. Turn left at NW 2nd St. and go 1½ blocks to NW 2nd Ave., turn right and park at the Metro-Dade Garage (50 NW 2nd Ave.). Bring ticket to lobby for validation.

SPANISH MONASTERY CLOISTERS, 16711 W. Dixie Hwy. at the corner of 167th St., North Miami Beach. Tel. 945-1462.

Did you know that the oldest building in the Western Hemisphere dates from A.D. 1141 and is located in Miami? It's true! The Spanish Monastery Cloisters were first erected in Segovia, Spain. Purchased by newspaper magnate William Randolph Hearst, the building was brought to America in pieces, and reassembled in 1954 on its present site!

Admission: $4 adults, $1 children 7–12, $2.50 seniors, under 7 free.

Open: Mon–Sat 10am–5pm, Sun noon–5pm. **Directions:** From Downtown, take U.S. 1 North and turn left onto 163rd St. Make the first right onto W. Dixie Hwy. The Cloisters are 3 blocks ahead on right.

VENETIAN POOL, 2701 DeSoto Blvd. at Toledo St., Coral Gables. Tel. 442-6483.

Miami's most unusual swimming pool, dating from 1924, is hidden behind pastel stucco walls, and is honored with a listing in the National Register of Historic Places. The free-form lagoon is fed by underground artesian wells, shaded by three-story Spanish porticos, and features both fountains and waterfalls. During summer months, the pool's 800,000 gallons of water are drained and refilled nightly, ensuring a cool, clean swim. Visitors are free to swim and sunbathe here, year-round, just as Esther Williams and Johnny Weissmuller did decades ago.

Admission: $4 adults, $3.50 children 13–17, $1.60 children under 13.

Open: June–Aug, Mon–Fri 11am–7:30pm; Sept–Oct and Apr–

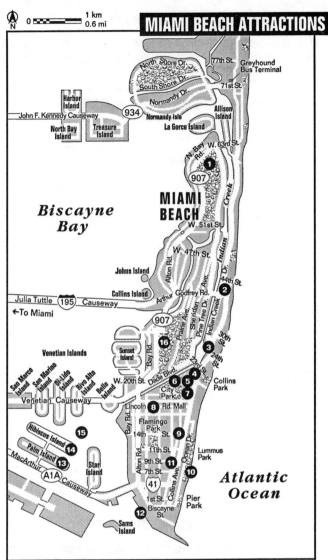

MIAMI BEACH ATTRACTIONS

Art Deco District **11**
Bass Museum of Art **4**
Bay Shore Golf Course **16**
City Hall **6**
Española Way **9**
Flagler Memorial Monument **15**
Fontainebleau Hilton **2**
Hibiscus Island **14**

Jackie Gleason Theatre of the Performing Arts (TOPA) **7**
La Gorce Country Club **1**
Lincoln Road Arts District & Mall **8**
Lummus Park **10**
Miami Beach Marina **12**
Palm Island **13**
Sightseeing Boats **3**
Stephen Moss Convention Center **5**

May, Tues–Fri 11am–5:30pm; Nov–Mar, Tues–Fri 11am–4:30pm; year round Sat and Sun 10am–4:30pm. **Closed:** Nov–May, Mon.

3. COOL FOR KIDS

Florida's vacationland has always been family oriented, and offers a host of programs and activities exclusively for children. Several beachfront resort hotels provide excellent supervised activities for kids, including the Sonesta Beach Hotel on Key Biscayne, and the Fontainebleau and Doral hotels in Miami Beach (see Chapter 5, "Miami Accommodations"). Information on these and other family packages is available from the Greater Miami Convention and Visitors Bureau (see "Information," Chapter 2).

TOP CITY ATTRACTIONS

For details of attractions listed here, see "Top Attractions," above.

THE MIAMI METROZOO *(see page 117)* This completely cageless zoo offers such star attractions as a monorail "safari" and a newly designed petting zoo. Especially fun for kids are the elephant rides.

MONKEY JUNGLE *(see page 121)* A zoo filled with monkeys, gorillas, and chimpanzees. Special shows are offered daily.

PARROT JUNGLE AND GARDENS *(see page 121)* For its roller-skating cockatoos, card-playing macaws, and lots of stunt-happy parrots.

MIAMI SEAQUARIUM *(see page 117)* Especially for performances given by Flipper, the original dolphin from the television series.

ANOTHER ATTRACTION

MIAMI MUSEUM OF SCIENCE AND SPACE TRANSIT PLANETARIUM, 3280 S. Miami Ave., Coconut Grove. Tel. 854-4247, general info; 854-2222, for planetarium show times.

The Museum of Science features over 150 hands-on exhibits that explore the mysteries of the universe. Live demonstrations and collections of rare natural history specimens make a visit here fun and informative.

The adjacent Space Transit Planetarium projects astronomy and laser shows. Most interesting, perhaps, is the in-house observatory, free and open to the public on weekend evenings.

Science Museum admission: $6 adults, $4 children 3–12

and seniors, under 3 free. **Planetarium admission:** $5 adults, $2.50 children and seniors. **Combined admission:** $8.50 adults, $5 children and seniors.

Open: Science Museum, daily 10am–6pm. Call for planetarium show times. **Closed:** Thanksgiving and Christmas. **Directions:** Take I-95 South to exit 1 and follow signs. Alternatively, ride the Metrorail to Vizcaya Station.

4. ORGANIZED TOURS

Similar to the tourist attractions, many of Miami's organized tours are interestingly offbeat. They are also fun and generally well priced. Always call ahead to check prices and times. Reservations are usually suggested.

BUS TOURS

OLD TOWN TROLLEY OF MIAMI. Tel. 374-8687.

Old Town's distinctive red and green "trolley" buses cruise the city's streets and causeways in a continuous 90-minute loop. You can stay aboard for the entire trip, or disembark at any one of a half-dozen stops, and reboard at your convenience. Trolleys depart every 30 minutes, and tickets are valid all day. Tours are completely narrated. Departure points include Bayside Marketplace and a dozen other locations. Call for information.

Admission: $14 adults, $5 children.
Open: Daily 10am–4pm.

WALKING TOURS

THE MIAMI DESIGN PRESERVATION LEAGUE, 1244 Ocean Dr., in the Leslie Hotel, South Miami Beach. Tel. 672-2014.

If you are lucky enough to be in Miami on a Saturday, don't miss this fascinating inside look at the city's historic art deco district. Tourgoers meet at South Beach's Welcome Center (address above) for a 1½-hour walk through some of America's most exuberantly "architectured" buildings. The Design Preservation League led the fight to designate this area a National Historic District, and is proud to share the splendid results with visitors.

Admission: $6 adults and children.
Times: Tours depart Saturday at 10:30am.

BOAT TOURS

HERITAGE *MIAMI II* TOPSAIL SCHOONER, Bayside Marketplace Marina, 401 Biscayne Blvd. (Downtown). Tel. 442-9697.

More adventure than tour, this relaxing ride aboard Miami's only tall ship is a fun way to see the city. Two-hour cruises pass by Villa Vizcaya, Coconut Grove, and Key Biscayne, and put you in sight of Miami's spectacular skyline. Cruises are offered September through May only. Call beforehand to make sure the ship is running on schedule.

Admission: $10 adults, $5 children under 12.

Times: Daily 1:30 and 6:30pm; Sat–Sun also 11am and 9pm.

BISCAYNE NATIONAL PARK TOUR BOATS, east end of SW 328th St., Homestead. Tel. 247-2400.

Biscayne National Park includes almost 200,000 acres of mangrove shoreline, barrier islands, and living coral reefs, which are all protected by the federal government. Tours of the area, aboard a 52-foot glass-bottom boat, cross the aquatic wilderness for a fish-eye view of some of America's most accessible coral reefs. Family snorkeling and canoe rentals are also offered.

Admission: $16.50 adults, $8.50 children under 13.

Times: Tours daily at 10am and 1:30pm. Reservations required.

RIVER QUEEN SIGHTSEEING, Eden Roc Yacht & Charter Center, 4525 Collins Ave. at 45th St., Miami Beach. Tel. 538-5380.

River Queen, an authentic Mississippi River–style paddlewheel boat, cruises up Indian Creek and out into Biscayne Bay. There are three daily sight-seeing tours.

Daily sight-seeing: $10 adults, $5 children under 12.

Times: Tours daily at 10am, 1pm, and 4pm. Hotel pickup is available.

HELICOPTER

DADE HELICOPTER, 950 MacArthur Causeway. Tel. 374-3737.

Miami by helicopter is the ultimate photo opportunity! Rides range in length from 7 to 20 minutes, and cost from $50 to $120 per person. There is a two-person minimum, and children under 12 ride for half price. The helipad is located on the south side of the MacArthur Causeway, between the mainland and Miami Beach.

5. SPORTS & RECREATION

SPECTATOR SPORTS

Miami's spectacular sports scene includes several major professional franchises, including football and basketball, and an eclectic variety of international games including cricket, soccer, and jai alai. Check the *Miami Herald*'s sports section for a daily listing of local events, and the paper's Friday "Weekend" section for comprehensive coverage and in-depth reports.

BASEBALL

BALTIMORE ORIOLES SPRING TRAINING, Miami Stadium, 2301 NW 10th Ave. Tel. 643-7100.

From mid-February until the season opener, Baltimore's best can be seen training in Miami. Practices are relaxed, fun, and free.

UNIVERSITY OF MIAMI HURRICANES, Mark Light Stadium, on the U of M's Coral Gables Campus. Tel. 284-2655, or toll free 800/GO-CANES in Florida.

UM's baseball Hurricanes play about 50 home games in their 5,000-seat stadium on the Coral Gables campus. The season lasts from February to May with both day and evening games scheduled.

Tickets: $3–$10.

Box office open: Mon–Fri 8am–6pm, Sat 8am–2pm.

BASKETBALL

MIAMI HEAT, Miami Arena, 721 NW 1st Ave. Tel. 577-HEAT.

The Heat made their debut in November 1988, and are one of the newest entries in the National Basketball Association. Predictably, they are also one of Miami's hottest tickets. The approximately 41-home game season lasts from November to April, with most games beginning at 7:30pm.

Tickets: $9–$29.

Box office open: Mon–Fri 10am–4pm (until 8pm on game nights). Tickets also available through Ticketmaster, tel. 358-5885.

DOG RACING

Greyhound racing is Miami's most popular spectator sport. The dogs circle the oval at speeds averaging 40 miles per hour. Similar to the horsetrack, betting is simple and track workers are willing to give you a hand. Note that racing is during winter months only.

FLAGLER GREYHOUND TRACK, 401 NW 38th Court at NW 33rd St., Tel. 649-3000.

This fun, high-stakes track features some of America's top dogs, with racing 6 days a week. The track hosts the $110,000 International Classic, one of the richest races on the circuit.

Admission: $1 general, $3 clubhouse. 50¢ Parking.

Post times: Mon–Sat 7:45pm; matinees Tues, Thurs, and Sat 12:30pm.

HOLLYWOOD GREYHOUND TRACK, 831 N. Federal Hwy. at Pembroke Rd., Hallandale. Tel. 758-3647.

An average crowd of 10,000 fans wager a collective $1 million nightly at this track, considered by experts to be one of the best in the country. If you've never been to the dog track before, arrive a half-hour early for a quick introduction to greyhound racing, shown on the track's television monitors.

Admission: 50¢ general, $1.50 clubhouse. $1 Parking.

Post times: Late Dec–late Apr Mon–Sat 7:30pm, Sun 7pm; matinees Mon, Wed, and Sat 12:30pm.

FOOTBALL

MIAMI DOLPHINS, Joe Robbie Stadium, 2269 NW 199th St. (Greater Miami North). Tel. 620-5000.

The city's National Football League franchise is Miami's most recognizable team and followed by thousands of "dolfans." About six home games are played during the season, most starting at 1pm.

Tickets: About $30.

Box office open: Mon–Fri 10am–6pm; also available through Ticketmaster, tel. 358-5885.

UNIVERSITY OF MIAMI HURRICANES, Orange Bowl Stadium, 1501 NW 3rd St. Tel. 284-2655, or toll free 800/GO-CANES in Florida.

The U of M football Hurricanes play at the famous Orange Bowl from September through November. The stadium is seldom full, and games here are really exciting. If you sit high up, you will have an excellent view over Miami. Call for schedule.

Tickets: $5–$12.

Box office open: Mon–Fri 8am–6pm and prior to all games.

HORSE RACING

GULFSTREAM PARK, U.S. 1 and Hallandale Beach Blvd., Hallandale. Tel. 944-1242.

Wrapped around an artificial lake, this suburban course is both pretty and popular. Large purses and important races are commonplace, and the track is often crowded.

Admission: $2 grandstand, $4.50 clubhouse. **Parking:** From $1. **Post times:** Jan 13–March 31, Tues–Sun at 1pm.

HIALEAH PARK, grandstand entrance at E. 2nd Ave. and 32nd St., Hialeah. Tel. 885-8000.

You've seen the park's pink American flamingos on *Miami Vice*, and indeed, this famous colony is the largest of its kind. This track, listed on the National Register of Historic Places, is one of the most beautiful in the world, featuring old-fashioned stands and acres of immaculately manicured grounds.

Admission: $2 grandstand, $4 clubhouse; children under 18 free with adult. **Parking:** From $1.50.

Open: Races mid-Nov–mid-May. Call for post times. Open year-round for sight-seeing Mon–Sat 10am–4pm.

JAI ALAI

Jai alai, sort of a Spanish-style indoor lacrosse, is popular around these parts, and regularly played in two Miami-area frontons. Players use woven baskets, called cestas, to hurl balls, pelotas, at speeds that sometimes exceed 170 miles per hour. Spectators, who are protected behind a wall of glass, place bets on the evening's players.

MIAMI JAI ALAI FRONTON, 3500 NW 37th Ave. at NW 35th St., Tel. 633-6400.

America's oldest jai-alai fronton dates from 1926 and schedules 13 games per night.

Admission: $1 grandstand, $5 clubhouse.

Open: Year-round, except for a 4-week recess in the fall. First game Mon–Sat 7:10pm; matinees Mon, Wed, and Sat at noon.

SOCCER

MIAMI FREEDOM, Milander Stadium, 4800 Palm Ave., Hialeah. Tel. 446-3136.

Representing yet another attempt to make soccer a viable spectator sport Miami Freedom has recently become incorporated. Games are played April through August, but as of this writing, the schedule has not yet been set.

Tickets: $8.50 adults, $3 children under 15.

Box office open: Mon–Fri 9am–5pm.

RECREATION

The climate in this southern city is perfectly suited for recreation, and there are a host of opportunities.

It should come as no surprise that the lion's share of participatory sports options here are water-related. **Penrod's Beach Club,** 1 Ocean Drive (tel. 538-1111), in South Miami Beach, offers a pool, a Jacuzzi, and a full day of activities for $39. This single, reasonable price includes use of beach bicycles, kayaks, Windsurfers, rafts, snorkeling equipment, "muscle beach" free weights, and fishing gear. It also includes continental breakfast, lunch, and three drinks. It's open Sunday to Thursday 10am to 2am, Friday to Saturday 10am to 5am.

BEACHES

In short, there are two distinct beach alternatives: Miami Beach and Key Biscayne. It's all explained below.

Miami Beach's Beaches

Collins Avenue fronts 10 miles of white sandy beach and blue-green waters from 1st to 192nd Street. Although most of this stretch is lined with a solid wall of hotels, beach access is plentiful, and you are free to frolic along the entire strip. There are lots of public beaches here, complete with lifeguards, toilet facilities, concession stands, and metered parking (bring lots of quarters). Miami Beach's beaches are both wide, and well maintained. Except for a thin strip close to the water, most of the sand here is hard-packed—the result of a $10-million Army Corps of Engineers Beach Rebuilding Project meant to protect buildings from the effects of eroding sand.

In general, the beaches on this barrier island become less crowded the farther north you go. A wooden boardwalk runs along the hotel side of the beach from 21st to 44th Street—about 1½ miles—offering a terrific sun and surf experience without getting sand in your shoes. Aside from the "Best Beaches" listed below, Miami Beach's public, lifeguard-protected beaches include: 21st Street, at the beginning of the boardwalk; 35th Street, popular with an older crowd; 46th Street, next to the Fontainebleau Hilton Hotel; 53rd Street, a narrower, more sedate beach; 64th Street, one of the quietest strips around; and 72nd Street, a local old-timers spot.

Key Biscayne's Beaches

If Miami Beach is not private enough for you, Key Biscayne might be more of what you had in mind. Crossing Rickenbacker Causeway ($1 toll) is almost like crossing into the Bahamas. The 5 miles of public beach here are blessed with softer sand, and are less developed and more laid-back than the hotel-laden strips to the north.

BEST PICNIC BEACH Bill Baggs Cape Florida State Park, on the south end of Key Biscayne, has barbecue grills and picnic tables shaded by a tall forest of trees. On weekends, the place really hops, primarily with partying families playing games, listening to music, and cooking up a storm. The adjacent, narrow, soft-sand beach is home to the picturesque Cape Florida Lighthouse, which has operated here since 1825. Admission is $2 per vehicle, $1 per passenger.

BEST SURFING BEACH The First Street Beach, at the bottom of Ocean Drive in South Miami Beach has Miami's "gnarliest" waves. No lifeguard.

BEST PARTY BEACH Crandon Park Beach, on Crandon Boulevard in Key Biscayne has 3 miles of oceanfront beach, 493 acres of park, 75 grills, three parking lots, several soccer and softball fields, and a public 18-hole championship golf course. The beach is particularly wide and the water is usually so clear you can see to the bottom. Admission is $2 per vehicle. It's open 8am to sunset.

BEST SWIMMING BEACH The competition is fierce, but my favorite is the chic Lummus Park Beach, which runs along Ocean Drive from about 6th to 14th Street, in South Miami Beach's art deco district. It's pretty, has plenty of metered parking, and is close to a number of restaurants with excellent happy hours.

BEST WINDSURFING BEACH Hobie Beach, beside the causeway leading to Key Biscayne, is not really a beach, but a quiet inlet with calm winds and a number of Windsurfer-rental places.

BEST SHELL-HUNTING BEACH Bal Harbour Beach, Collins Avenue at 96th Street, is just a few yards north of Surfside Beach.

There's an exercise course, good shade, and usually plenty of colorful shells. No lifeguard.

BINGO

Well, why not? This is Miami after all. **North Collins Bingo,** 18288 Collins Ave., Sunny Isles (tel. 932-7185), features games every day from noon to midnight (with a break from 4 to 7pm), and in the afternoon you get 6 cards for just 25¢; $15–$65 at night. There are nonsmoking areas, door prizes nightly, and "the largest cash prizes allowed by law."

BOATING/SAILING

Sailboats and catamarans are available through the beachfront concessions desk of several top resorts. They are listed under the appropriate hotels in Chapter 5. Other private rental places include:

BEACH BOAT RENTALS, 2380 Collins Ave., Miami Beach. Tel. 534-4307.

These 50-horsepower 18-foot power boats rent for some of the best rates on the beach. Cruising is exclusively in and around Biscayne Bay, as ocean access is prohibited. Renters must be over 21 years old, and must present a current passport or driver's license. The rental office is at 23rd Street, on the inland waterway in Miami Beach.

Rates: $45 one hour, $120 four hours, $175 eight hours. AE, MC, V.

Open: May–Oct, daily 9am–6pm, Nov–Apr, daily 9am–5pm (weather permitting).

CLUB NAUTICO OF COCONUT GROVE, 2560 S. Bayshore Dr., Coconut Grove. Tel. 858-6258.

High-quality power boats are rented for fishing, waterskiing, diving, and cruising in the bay or ocean. All boats are Coast Guard–equipped with VHF radios and safety gear.

Two other locations include Biscayne Bay Marriot Hotel, 1633 North Bayshore Drive (Downtown, tel. 371-4252); and Miami Beach Marina, Pier E, 300 Alton Road (South Miami Beach, tel. 673-2502).

Rates: 4 hours from $150, 8 hours from $249.

Open: Daily 8am–5:30pm (weather permitting).

FISHING

Bridge fishing is popular in Miami; you'll see people with poles over most every waterway.

Some of the best surf casting in the city can be had at Haulover Beach Park, at Collins Avenue and 105th Street, where there is a bait and tackle shop right on the pier. South Pointe Park, at the southern tip of Miami Beach, is another popular fishing spot, and features a long pier, comfortable benches, and a great view of the ships passing through Government Cut. A number of deep-sea fishing opportunities are also on offer, including:

KELLEY FISHING FLEET, Haulover Marina, 10800 Collins Ave. at 108th St., Haulover (Miami Beach). Tel. 945-3801.

Half-day, full-day, and night fishing aboard diesel-powered "party boats" lures in fish like snapper, sailfish, and mackerel. The fleet's emphasis on drifting is geared toward trolling and bottom fishing. Reservations recommended.

Cost: $18.75 adult, $11.75 children half-day and night fishing; $28.75 adult, $17.50 children full-day; $3.75 rod and reel rental.

Sailing: Half-day daily 9am–12:30pm and 1:45pm–5:30pm; full-day Wed, Sat, and Sun 9am–4pm; nightly 8pm–midnight.

CHARTER BOAT *HELEN C*, Haulover Marina, 10800 Collins Ave., Haulover (Miami Beach). Tel. 947-4081.

Although there is no shortage of private charter boats here, Capt. John Callan is a good pick, since he puts individuals together to get a full boat. His *Helen C* is a twin-engine 55-footer, equipped for big game "monster" fish like marlin, tuna, dolphin, and bluefish. Call for reservations.

Cost: $60 per person.

Sailing: Daily 8am–noon or 1–5pm.

GOLF

There are dozens of golf courses in the Greater Miami area, many of which are open to the public. Contact the Greater Miami Convention and Visitors Bureau (see "Information" in Chapter 2) for a complete list of courses and costs.

THE BAYSHORE GOLF COURSE, 2301 Alton Rd., Miami Beach. Tel. 532-3350.

This Miami Beach park has an 18-hole green and a lighted driving range for night swings.

Admission: $25 per person during the week, $15 after 4pm; $26 on the weekends, $20 after 4pm. Florida residents save $5.

Open: Daily 6:30am–dusk.

KEY BISCAYNE GOLF COURSE, 6700 Crandon Blvd., Key Biscayne. Tel. 361-9129.

Key Biscayne Golf Course is the number-one ranked municipal course in the state, and one of the top five in the country. The park is situated on 200 bayfront acres, and offers a pro shop, rentals, lessons, carts, and a lighted driving range.

Admission: $55–$60 per person Thanksgiving to Easter, $35 per person the rest of the year. Carts ($25 for 2 people) are required until 1pm.

Open: Daily dawn–dusk.

HEALTH CLUBS

BARCADO BEACH CLUB GYMNASIUM, 2377 Collins Ave., between 23rd and 24th Sts., on the ground floor of Roney Plaza, Miami Beach. Tel. 531-7357.

Although there are some bicycles and Universal-type pulley systems here, the Barcado's workout room is primarily a free-weight facility. Not fancy, but well equipped, and visitors have free access to a nearby swimming pool.

Admission: $6 per day.

Open: Mon–Fri 7am–10pm, Sat 9am–8pm, Sun 9am–1pm.

JET SKIS

Tony's Jet Ski Rentals, 3601 Rickenbacker Causeway, Key Biscayne (tel. 361-8280), rents jet skis, Yamaha Wave Runners, and Kawasaki two-seaters. This is the city's largest rental shop, located on a private beach in the Miami Marine Stadium lagoon. The cost is from $45 per hour. Wave Runners rent for $60 per hour. It's open daily 11am to dusk.

SCUBA DIVING/SNORKELING

In 1981, the government began a wide-scale project designed to increase the number of habitats available to marine organisms. One of the program's major accomplishments has been the creation of nearby artificial reefs, which have attracted all kinds of tropical plants, fish, and animals. An excellent reef guide is available free from Biscayne National Park, Box 1369, Homestead, FL 33090 (tel. 530-9955).

Several dive shops around the city offer organized weekend outings, either to these reefs, or to one of over a dozen old shipwrecks around Miami's shores. Check "Divers" in the "Yellow Pages" for rental equipment, and for a full list of undersea tour operators.

Divers by the Bay, 2550 S. Bayshore Dr., Coconut Grove (tel. 530-9955) offers some of the best dive trips. Experienced guides and quality equipment are provided to adventurers on their multipassenger vessels. Reservations are required. You pay $25 per person and rentals are additional. Sails daily 8am and 1pm.

TENNIS

In addition to hotel tennis facilities, about 500 public courts are available free or for a minimal charge. Some of the best tennis courts are located in Miami Beach. For information on courts closest to you, contact the **Metro-Dade County Parks and Recreation Department** (tel. 579-2676), weekdays between 8am and 5pm.

The Flamingo Park Center, 1245 Michigan Ave, at 12th St., South Miami Beach (tel. 673-7761), is the city's largest facility, with 20 clay courts. Open Mon to Fri 9am to 8pm, Sat to Sun 9am to dusk.

The Bayshore Golf Course, 2301 Alton Rd., Miami Beach (tel.

532-3350), has two hard courts and is open daily during daylight hours.

WINDSURFING

Sailboards Miami, Rickenbacker Causeway, Key Biscayne (tel. 361-SAIL), operates out of big yellow trucks on Hobie Beach (see "Beaches," above), the most popular windsurfing spot in the city. Rentals are by the hour or day, and lessons are given throughout the day. You pay $15 per hour, $45 per day; 2-hour lesson and rental package is $39. It's open daily 9am to 6pm.

CHAPTER 8

DRIVING & WALKING AROUND MIAMI

1. **MIAMI PANORAMA**
2. **DOWNTOWN, COCONUT GROVE & CORAL GABLES**
3. **SOUTH MIAMI BEACH**

Miami is famous for its great weather and natural surroundings. So understandably, with few exceptions, Miami's best sights are outdoors. The city's beautiful buildings and beaches tend to be far away from each other, so driving is definitely in order. But Miami is relatively easy to negotiate; you can't get too lost. And, if you do, chances are you'll stumble onto a special find of your own.

The following tours are designed to give you a feel for the city in a relatively short time. If you have more time to spare, don't hesitate to follow a hunch or turn down a street that is beckoning for your attention. Have fun!

DRIVING TOUR 1 — Miami Panorama

Start and Finish: Bayside Marketplace, 401 Biscayne Blvd. (Downtown).
Time: Approximately 1 hour, excluding stops, and allowing for light traffic.
Best Times: Weekday working hours when the roads tend to be less busy.
Worst Times: Rush hour, weekdays 8–10am and 4–6pm.

Miami's ethnic and cultural diversity is its most important asset. The following circular route will give you a good feel for the city in general, including all its divergent parts. Start at the:

1. **Bayside Marketplace** (401 Biscayne Blvd.). This Rouse Company development occupies a beautiful shorefront location, and encompasses dozens of retail shops and eateries.

   Drive north along U.S. 1 (Biscayne Blvd.) about 10 blocks, and turn east onto the MacArthur Causeway (Rte. 41). When crossing the bridge, look back toward Downtown and you will see one of the prettiest cityscapes in the world. To your right you can see the:

2. **Port of Miami,** just across a thin strip of water. If they are not out at sea, several large cruise ships will be docked here; so close

it seems like you can almost touch them. Once the causeway reaches Miami Beach, stay in the right lane, and continue straight onto 5th Street, the southern boundary of South Miami Beach's art deco district. Fifth Street terminates at:

3. Ocean Drive, the deco district's most celebrated strip. Turn left and drive slowly. Lined with pretty hotels, tall palm trees, and a long stretch of beach, this unusual road offers some of the best people-watching in Miami. For a more in-depth look at this historic area, see "A Walking Tour," below.

A REFUELING STOP   Take a break from your tour to relax at the **4. News Café,** 800 Ocean Dr. (tel. 538-NEWS). This cheap and trendy sidewalk café is just across from the beach and features terrific soups, salads, sandwiches, and the like. Excellent breakfasts are also available, along with good coffee and herbal teas. (See Chapter 6, "Miami Dining".)

At 15th Street you will be forced to turn left. Make the turn, drive one block, and turn right onto Collins Avenue. You are now heading north along Miami Beach's most celebrated street, which will give you a good perspective on the diversity of the beach. On your right, take time to admire the:

5. Deco hotels like the Delano, National, and Shelborne (1685, 1687, and 1801 Collins Ave.). These are some of the region's prettiest early skyscrapers. On the northwest corner of Collins Avenue and Lincoln Road is:

6. Burger King, Miami's most popular fast-food joint, complete with a blue and yellow tropical exterior, and trademark art deco curves.

Continue north, past the huge hotels and condominiums, and you will soon see a lush tropical garden behind huge Roman-style columns. This fancy greenery is just an illusion; it's really the:

7. Fontainebleau Mural at Collins Avenue and 44th Street. The lagoon and waterfalls pictured actually exist behind the wall in the rear of the famous Fontainebleau Hotel (4441 Collins Ave.). Stop by and take a look.

Farther along Collins Avenue, you will pass the:

8. Eden Roc (4525 Collins Ave.), **Doral** (4833 Collins Ave.), and many more of Miami Beach's monolithic hotels. Continue north and turn left onto 71st Street. You are now heading toward the 79th Street Causeway, named for its terminus on the mainland. You will see:

9. Normandy Isles, as the route to the causeway winds its way through. This is an exclusive and pretty Biscayne Bay enclave riddled with French-sounding street names. In the middle of the bay, the causeway crosses:

10. North Bay Village, a couple of residential islands built from the soil dredged from Biscayne Bay.

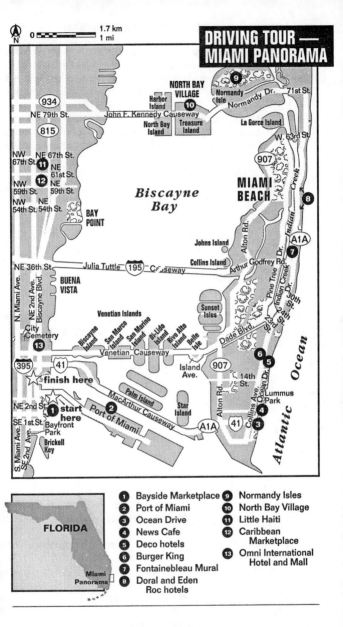

**DRIVING TOUR —
MIAMI PANORAMA**

1. Bayside Marketplace
2. Port of Miami
3. Ocean Drive
4. News Cafe
5. Deco hotels
6. Burger King
7. Fontainebleau Mural
8. Doral and Eden Roc hotels
9. Normandy Isles
10. North Bay Village
11. Little Haiti
12. Caribbean Marketplace
13. Omni International Hotel and Mall

FLORIDA

Miami Panorama

Once back on the mainland, continue straight, about 6 blocks past Biscayne Boulevard, and turn left onto NE 2nd Avenue. You are now driving through the heart of:

11. Little Haiti. This region's main thoroughfare contains dozens of stores with signs announcing their goods in Creole, French, and sometimes English. Drive south until you reach the:

12. **Caribbean Marketplace,** located at the corner of 60th Street. The colorful, new building's architecture is based on the Iron Market in Port-au-Prince, and contains a number of shops selling traditional foods and merchandise (see "Neighborhoods in Brief" in Chapter 4).

After seeing the Caribbean Marketplace, turn left on any street and make your way back to U.S. 1. Turn right and head south. This relatively tame-looking main thoroughfare is, by night, one of Miami's seediest strips. After dark, prostitutes walk the streets and numerous police actions take place. Keep your eyes open during the day, too. In addition to a terrific variety of fast-food joints, cheap motels, and annoying traffic lights, there are also some good restaurants and interesting shops.

13. **The Omni International Hotel and Mall** (1601 Biscayne Blvd.) will soon appear on your left, after which you will drive under the bridge leading to the MacArthur Causeway and end up back at the Bayside Marketplace.

DRIVING TOUR 2 — Downtown, Coconut Grove & Coral Gables

Start and Finish: Bayside Marketplace, 401 Biscayne Blvd. (Downtown).
Time: Approximately 1½ hours, excluding stops.
Best Times: Two hours before sunset, when the city will be breathtakingly illuminated.
Worst Times: Weekdays 8–10am.

After driving past the skyscrapers of the city's Downtown, this tour will take you through two of Miami's oldest and best-known neighborhoods.

Coconut Grove, annexed by the City of Miami in 1925, was established by Northeastern artists and writers, and built a reputation as being an "in" spot for bohemian-minded intellectuals. The first hotel in the area was built in 1880.

Coral Gables, one of Miami's first planned developments, was created by developer George Merrick in the early 1920s. Many of the houses were built in a Mediterranean style along lush tree-lined streets that open onto beautifully carved plazas. The best architectural examples of the era have Spanish-style tiled roofs and are built from Miami oolite, a native limestone, commonly called "coral rock." (See "Neighborhoods in Brief" in Chapter 4.) Start at the:

1. **Bayside Marketplace** (see "Driving Tour 1," above) and drive south along Biscayne Boulevard. Take note of the:
2. **Southeast Financial Center** (200 S. Biscayne Blvd.). This 55-story steel and glass tower is the tallest building east of Dallas

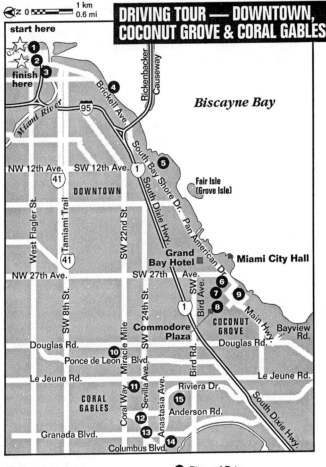

1 Bayside Marketplace
2 Southeast Financial Center
3 CenTrust Tower
4 The Palace, The Imperial, The Atlantis, and Villa Regina
5 Vizcaya
6 Grand Bay Hotel and Miami City Hall
7 Coconut Grove business district
8 Pita and Eats
9 The Barnacle
10 "Miracle Mile"
11 Granada Golf Course
12 Venetian Pool
13 DeSoto Plaza
14 Biltmore Hotel
15 Palermo, Catalonia, and Malaga avenues

and south of Manhattan. At its bottom, Biscayne Boulevard doglegs and reveals the:

3. CenTrust Tower (100 SE 1st St.). Designed by celebrated architects I. M. Pei & Partners, this spectacular wedge-shaped building is particularly eye-catching when illuminated at night.

Stay in the left lane and cross the drawbridge over the Miami

River; the mainland's most beautiful waterway and a sewer of illegal activities. Be patient—the bridge regularly opens to let tugboat-led barges through.

You are now on Brickell Avenue, home to the largest concentration of international banks in the United States. Drive slowly. Each one of these architectural masterpieces deserves equal attention.

South of SE 15th Street, Brickell Avenue becomes residential, and an equally extraordinary block of condominiums rises up along the avenue's east side. Lush foliage makes it hard to see these palaces, so you might want to stop your car for a better view. Three of these apartment buildings, including:

4. The Palace (1541 Brickell Ave.), **The Imperial** (1617 Brickell Ave.), and **The Atlantis** (2025 Brickell Ave.) were designed by Arquitectonica, Miami's world-famous architectural firm. The latter sports a square hole in its center, and is one of the city's most famous structures. **Villa Regina** (1581 Brickell Ave.) would almost be a plain-looking building if it were not for its spectacular rainbow colored exterior, painted by Israeli artist Yacov Agam.

A few blocks past the turn-off toward Key Biscayne you will come to a second set of traffic lights. Bear left onto South Miami Avenue, which quickly becomes South Bayshore Drive. This two-lane road runs along Biscayne Bay, on the southern edge of Coconut Grove. Look out on your left for the entrance to:

5. Villa Vizcaya (3251 South Miami Ave.), the elegant and opulent estate of International Harvester pioneer James Deering. Think about visiting the magnificent house and grounds (see "The Top Attractions" in Chapter 7).

Continuing along tree-covered South Bayshore Drive, you'll pass:

6. Grand Bay Hotel (2669 South Bayshore Dr.) on your right, and **Miami City Hall,** at the end of Pan American Drive, on your left.

At its end, South Bayshore Drive turns right, into McFarlane Road, a short street that terminates at Coconut Grove's most important intersection. Make a sharp left onto Main Highway and cruise slowly. This is the heart of the:

7. Grove's business district, and home to dozens of boutiques and cafés. You may wish to walk around and explore.

A REFUELING STOP For a light snack or a long lunch, there are plenty of places to choose from. But, **8. Pita and Eats** is a good choice for inexpensive grazing on one of the area's most central streets. Pita sandwiches, salads, and other light foods are available to eat inside, or on the steps, watching the street scene below. (See Chapter 6, "Miami Dining.")

Two blocks south of Commodore Plaza, you will see the entrance to:

9. The Barnacle, 3485 Main Hwy. (tel. 448-9445). This former home of navel architect and early settler Ralph Middleton Munroe is now a museum and open to the public. Tours are given Thursday through Monday at 9am, 10:30am, 1pm, and 2:30pm. Admission is $2. (See "More Attractions" in Chapter 7.)

On the next block, on your right, is the Coconut Grove Playhouse (3500 Main Hwy.). Built as a movie theater in 1926, it is one of the oldest showplaces in Miami (see "The Performing Arts" in Chapter 10).

Main Highway ends at Douglas Road (SW 37th Ave.). Turn right, drive north about 10 miles, and make a left onto Coral Way (SW 22nd St.). You are now entering Coral Gables via the village's most famous thoroughfare. Dubbed:

10. "Miracle Mile," this stretch of shops and eateries dates from the development's earliest days, and is the heart of the Gables' downtown. To your right, on the corner of Ponce de Leon Boulevard, stands the Colonnade Building (133–169 Miracle Mile), a structure that once housed George Merrick's sales offices, and has recently been rebuilt into a top hotel, the Colonnade (see Chapter 5, "Miami Accommodations"). Coral Gables City Hall (405 Biltmore Way), with its trademark columned rotunda, is at the end of the Miracle Mile, and can be visited free weekdays from 8am to 5pm.

Follow Coral Way to the right of City Hall, and past the:

11. Granada Golf Course, one of two public teeing grounds in Coral Gables. After 4 blocks, turn left onto DeSoto Boulevard, and look for the:

12. Venetian Pool (2701 DeSoto Blvd.) on your left. Miami's most unusual swimming pool, dating from 1924, is hidden behind pastel stucco walls, and is honored with a listing on the National Register of Historic Places. It costs $4 to swim and sunbathe, but if you just want to look around for a few minutes, the cashier may let you in free. See Chapter 7 for more information.

One block farther along DeSoto Boulevard is the:

13. DeSoto Plaza and Fountain, one of Coral Gables' most famous traffic circles. Designed by Denman Fink in the early 1920s, the structure consists of a column-topped fountain, surrounded by a footed basin that catches water flowing from four sculptured faces.

DeSoto Boulevard picks up again on the other side of the fountain, and continues for about 4 blocks to its end at Anastasia Avenue, in front of the:

14. Biltmore Hotel (1200 Anastasia Ave.). This grand hotel is one of Miami's oldest and prettiest properties. Its 26-story tower is a replica of the Giralda Bell Tower of the Cathedral of Seville in

Spain. The enormous cost of operating this queen has forced the hotel through many hands in recent years. Bankruptcy shut the hotel in 1990, but the Biltmore may once again be open by the time you visit. If it is, go inside and marvel at the ornate marble and tile interior, outfitted with mahogany furniture and a medieval fireplace.

Out back, the hotel's 1.25 million-gallon swimming pool is the largest of its kind in America. Just beyond is the Biltmore Golf Course, challenging and beautiful.

The fastest way back to Downtown Miami is to continue east to the end of Anastasia Avenue, turn right on LeJeune Road, and then left onto U.S. 1. Take a detour on your way home to sightsee on:

15. **Palermo, Catalonia, Malaga,** and other interesting avenues. Houses in this area, along tree-canopied streets, are delightful to look at.

A WALKING TOUR — South Miami Beach

Start and Finish: South Miami Beach Welcome Center, 1244 Ocean Dr., Miami Beach.
Time: Allow approximately 1½ hours, not including browsing in galleries.
Best Times: Monday through Saturday between noon and 5pm.
Worst Times: Nights and Sundays, when galleries are closed and the buildings are dark.

After years of neglect and calls for the wholesale demolition of its buildings, South Miami Beach got a new lease on life in 1979. Under the leadership of the Miami Design Preservation League, an approximate square mile of South Beach was granted a listing on the National Register of Historic Places. Thus the art deco district was born.

Leonard Horowitz, a gifted young designer, began to cover the buildings' peeling beige paint with his now-famous flamboyant colors. Long-lost architectural details were highlighted with soft sherbets, and the colors of peach, periwinkle, turquoise, and purple received worldwide attention. Developers soon moved in and the full-scale refurbishment of the area's hotels was underway.

Today, new hotels, restaurants, and nightclubs continue to open, and South Beach, or "SoBe," as it is more chicly known, is on the cutting edge of Miami's cultural and nightlife scene. A stroll around the art deco district—a vibrant architectural museum—is a fun and fascinating way to spend a day.

If you are lucky enough to be in Miami on a Saturday, don't miss the fascinating art deco district guided walking tour offered by **The Miami Design Preservation League** (tel. 672-2014). Tours

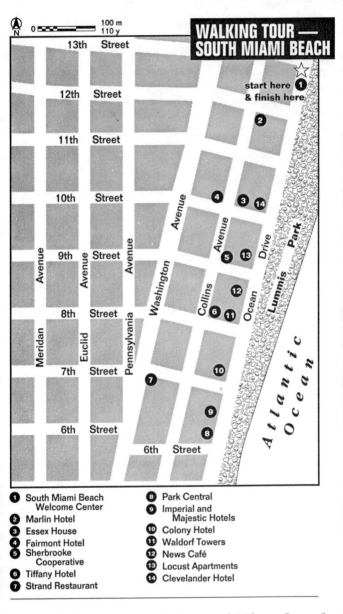

depart at 10:30am from the South Miami Beach Welcome Center, (in the Leslie Hotel, 1244 Ocean Dr.). Cost is $6 per person, and tours last about an hour and a half.

You don't have to be an architect to enjoy the fanciful styles that are so prevalent in these parts; the intrinsic beauty of these buildings is easy to see. Still, knowing what to look for will increase your appreciation for this special area. Here are some hints:

Eyebrows Colorfully painted cantilevered window shades are a common ornament on Streamline Moderne buildings.

Etched Glass Flamingos, fish, palm trees, and other tropical motifs are found in many area lobbies.

Finial, Spire, or Trylon A futuristic-looking vertical ornament located atop a building's highest point.

Neon Light The trademark of some of the area's prettiest buildings.

Porthole Windows Nautical imagery is one of South Miami Beach's most important motifs.

Rounded Corners The most obvious aspect of the influence of airplanes, automobiles, trains, and ships on Streamline Moderne architecture. Fast, sleek aerodynamic designs looked futuristic in the 1930s and '40s.

Terrazzo Composite flooring frequently arranged in geometric patterns.

Ziggurat or Stepped Pediment Seen on roofs and incorporated into other areas, this Egyptian style is common in art deco design.

The Miami Beach Historic District is roughly bounded by the Atlantic Ocean on the East, Alton Road on the West, 6th Street on the South, and Dade Boulevard (along the Collins Canal) to the North. The South Miami Beach Welcome Center (tel. 672-2014) can suggest several walking and driving routes, highlighting a variety of architectural styles. One general tour is offered below. Start at the:

1. **South Miami Beach Welcome Center** (1244 Ocean Dr.). This storefront inside the Leslie Hotel has several informative giveaways, including maps and art deco architecture information. Art deco books, T-shirts, postcards, mugs, car sunshades, and other similarly styled items are sold. It's open Monday to Saturday from 9am to 6pm, sometimes later.

    Walk south (with the ocean on your left) and turn right onto 12th Street. One block ahead, on the corner of Collins Avenue, you will see the:

2. **Marlin Hotel** (1200 Collins Ave.), one of South Beach's newest deco renovations. Owned by former Island Records president Chris Blackwell, this eye-catching pastel-blue building encompasses a hotel, restaurant/bar, and recording studio. Topped by a regal spire, the Marlin was redesigned by local artist Barbara Hulanicki, who is responsible for both the clean Disneyesque exterior, and the more gritty bar area.

    Continue south, walking two blocks down Collins Avenue. Many of the buildings on this street feature corner entrances, and the beautiful:

3. **Essex House** (1001 Collins Ave.), on the corner of 10th Street, is no exception. Built in 1938, the Essex is an excellent example of Nautical Moderne, complete with octagonal porthole windows, a curved design, and sleek "racing stripes" along its sides.

Explore the lobby, which features etched glasswork and detailed crown moldings.

Across the street is the pink and yellow:

4. **Fairmont Hotel** (1000 Collins Ave.), best known for its extremely stylish garden restaurant just beside it. Although the restaurant's angles and colors blend in with the surroundings, its decorations are contemporary.

Continue down Collins Avenue to the:

5. **Sherbrooke Cooperative** (901 Collins Ave.), which has a beautiful porch railing, porthole windows, and multilevel rounded eyebrows that give elegance to an otherwise simple design.

On the corner of 8th Street is the:

6. **Tiffany Hotel** (801 Collins Ave.), an attractive building boasting an imposing metal spire. Now painted plain white, the hotel would benefit from a color scheme that highlighted its special design.

Turn right onto 8th Street, walk one block, and make a left onto Washington Avenue. Most of the storefronts along this street are original commercial exteriors. Like many establishments on the block, the aqua-colored:

7. **Strand Restaurant** (671 Washington Ave.) features ornate moldings and a ziggurat roofline. Formerly the Famous, a popular Jewish restaurant, the Strand has maintained the original wide-open, but warm interior.

Walk south, turn left on 6th Street, and continue two blocks to the beach. Make a left on Ocean Drive, and stroll along one of South Beach's most beautiful strips. Most of the buildings on this stretch are hotels built in the late 1930s, and early '40s. The:

8. **Park Central** (640 Ocean Dr.) is one of the street's most successful designs, flaunting a fluted tin eave, etched-glass windows, and a geometric guardrail. The:

9. **Imperial** and **Majestic Hotels** (650 and 660 Ocean Dr.) are also excellent examples of the period. Like many hotels in the area, these buildings are cantilevered over their front terraces and are supported by columns.

On the next block, the:

10. **Colony Hotel** (736 Ocean Dr.) stands out because of the huge neon sign affixed to its curved-entry overhang. The:

11. **Waldorf Towers** (860 Ocean Dr.) is a corner building with a cylindrical turret capped by a rooftop tower. Glass bricks and eyebrows are also incorporated into the building's design. At night, a spectacular neon light sculpture shines in the uppermost windows.

A REFUELING STOP Take a break from your tour to relax at the **12. News Café,** 800 Ocean Dr. (tel. 538-NEWS). See "A Refueling Stop" in "Driving Tour 1," above.

Having regained your energy after that refreshing pause, walk a little farther along the same street to the:

13. Locust Apartments (918 Ocean Dr.), the only Mediterranean Revival building on the street. It features attractive pointed-arch windows reminiscent of those found in medieval Venetian edifices. On the ground floor is the Café des Arts restaurant (see Chapter 6, "Miami Dining").

14. Clevelander Hotel (1020 Ocean Dr.) is one of the few in the area with an original swimming pool and deco-style sun deck area. The huge outdoor stage, located behind the pool, hosts live rock and reggae bands most every night, when the Clevelander becomes one of the liveliest locales on the beach.

Continue along Ocean Drive, and you will return to the South Miami Beach Welcome Center. Stop in and ask any questions you might have. Think about touring other parts of the Historic District. Lincoln Road, the area's art center, and Espanola Way, a pretty street with Mediterranean-revival architecture are excellent bets.

CHAPTER 9

MIAMI SHOPPING

1. THE SHOPPING SCENE
2. SHOPPING A TO Z

With few exceptions, Miami's main shopping areas are not streets, but malls—a reminder of the city's strong suburban bent. Most, like Dadeland Mall and The Mall at 163rd Street, are unabashedly straightforward about their identities, and look pretty much like thousands of other shopping centers all across America. Other arcades, like the Bal Harbour Shops and Bayside Marketplace, are more coyly named, as they shy away from the "mall's" middle-class connotations. Whatever the shopping centers call themselves, some retailers believe that there are too many of them. South Florida's gaggle of galleries has created stiff competition, a situation that keeps shoppers happy with good values and lots of choices.

1. THE SHOPPING SCENE

SHOPPING AREAS

Almost every major street in Miami is lined with an infinite variety of small stores, restaurants, motels, and fast-food joints. Some of the city's best shops and shopping areas are outlined below under "Shopping A to Z," but you are bound to make your own finds. Keep your eyes open and stop at shops that interest you.

COCONUT GROVE

Downtown Coconut Grove is one of Miami's few pedestrian-friendly zones. Centered around Main Highway and Grand Avenue, and branching onto the adjoining streets, the Grove's wide, café- and boutique-lined sidewalks provide hours of browsing pleasure. You can't escape Miami's ubiquitous malls, however—there's one near this cozy village center (see "Mayfair Shops," under "Malls" below). Coconut Grove is best known for its dozens of avant-garde clothing stores, funky import shops, and excellent sidewalk cafés. See "City Layout," in Chapter 4, for more information about this area.

CORAL GABLES — MIRACLE MILE

Actually only a half mile, this central shopping street was an integral part of George Merrick's original city plan (see "Neighborhoods in Brief," in Chapter 4). Today, the strip's importance seems slightly more historical than commercial. Lined primarily with small, 1970s storefronts, the Miracle Mile, which terminates at the

SHOPPING CENTERS AND AREAS:

Aventura Mall ①
Bal Harbour Mall ③
Bayside Marketplace ⑨
Cutler Ridge Mall ⑮
Dadeland Mall ⑬
The Falls ⑭
Fashion District ⑥
Lincoln Road Mall ⑩
Mayfair Mall ⑫
Miami International Mall ⑤
Midway Mall ⑧
Miracle Mile ⑪
Omni International Mall ⑦
163rd Street Mall ②
Westland Mall ④

Mediterranean-style City Hall rotunda, also features several good and unusual restaurants (see Chapter 6, "Miami Dining"), and is worth a stop on your tour of Coral Gables.

SOUTH MIAMI BEACH — LINCOLN ROAD

The Lincoln Road Mall is an 8-block pedestrian zone near the north end of Miami Beach's art deco district. The hip but struggling area stretches from Washington Avenue to Alton Road, and is the center of the city's most exciting art scene. There is a unique assortment of art galleries, antique stores, and furniture shops, as well as the studios of the Miami City Ballet. Surrounding streets, including Washington and Collins avenues, are rife with funky thrift stores, eateries, and T-shirt shops. See "City Layout," in Chapter 4 for more information about this area.

HOURS, TAXES & SHIPPING

For most shops around the city **open hours** are Monday through Saturday from 10am to 6pm, and Sunday from noon to 5pm. Many stay open late (usually until 9pm) one night of the week (usually Thursday). Shops in trendy Coconut Grove are open until 9pm Sunday through Thursday, and even later on Friday and Saturday nights. Department stores and shopping malls keep longer hours, staying open from 10am to 9 or 10pm Monday to Saturday, noon to 6pm on Sunday.

The 6% Florida state **sales tax** is added to the price of all nonfood purchases.

Most Miami stores can wrap your purchase and **ship** it anywhere in the world via the United Parcel Service (UPS). If they can't, you can send it yourself, either through UPS (tel. 238-0134) or through the U.S. Mail (see "Fast Facts" in Chapter 4).

BEST BUYS

Locally produced and widely distributed goods are easily Miami's best buys. Not surprisingly, local seafood and citrus products are some of the city's most important exports. Other high-quality items are available in Miami, but fruit and fish are the region's specialties, and nowhere will you find them fresher.

Downtown Miami is the best district to visit for discounts on all types of goods, from watches and jewelry, to luggage and leather. Inexpensive electronics and discount clothing can also be found, often from shops with a heavy Hispanic influence. Look around Flagler Street and Miami Avenue for all kinds of cluttered bargain stores. Most of the signs around here are printed in both English and Spanish, for the benefit of locals and tourists alike.

CITRUS FRUIT

There was a time when it seemed as though almost every other store was shipping fruit home for tourists. Today such stores are a dying breed, but a few high-quality operations still send the freshest oranges and grapefruit. **Todd's Fruit Shippers,** 221 Navarre Ave. (tel. 448-5215), can take your order over the phone, and charge it to American Express, MasterCard, or VISA. Boxes are sold by the bushel or fractions thereof, and start from about $17.

SEAFOOD

East Coast Fisheries, 360 W. Flagler St., Downtown (tel. 373-5516), a retail market and restaurant (see Chapter 6, "Miami Dining"), has shipped millions of pounds of seafood worldwide from its own fishing fleet. They are equipped to wrap and send 5- or 10-pound packages of stone crab claws, Florida lobsters, Florida Bay pompano, fresh Key West shrimp, and a variety of other local delicacies to your door via overnight mail.

Miami's most famous restaurant is **Joe's Stone Crab,** located at 227 Biscayne St., South Miami Beach (tel. 673-0365 or toll free 800/780-CRAB). Joe's makes overnight air shipments of stone crabs to anywhere in the country. Joe's is only open during crab season (from October through May).

2. SHOPPING A TO Z

ANTIQUES

The best collection of antiques shops in the city is located in the art deco district of South Miami Beach. They are usually open Tuesday through Saturday afternoons. A full list of offerings with their specific operating hours can be obtained free from the **South Beach Welcome Center,** 1244 Ocean Dr., in the Leslie Hotel, South Miami Beach (tel. 672-2014). Two good choices are:

DECOLECTABLE, 233 14th St., South Miami Beach. Tel. 674-0899.
This store sells art deco furniture, radios, clocks, and lighting.

ONE HAND CLAPPING, 432 Espanola Way, South Miami Beach. Tel. 532-0507.
This is another excellent find, featuring a broad range of art, antiques, and collectibles from this and previous centuries.

BEACHWEAR

In addition to stores in all of the area shopping malls, try the following:

TOO COOL OCEAN DRIVE, 504 Ocean Dr., South Miami Beach. Tel. 538-5101.

If it has to do with the beach, it's here: swimsuits, T-shirts, shorts, thongs, floats, beach chairs, towels, umbrellas, tanning lotions, and more.

BOOKS

B. DALTON, in the Bayside Marketplace, 401 Biscayne Blvd. (Downtown). Tel. 579-8695.

Like others in the chain, this B. Dalton has a wide selection of general-interest books.

A second bookshop is located in the Omni International Mall, 1601 Biscayne Blvd. (Downtown). Tel. 358-1895.

BOOKS & BOOKS, 296 Aragon Ave., Coral Gables. Tel. 442-4408.

✪ This is one of the best book shops to be found anywhere. It's not particularly big, but B&B stocks an excellent collection of new, used, and hard-to-find books on all subjects. They have a particularly strong emphasis on art and design, as well as alternative literature, and the shop hosts regular, free lectures by noted authors and experts. For a recorded listing of upcoming events, dial 444-POEM.

A second Books & Books is located at 933 Lincoln Road in South Miami Beach (tel. 532-3222).

BOOKWORKS II, 6935 Red Rd. Tel. 661-5080.

This is one of Miami's most upscale bookshops, located between Coconut Grove and Coral Gables. Bookworks has long featured works from both national and local publishers.

DOUBLEDAY BOOK SHOP, in the Bal Harbour Shops, 9700 Collins Ave. Tel. 866-2871.

Located in one of the city's most upscale shopping centers, this Doubleday is known for its good variety of titles, and a particular emphasis on books of local interest.

DOWNTOWN BOOK CENTER, 247 SE 1st St. (Downtown). Tel. 377-9939.

Downtown Books is the city's best commercial area store, and is a great place to browse. This long-established shop is known for both its good service and wide selection. They have a second location at 215 NE 2nd Ave. (tel. 377-9938).

WALDENBOOKS, Omni International Mall, 1601 Biscayne Blvd. tel. 358-5764.

Waldenbooks is a good place for the latest titles, as well as good classics and light beach reading.

CRAFTS

GALLERY ANTIGUA, Boulevard Plaza Building, 5318 Biscayne Blvd. Tel. 759-5355.

One of the more unusual specialty shops, featuring African-American and Caribbean art, Gallery Antigua frequently offers individual original works as well as complete art installations.

DEPARTMENT STORES

Department stores are often the primary "anchors" for Miami's many malls. The biggest include:

BURDINES, 22 E. Flagler St., Downtown Miami. Tel. 835-5151.

One of the oldest and largest department stores in the state, Burdines specializes in high-quality, middle-class home furnishings and fashions.

Additional stores are located in the Dadeland Mall and at 1675 Meridian Avenue in Miami Beach. All stores may be reached at the number above. Check the "White Pages" for additional locations.

SEARS ROEBUCK & COMPANY, Aventura Mall, 19505 Biscayne Blvd., Aventura. Tel. 937-7500.

This common store has all the usual fashions and furnishings, plus appliances, insurance, and financial services.

There is also a Sears at 3655 Coral Way (tel. 460-3400), next to the Miracle Center just east of Coral Gables.

ELECTRONICS

BEYOND, Bayside Marketplace, 401 Biscayne Blvd. Tel. 592-1904.

Beyond features the latest in consumer electronics. Futuristic portable stereos, televisions, telephones, and the like are all offered at reasonable rates. Other stores are located at Cocowalk, Dadeland, Aventura, and The Falls shopping malls.

SPY SHOPS INTERNATIONAL, INC., 2900 Biscayne Blvd. Tel. 573-4779.

Farther up the street, this store sells real-life James Bond–style gadgets like night-vision binoculars, bulletproof briefcases, "bug" detectors, and other expensive gizmos. This is a serious store, not a museum, so look like you intend to buy.

FASHION

Over 100 retail outlets are clustered in Miami's mile-square Fashion District just north of Downtown. Surrounding Fashion Avenue (NW 5th Avenue), and known primarily for swimwear, sportswear, high-fashion children's clothing, and glittery women's dresses, Miami's fashion center is second in size only to New York's. The district features European- and Latin-influenced designs with tropical hues and subdued pastels. Most stores offer high-quality clothing at a 25% to 70% discount, and on-site alterations. Most are open Monday through Friday from 9am to 5:30pm.

FOOD

EPICURE MARKET, 1656 Alton Rd., South Miami Beach. Tel. 672-1861.

This is the place to go for prime meats, cheeses, and wines. Cooked foods include strictly gourmet hors d'oeuvres, pâtés, and desserts. The shop also sells homemade breads and soups, along with a variety of freshly made hot items that are ready to eat.

GIFTS & SOUVENIRS

DAPY, BAYSIDE MARKETPLACE, 401 Biscayne Blvd. Tel. 374-3098.

Gift shops are located all over town and in almost every hotel, but Dapy is tops if you're in the market for high-tech watches, rubber coasters, Technicolor trash cans, oversized calculators, Lucite televisions, and the like. If it's cool, it's here. New Wave Japanese and European fads and gifts cost from just a few cents to hundreds of dollars.

HOUSEWARES

Miami's design district shops are also some of the best in the country. Strongly influenced by Latin American markets, outlets feature the latest furniture and housewares, all at discount prices. Not all stores are open to the public, but those that are offer incredible bargains to the savviest of shoppers. The district runs north along NE 2nd Avenue, beginning at 36th Street.

JEWELRY

THE SEYBOLD BUILDING, 3601 NE 1st St., Downtown. Tel. 377-0122.

This is the best place in Miami for discount diamonds and jewelry. The building is located right in the middle of Downtown, and houses a large variety of retail shops.

LINGERIE

LINGERIE BY LISA, 3000 McFarlane Rd., (Coconut Grove). Tel. 446-2368.

Coconut Grove's best lingerie shop features a huge selection of bras, panties, teddies, and camisoles. Located on the corner of Main Highway, this store includes lots of items you'll never see in a national catalog. On weekends, a live model poses in the window.

LUGGAGE

BENTLEY'S, in the Bayside Marketplace, 401 Biscayne Blvd., Downtown. Tel. 372-2907.

Carrying a large selection of luggage and travel-related items, this store also features leather cases and business accessories. Bentley's also makes expert repairs.

MALLS

There are so many shopping centers in Miami that it would be impossible to mention them all, but here is a list of the biggest and the best:

AVENTURA MALL, 19501 Biscayne Blvd., Aventura. Tel. 935-4222.

Enter this large, enclosed mall, located at Biscayne Boulevard and 197th Street near the Dade-Broward county line, and it's easy to imagine you're on the outskirts of Omaha . . . or anywhere else in America for that matter. Over 200 generic shops are complemented by the megastores J.C. Penney, Lord & Taylor, Macy's, and Sears. Parking is free.

BAL HARBOUR SHOPS, 9700 Collins Ave., Bal Harbour. Tel. 866-0311.

There's not much in the way of whimsy here, just the best quality goods from the fanciest names. AnnTaylor, Fendi, Krizia, Rodier, Gucci, Brooks Brothers, Waterford, Cartier, H. Stern, Tourneau . . . the list goes on and on. The Bal Harbour Shops are the fanciest in Miami. With Neiman Marcus at one end and Saks Fifth Avenue at the other, the mall itself is a pleasant open-air emporium, with covered walkways and lush greenery. The Bal Harbour Shops are located at 97th Street, just opposite the tall Sheraton Bal Harbour hotel. Parking is $1.

BAYSIDE MARKETPLACE, 401 Biscayne Blvd. (Downtown). Tel. 577-3344.

Miami's successful Rouse Company development has taken over a stunning location—16 beautiful waterfront acres in the heart of Downtown—and turned it into a lively and exciting shopping place. Downstairs, about 100 shops and carts sell everything from plastic fruit to high-tech electronics (some of the more unique specialty shops are listed separately). The upstairs eating arcade is stocked with dozens of fast-food choices, offering a wide variety of inexpensive international eats. (See Chapter 6, "Miami Dining.") Some restaurants stay open later than the stores, which close at 10pm Monday to Saturday, 8pm Sunday. Parking is $1 per hour.

DADELAND MALL, 7535 North Kendall Dr., Kendall. Tel. 665-6226.

The granddaddy of Miami's suburban mall scene, Dadeland features more than 175 specialty shops, anchored by five large department stores—Burdines, J.C. Penney, Jordan Marsh, Lord & Taylor, and Saks Fifth Avenue. Sixteen restaurants serve from the adjacent Treats Food Court. The mall is located at the intersection of U.S. 1 and SW 88th Street, 15 minutes south of Downtown. Parking is free.

THE FALLS, 8888 Howard Dr. (Kendall area). Tel. 255-4570.

Tropical waterfalls are the setting for this outdoor shopping center with dozens of moderately priced, slightly upscale shops. Miami's only Bloomingdale's is here, as are Polo Ralph Lauren, Godiva, Caswell-Massey, and over 60 other specialty shops. The Falls is located at the intersection of U.S. 1 and 136th Street, about 3 miles south of Dadeland Mall. Parking is free.

THE MALL at 163rd Street, 1421 NE 163rd St., North Miami Beach. Tel. 947-9845.

This 3-story megamall, between U.S. 1 and I-95, in Greater Miami North, is protected by the world's first Teflon-coated fiberglass roof. Beneath it are 150-plus middle American shops including Burdines, Mervyn's, and Marshalls department stores. Parking is free.

MAYFAIR SHOPS IN THE GROVE, 2911 Grand Avenue, Coconut Grove. Tel. 448-1700.

The small and labyrinthine Mayfair Shops complex, just a few blocks east of Commodore Plaza, conceals several top-quality shops, restaurants, art galleries, and nightclubs. The emphasis is on chic, expensive elegance, and intimate, European-style boutiques are featured. Valet parking is $5.

MARKETS

THE OPA-LOCKA/HIALEAH FLEA MARKET, 12705 NW 42nd Ave. (LeJeune Rd.), near Amelia Earhart Park. Tel. 688-0500.

Featuring over 1,000 merchants this flea market sells everything from plants and pet food to luggage and linen. This indoor/outdoor weekend market is one of the largest of its kind in Florida. There are no real antiques here. Almost everything is brand new (though of suspect quality and origin) and dirt cheap.

It's open from 5am to 6pm, Friday to Sunday. Admission and parking are free.

PERFUMES & BEAUTY SUPPLIES

PERFUMANIA, in the AmeriFirst Building, 1 SE 3rd Ave., Downtown. Tel. 358-3224.

Perfumania sells skin products, as well as designer fragrances, at 10% to 60% below normal retail prices. The shop is in the heart of Downtown Miami.

Other locations include 223 Miracle Mile, Coral Gables (tel. 529-0114); and 1604 Washington Avenue, South Miami Beach (tel. 534-7221).

TOYS

FUNWORLD TOYS & HOBBIES, 145 E. Flagler St., Downtown. Tel. 374-1453.

This large store features all the hits, including Legos, Sega electronics, Mattel cars and toys, and remote-control boats, cars, and airplanes. Fisher Price and other toddlers' toys are also available.

WINES

In addition to the Epicure Market (see "Food," above), wine lovers should visit the following:

THE ESTATE WINES & GOURMET FOODS, 92 Miracle Mile, Coral Gables. Tel. 442-9915.

This exceedingly friendly storefront in the middle of Coral Gables' main shopping street offers a small, but well-chosen selection of vintages from around the world. Every Thursday, from 5 to 8pm, the store's knowledgeable owner hosts a wine tasting and lecture, at which vineyard representatives are present. Tastings cost $5, and are open to the public.

CHAPTER 10

MIAMI NIGHTS

1. THE PERFORMING ARTS
2. THE CLUB & MUSIC SCENE
3. THE BAR SCENE
4. MORE ENTERTAINMENT

One of the most striking aspects of the city is the recent growth of world-class music, dance, and theater. Miami proudly boasts a top opera and symphony orchestra, as well as respected ballet and modern dance troupes. The most unique performances have a strong ethnic influence. Both Western and nontraditional choices are listed below.

South Florida's late-night life is abuzz, with South Miami Beach at the center of the scene. The **art deco district** is the spawning ground for top international acts including Latin artist Julio Iglesias, controversial rappers 2 Live Crew, jazz man Nestor Torres, and rockers Expose, Nuclear Valdez, and of course Gloria Estefan and the Miami Sound Machine. It's no secret that Cuban and Caribbean rhythms are extremely popular, and the sound of the conga, inextricably incorporated into Miami's club culture, makes dancing irresistible.

If you're not sure where to spend an evening, you can't go wrong by heading into downtown **Coconut Grove.** In the heart of this otherwise quiet enclave, music clubs blast their beats, and sidewalks are perpetually crowded with outdoor café tables. There is not a lot of professional entertainment in the Grove; the main show is always on the street, where crowds gather to see and to be seen. (See "Neighborhoods in Brief" in Chapter 4.)

New Times is the most comprehensive of Miami's free weekly newspapers. Available each Wednesday, this newspaper prints articles, previews, and advertisements on upcoming local events. Several **telephone hotlines**—many operated by local radio stations—give free recorded information on current events in the city. These include: WTMI Cultural Arts Line (tel. 550-9393), Love 94 Concert Hotline (tel. 654-94FM), PACE Free Concert (tel. 237-1718), Song & Dance Concerts (tel. 947-6471), 24-Hour Cosmic Hotline (tel. 854-2222), and the UM Concert Hotline (tel. 284-6477). Other information-oriented telephone numbers are listed under the appropriate headings, below.

1. THE PERFORMING ARTS

Tickets for most performances can be purchased by phone through **Ticketmaster** (tel. 358-5885). The company accepts all major credit cards and has phone lines open 24 hours. If you want to

MAJOR CONCERT & PERFORMANCE HALL BOX OFFICES

Colony Theater, 1040 Lincoln Rd., South Miami Beach. Tel. 674-1026.

Dade County Auditorium, 2901 W. Flagler St. (Downtown). Tel. 545-3395.

Gusman Center for the Performing Arts, 174 E. Flagler St. (Downtown). Tel. 372-0925.

Gusman Concert Hall, 1314 Miller Dr., Coral Gables. Tel. 284-2438.

Jackie Gleason Theater of the Performing Arts (TOPA), 1700 Washington Ave., South Miami Beach. Tel. 673-8300.

pick up your tickets from a Ticketmaster outlet, call for the location nearest you. Outlets are open Monday to Saturday 10am to 9pm, Sunday noon to 5pm. There is a small service charge.

MAJOR MULTIPURPOSE PERFORMANCE & CONCERT HALLS

COLONY THEATER, 1040 Lincoln Rd., South Miami Beach. Tel. 674-1026.

After years of decay and a $1-million face-lift, the Colony has become an architectural showpiece of the art deco district. This multipurpose, 465-seat theater stages performances by the Miami City Ballet and the Ballet Flamenco La Rosa, as well as various special events.

DADE COUNTY AUDITORIUM, 2901 W. Flagler St. (Downtown). Tel. 545-3395.

Performers gripe about the lack of space, but for patrons, this 2,500-seat auditorium is comfortable and intimate. It's home to the city's renowned Greater Miami Opera, and stages productions by the Miami Ballet Company and the Concert Association of Greater Miami.

GUSMAN CENTER FOR THE PERFORMING ARTS, 174 E. Flagler St. (Downtown). Tel. 372-0925.

Seating is tight, but sound is good at this 1,700-seat Downtown theater. In addition to providing a regular stage for the Philharmonic Orchestra of Florida and the Ballet Theatre of Miami, the Gusman Center also features pop concerts, plays, film festival screenings, and special events.

The auditorium itself was built as the Olympia Theater in 1926, and its ornate palace interior is typical of the era, complete with fancy columns, a huge pipe organ, and twinkling "stars" on the ceiling.

GUSMAN CONCERT HALL, 1314 Miller Dr., Coral Gables. Tel. 284-2438.

Not to be confused with the Gusman Center, above, this roomy 600-seat hall gives a stage to the Miami Chamber Symphony and a varied program of university recitals.

JACKIE GLEASON THEATER OF THE PERFORMING ARTS [TOPA], 1700 Washington Ave., South Miami Beach. Tel. 673-8300.

It has become tradition for the American Ballet Theatre to open their touring season here during the last two weeks of January, after which TOPA is home to big-budget Broadway shows, classical music concerts, opera, and dance performances. This 2,705-seat hall has been newly renovated in order to improve the acoustics and sightlines.

MIAMIWAY THEATER, 12615 W. Dixie Hwy. (North Miami). Tel. 893-0005.

Owned by actor Philip Michael Thomas of *Miami Vice* fame, this high-tech performing arts complex features a state-of-the-art sound system in a 435-seat theater. Keep an eye out for interesting alternative productions as well as various live performances.

Prices: Depend on production.
Performances: Call for schedule.

MINORCA PLAYHOUSE, 232 Minorca Ave., Coral Gables. Tel. 446-1116.

The Florida Shakespeare Theater calls Minorca home. At other times, traveling dance and theater companies perform here. Performances are usually held Tuesday through Saturday evenings, as well as Wednesday, Saturday, and Sunday matinees throughout the year.

Prices: $18 and $20; $10 and $15 for students and seniors.
Box office open: Mon–Sat 10am–8pm, Sun noon–4pm.

THE RING THEATRE, on the University of Miami Campus, 1380 Miller Dr., entrance #6, Coral Gables. Tel. 284-3355.

The University's Department of Theater Arts uses this stage for advanced student productions of comedies, dramas, and musicals. Faculty and guest actors are regularly featured, as are contemporary works by local playwrights. Performances are usually scheduled Tuesday through Saturday during the academic year only.

Prices: $3–$10.
Box office open: Mon–Fri 9am–5pm, and before show time.

A MAJOR PERFORMING-ARTS COMPANY

ACME ACTING COMPANY, P.O. Box 402917, Miami Beach. Tel. 372-1718.

Miami's closest approximation to New York's off-off Broadway is embodied in this single local troupe. Lively productions of contemporary plays are most often performed at The Colony Theater in South Beach.

Performances: Wed–Sat 8:15pm, Sun 7:15pm.

Prices: $15 Wed–Fri and Sun, $17 Sat, $13 students and seniors.

THEATERS

COCONUT GROVE PLAYHOUSE, 3500 Main Hwy., Coconut Grove. Tel. 442-4000.

The Grove Theater, as it was originally called, opened as a movie house in 1927. Thirty years later, real estate developer George Engle bought this beautiful Spanish rococo palace and, after a $1-million renovation, staged one of the first major productions of Tennessee Williams' *A Streetcar Named Desire*.

Today this respected playhouse is known for its original and innovative staging of both international and local plays. Dramas and musicals receive equal attention on the theater's main stage, while the house's second, more intimate Encore Room is well suited to alternative and experimental productions. The theater's play season lasts from October through June.

Prices: $8–$35.

Box office open: Tues–Sat 10am–9pm, Sun–Mon 10am–6pm; tickets also available through Ticketmaster.

Main stage performances: Tues–Sat 8:15pm; matinees Wed, Sat, and Sun 2pm. **Encore Room performances:** Tues–Sat 8:30pm, matinees Wed, Thurs, and Sun 2:15pm. Schedules differ during previews.

CLASSICAL MUSIC & OPERA

In addition to a number of local orchestras and operas, which regularly offer high-quality music and world-renowned guests, each year brings with it a slew of special events and touring artists. One of the most important and longest-running series is produced by the **Concert Association of Florida (CAF),** 555 17th St., South Miami Beach (tel. 532-3491). Known for almost a quarter of a century for their high-caliber, star-packed schedules, CAF regularly arranges the best "serious" music concerts for the city. It's not just traveling symphony orchestras either. Season after season the schedules are punctuated by world-renowned dance companies and seasoned virtuosi like Itzhak Perlman, Andre Watts, and the Labeque sisters.

CAF does not have its own space. Performances are usually scheduled either in the Dade County Auditorium or the Jackie Gleason Theater of the Performing Arts (see "Major Multipurpose Performance and Concert Halls," above). Their performance season lasts from October through April, and ticket prices range from $15 to $52.

GREATER MIAMI OPERA ASSOCIATION, 1200 Coral Way, Coral Gables. Tel. 854-1643.

The 50th anniversary of the Miami Opera was in 1991. It's a world-class company that regularly features singers from America's and Europe's top houses. All productions are sung in their original language and staged with projected English supertitles. Tickets become scarce when Placido Domingo or Luciano Pavarotti (who made his American debut here in 1965) come to town.

The opera's season runs roughly from January through April only, with performances four days per week. Most productions are staged in the Dade County Auditorium (see "Major Multipurpose Performance and Concert Halls," above).

Prices: $13–$50. Student and senior discounts available.

THE NEW WORLD SYMPHONY, 541 Lincoln Rd., South Miami Beach. Tel. 673-3331.

Alternating performances between Downtown's Gusman Center for the Performing Arts and South Beach's Lincoln Theatre, this 5-year-old advanced training orchestra is a major stepping-stone for gifted young musicians seeking a professional career. Accepting artists on the basis of a 3-year fellowship, and led by artistic advisor Michael Tilson Thomas, the orchestra specializes in ambitious, innovative, energetic performances, and often features guest soloists and renowned conductors. The symphony's season lasts from October through April.

Prices: $10–$40. Student and senior discounts available.

FLORIDA PHILHARMONIC ORCHESTRA, Dade County Office, 836 Biscayne Blvd. (Downtown). Tel. 800/226-1812.

South Florida's premier symphony orchestra, under the direction of James Judd, presents a full season of mainstream and pops programs interspersed with several children's and contemporary popular music dates. The Philharmonic performs Downtown in the Gusman Center for the Performing Arts, the Jackie Gleason Theater of the Performing Arts, and the Dade County Auditorium (see "Major Multipurpose Performance and Concert Halls," above).

Prices: $11–$35.

MIAMI CHAMBER SYMPHONY, 5690 N. Kendall Dr. (Kendall). Tel. 662-6600.

Renowned international soloists regularly perform with this professional orchestra. The symphony performs October through May, and most concerts are held in the Gusman Concert Hall, on the University of Miami campus (see "Major Multipurpose Performance and Concert Halls," above).

Prices: $12–$25.

DANCE

Several local dance companies train and perform in the Greater Miami area. In addition, top traveling troupes regularly pass through the city, stopping at the venues listed above. Keep your eyes open for special events and guest artists.

BALLET FLAMENCO LA ROSA, 1008 Lincoln Rd., South Miami Beach. Tel. 672-0552.

This year marks the ballet's first season in their new home in South Miami Beach. Although other styles are danced, the company is primarily influenced by the flamenco and Latin style.

In addition to performances, which are held primarily in South Beach's Colony Theater, the Flamenco La Rosa also offers dancing lessons. They cost $8 each, and are held at their Lincoln Road studio. The ballet season runs from March through October.

Prices: $15–$20.

MIAMI CITY BALLET, 905 Lincoln Rd. Mall, South Miami Beach. Tel. 532-4880.

Headquartered behind a storefront in the middle of the art deco district (see "A Walking Tour" in Chapter 8), and directed by Edward Villella, this 7-year-old Miami company has quickly emerged as a top troupe, performing both classical and contemporary works. The artistically acclaimed and innovative company features a repertoire of more than 60 ballets, many by George Balanchine, and more than 20 world premieres. The City Ballet season runs from October through March, with performances both at the Dade County Auditorium and in South Beach at the Lincoln Theater (see "Major Multipurpose Performance and Concert Halls," above).

Prices: $17–$44.

MIAMI BALLET COMPANY [MBC], 2901 W. Flagler St. Tel. 667-5985.

Because MBC is an amateur troupe, all the performers' energy is fueled by the dream of going pro. Established in 1951, the company has a reputation for working with the most talented young performers, as well as top guest dancers from around the world. The 1992–93 season features Miami performances in October, November, January, and May. MBC usually performs in the Dade County Auditorium (see "Major Multipurpose Performance and Concert Halls," above).

Prices: $11–$38.

BALLET THEATRE OF MIAMI, 1809 Ponce de Leon Blvd., Coral Gables. Tel. 442-4840.

The Ballet Theatre is a professional troupe under the artistic direction of Lizette Piedra and Tony Catanzaro, formerly of the Boston Ballet. Beautifully staged performances of traditional and avant-garde dances have earned critical acclaim. Performances are held from October through June in the Gusman Center for the Performing Arts (see "Major Multipurpose Performance and Concert Halls," above).

Prices: $12–$40.

2. THE CLUB & MUSIC SCENE

COMEDY CLUBS

COCONUTS COMEDY CLUB, in the Peacock Café, 2977 McFarlane Rd., Coconut Grove. Tel. 446-2582.

Coconuts, which opened in spring 1990, has quickly become Miami's premier comedy room, mostly due to its great location. Like other Coconuts clubs, this one has become a major stop on the comedy circuit, showcasing all the names you might very well see on television. Obviously, acts vary.

Show times: Sun–Thurs 9pm, Fri–Sat 8 and 11pm. Reservations recommended.

Admission: $6 Wed–Sun, $10 Fri–Sat, plus two-drink minimum.

LIVE REGGAE

Lots of local clubs regularly feature live and recorded reggae. Some are authentic Jamaican joints, while others play the music to round out their island motifs. Check the local listings for the latest.

THE HUNGRY SAILOR, 3064 Grand Ave., Coconut Grove. Tel. 444-9359.

This small, wood-paneled, English-style "pub," has Watneys, Bass, and Guinness on draught, and reggae regularly on tap. The club attracts an extremely mixed crowd. There is a short British menu and high-quality live music Tuesday through Saturday.

Open: Sun–Thurs noon–midnight, Fri–Sat noon–2:30am.
Admission: Free, except Fri and Sat $2.

SUNDAYS ON THE BAY, 5420 Crandon Blvd., Key Biscayne. Tel. 361-6777.

Terrific happy hours are followed by dockside disco nights. Sundays has a great party atmosphere, fantastic water views, and good tropical food (see Chapter 6, "Miami Dining").

Sundays' sister restaurant, Salty's (tel. 945-5115), also occupies a terrific location, in Haulover Park at Collins Avenue and 108th Street in Miami Beach.

Open: Sun–Wed 11am–2am, Thurs–Sat 11am–2:30am.
Admission: Free.

ROCK/COUNTRY/FOLK

Rock clubs often overlap with dance spots (see below) which also sometimes offer live rock bands. For up-to-date listings, check the papers, WGTR-FM Concertline (tel. 284-6477), and the ZETA Link (tel. 620-3600).

Along with the venues listed below, free rock concerts are held every Friday throughout the winter in South Miami Beach's South

Pointe Park. The shows feature the best local bands and start at 8pm.

Many area clubs book country bands and folk musicians, but not regularly enough to be included here. Check the Folk Hotline (tel. 531-3655), scan the free weekly *New Times,* and keep your eyes and ears open for current happenings.

CACTUS CANTINA GRILL, 630 6th St. just west of Washington Ave., South Miami Beach. Tel. 532-5095.

This Los Angeles–style cantina is one of South Beach's hottest finds. Gritty to the max, the Cactus features music that's live and loud almost every night. Styles range from jazz and blues to country, rockabilly, and soul. A huge, excellent, and inexpensive Cal-Mex menu is complemented by killer margaritas and a well-stocked tequila bar. Highly recommended.

Open: Daily 5pm–5am.
Admission: Free, except for occasional special events.

FIREHOUSE FOUR, 1000 South Miami Ave. (Downtown). Tel. 379-1923.

Miami's oldest fire station is now a popular restaurant and club. Live new rock music is featured on Fridays or Saturdays and there's usually a spirited crowd nightly. The club sometimes hosts folk artists on Thursday. (See "Happy Hours," below, for further information.)

Open: Mon–Thurs noon–midnight, Fri–Sat noon–3am.
Admission: Free–$5.

PENROD'S, 1 Ocean Dr., South Miami Beach. Tel. 538-1111.

South Miami Beach's jack-of-all-trades also books bands. On weekends, there is straightforward rock music all day. Drink and snack specials are common in this multilevel, sports-oriented club.

Open: Sun–Thurs 10am–2am, Fri–Sat 10am–5am.
Admission: $3–$6 after 10pm.

THE SPOT, 218 Espanola Way, South Miami Beach. Tel. 532-1682.

Brand-new and red-hot, Mickey Rourke's club is yet another celeb-owned spot in the city's trendiest quarter. Lines can be vicious, especially on weekends, but once inside, the crowd is mellower, and surprisingly unpretentious. The large drinking room features a full bar and good music that's often even danceable.

Admission: Free.
Open: Daily 9pm–5am.

WASHINGTON SQUARE, 645 Washington Ave., between 6th and 7th Sts., South Miami Beach. Tel. 534-1403.

Rock, blues, jazz, and D.J.'s all converge on this small, hip club in the heart of the art deco district. Washington Square has a stage at one end, an island bar in the middle, and an artsy late-night crowd all around.

Open: Nightly 10pm–5am.
Admission: Free–$3.

THE WHISKEY, 1250 Ocean Dr., South Miami Beach. Tel. 531-0713.
Sure, it's got a good beachfront location, but it's the reputation of co-owner Matt Dillon that helps pack 'em into this rather regular pool table, jukebox, drinking bar. Live bands sometimes perform. It's a worthy part of any Ocean Drive crawl.
Admission: Free–$10.
Open: Daily 9:30pm–2am.

JAZZ/BLUES

South Florida's jazz scene is very much alive with traditional and contemporary performers. Keep an eye out for guitarist Randy Bernsen, vibraphonist Tom Toyama, and flutist Nestor Torres, young performers who lead local ensembles. The University of Miami has a well-respected jazz studies program in their School of Music (tel. 284-6477), and often schedules low- and no-cost recitals. Frequent jazz shows are also scheduled at the Miami Metrozoo (see "Top Attractions" in Chapter 7). The lineup changes frequently, and it's not always jazz, but the quality is good, and concerts are included with zoo admission.

Additionally, many area hotels feature cool jazz and light blues in their bars and lounges. Schedules are listed in newspaper entertainment sections. Finally, some of the rock clubs, listed above, also feature blues bands. Try calling the **Blues Hotline** (tel. 666-MOJO), and the **Jazz Hotline** (tel. 382-3938) for the most up-to-date bookings in Miami's jazz rooms.

Perhaps because the area itself is reminiscent of the Jazz Age, the bulk of the listings below are clustered in the art deco district of South Miami Beach, making it easy to plan an evening walking tour of some of the city's best clubs.

5TH STREET, 429 Lenox St. at the corner of 5th St., South Miami Beach. Tel. 531-1910.
The deco district's best alternative video and dance club is also the premier place to listen and dance to jazz, reggae, calypso, house, and blues. Often packed into the wee hours, 5th Street features live music six nights a week, and a moderately priced Southern-style menu that includes jerk chicken wings, blackened dolphin, collard greens, and black-eyed peas. Reservations are sometimes necessary on special nights.
Open: Wed–Sun 9pm–4am, and every other Mon 8–11:30pm.
Closed: Tues.
Admission: Free–$10.

CAFE AVALON, in the Avalon Hotel, 700 Ocean Dr. at the corner of 7th St., South Miami Beach. Tel. 538-0133.
One of the beach's most stunning art deco hotels has jazz and

other live music Thursday through Sunday in their lobby restaurant/
bar.
  Open: Daily dawn–midnight or 2am.
  Admission: Free.

CLEVELANDER RESTAURANT, in the Clevelander Hotel, 1020 Ocean Dr. at 10th St., South Miami Beach. Tel. 531-3485.

  Often offering live jazz, rock, or reggae almost every night, the
Clevelander is another good choice along South Beach's most
popular strip.
  Open: Daily 5pm–3am.
  Admission: Free.

LET'S MAKE A DAIQUIRI, in the Bayside Marketplace, 401 Biscayne Blvd. (Downtown). Tel. 372-5117.

  Right smack in the middle of the mall is this outdoor bar with one
of the best views in town. Live jazz, rock, reggae, and calypso are
featured almost nightly, and you don't even have to order a drink.
  Open: Sun–Thurs 9am–midnight, Fri–Sat 9am–2am. Music
ends 1 hour before closing.
  Admission: Free.

SCULLY'S TAVERN, 9809 Sunset Dr. (South Miami). Tel. 271-7404.

  Excellent local bands, most often jazz and blues oriented,
frequent Sully's, a sports-type bar, with pool tables and television
monitors. There is live music every night except Monday.
  Open: Sun–Wed 11am–11pm, Thurs 11am–midnight, Fri–Sat
11am–3am.
  Admission: Free.

TOBACCO ROAD, 626 S. Miami Ave. (Downtown). Tel. 374-1198.

  Featuring live music nightly, Tobacco Road sports an eclectic
menu of new and local jazz, rock, and blues. On weekends, two
stages, one up and one down, heat up simultaneously. This is a great
place to dance.
  Open: Daily noon–5am.
  Admission: Free–$6.

DANCE CLUBS

In addition to quiet cafés and progressive poolside bars, Miami Beach
pulsates with one of the liveliest night scenes in the city. Several loud
dance clubs feature live bands as well as D. J. dancing.

FACADE, in the Intracoastal Mall, 3509 NE 163rd St., just east of U.S. 1, North Miami Beach. Tel. 948-6868.

  Modern and classical designs are so deftly styled here that even
the American Society of Interior Designers called it "spectacular."
Ultraflashy features include contemporary lines adjacent to ancient
Grecian murals, as well as floor-to-ceiling steel and stone columns
around an immense sunken dance floor. Pop dance disks are

regularly interrupted for performances by the club's 10-piece band and professional dancers. Expect the usual million-dollar light show.

Open: Tues–Sun 9pm–6am.
Admission: Free–$15.

THE ISLAND CLUB, 701 Washington Ave. at 7th St., South Miami Beach. Tel. 538-1213.

Located on one of Miami's most progressive corners, this is a local tavern that attracts chic visitors from the city's "underground." The club is unusually lively on Monday nights when the D.J. kicks in and the Ping-Pong table is put away to accommodate the crowds.

Open: Nightly 8pm–4am.
Admission: Free.

THE KITCHEN CLUB, CLUB BEIRUT, and REGGAE DIRECTORY, 100 21st St. at the beach, South Miami Beach. Tel. 538-6631.

The same space adopts different personas on alternate nights of the week. The Kitchen is a D.J. dance joint featuring the newest wave grooves. Beirut is generally a live music venue where cutting-edge bands are given a stage. Reggae Directory features new Jamaican sounds.

Open: Call for times and schedules.
Admission: Free–$10.

STUDIO ONE 83, 2860 NW 183rd St. (Carol City). Tel. 621-7295.

This African-American–oriented disco with occasional Caribbean bands, also features live jazz in the Jazz Room daily. Special live concerts are also booked.

Open: Daily 5pm–5am; happy hour daily 5–8pm.
Admission: Free–$5.

VAN DOME, 1532 Washington Ave., South Miami Beach. Tel. 534-4288.

South Beach's star of the moment is a very impressive New York–style dance club, located behind the carved stone walls of a former Jewish synagogue. Gothic styling and a wraparound second-floor ambulatory have attracted trendies, while an excellent sound system, late-night snack/raw bar, and quiet-enough tables combine to give this place some staying power.

Admission: $5–$15.
Open: Thurs–Sat 10pm–5am.

3. THE BAR SCENE

In addition to the many music clubs listed above, Miami's bars and lounges are noted for their spirited happy hours. In addition, several unique "theme" bars offer fun and adventure.

HAPPY HOURS

Miami is a happy-hour heaven. For tourists and locals alike, few things are more relaxing than sitting down with food, drinks, and friends, in a casual atmosphere.

Most hotel bars and many restaurants—especially in South Miami Beach and Coconut Grove—offer discounted drinks and food served just around sunset. Some are in sight of spectacular waterfront views. Many establishments offering special happy hours are listed with the restaurants in Chapter 6. Others are listed in this chapter under various club headings, and the rest are listed below.

ALCAZABA, in the Hyatt Regency Hotel, 50 Alhambra Plaza, Coral Gables. Tel. 441-1234.

The Hyatt's Top-40 lounge exudes a Mediterranean atmosphere that mixes fantasy with reality. Tropical drinks and authentic tapas are on the menu. Happy hour, Wednesday to Friday 5 to 7pm and Saturday 9 to 11pm offers half-price beer, wine, and well drinks plus a free buffet.

COCO LOCO'S, in the Sheraton Brickell Point Hotel, 495 Brickell Avenue (Downtown). Tel. 373-6000.

Coco Loco's offers one of the best happy-hour buffets in town, with hot hors d'oeuvres like chicken wings and pigs-in-blankets. On Fridays, there's an extra-special buffet. There is a $1 plate charge. Happy hour is Monday to Friday 5 to 8pm.

CRAWDADDY'S, South Pointe Park, 1 Washington Ave., South Miami Beach. Tel. 673-1708.

The mood is casual, and the scenery breathtaking with views overlooking the Atlantic Ocean and Government Cut. This is a great place to "kick back," especially on Fridays, when the cruise ships pass by on their way out to sea. Happy hour is Monday to Friday 5 to 7pm. There is a free buffet.

DOC DAMMERS SALOON, in the Colonnade Hotel, 180 Aragon Ave., Coral Gables. Tel. 441-2600.

A well-stocked mahogany bar and an easygoing 1920s motif are the hallmarks of this 30-something hangout. The light menu features dozens of upscale appetizers, gourmet pizzas, and alligator burgers. Happy hour is Monday to Friday 5 to 8pm. Specials include $2.50 beer, wine, and drinks plus a free buffet on Friday; look for $1-drink "Ladies' Nights."

FIREHOUSE FOUR, 1000 S. Miami Ave. (Downtown). Tel. 379-1923.

Burgers, fries, and crunchy conch fritters make great beer companions (see "Rock/Country/Folk," above). Happy hour is Monday to Friday 5 to 8pm. Specials include $2 drinks and a free hot buffet.

MONTY'S RAW BAR, 2560 S. Bayshore Dr., Coconut Grove. Tel. 858-1431.

This tropical-looking, outdoor, pier-top bar offers the Grove's most swinging happy hour, with beautiful sea views and rocking island music. Fresh oysters, chowders, and fritters are available. Happy hour is Monday to Friday 4 to 8pm.

TOBACCO ROAD, 626 S. Miami Ave. (Downtown). Tel. 374-1198.

Home of Miami's first liquor license, Tobacco Road still offers good music, great burgers (cheese, mushroom, chili), and wonderful homemade ice cream. Happy hour is Monday to Friday 5 to 8pm. Specials include drink discounts and $1 appetizer plates.

THEME BARS

PENROD'S BEACH CLUB, 1 Ocean Dr., South Miami Beach. Tel. 538-1111.

Earning a listing here for its party-happy evenings and frequent special events, Penrod's is always chock full of surprises. Almost every night it has a featured attraction, like drink and food specials, dance and bathing-suit contests, barbecues, laser shows, and live bands.

Open: Sun–Thurs 10am–3am, Fri–Sat 10am–5am.
Admission: $3–$6 after 10pm.

MIAMI BREWPUB, in Zum Alten Fritz Restaurant, 1840 NE 4th Ave. (Downtown). Tel. 538-8640.

It's Oktoberfest nightly at the city's only brewpub; an establishment that makes its own barley malt right on the premises. The beer is the freshest in Miami, and several varieties (including Miami Weiss) are really top-notch. The restaurant is also worth visiting (see Chapter 6, "Miami Dining").

Open: Mon–Thurs 11am–10pm, Fri 11am–midnight, Sat 3pm–midnight, Sun 3pm–midnight.
Admission: Free.

4. MORE ENTERTAINMENT

SUPPER CLUBS

After their heyday in the 1950s, Miami's many dinner shows fell upon difficult times. Today, however, they are experiencing a renaissance. Meals are served at all the establishments listed below, but you don't have to eat. After paying the cover charge, you can decide to just have drinks or coffee and dessert. Reservations are always recommended.

CLUB TROPIGALA, in the Fontainebleau Hilton Hotel, 4441 Collins Ave., Miami Beach. Tel. 538-2000.

Extravagant costumes on shapely showgirls are the hallmark of this glitzy hotel's tropical-theme nightclub. Musical reviews change, but all include huge casts, overdone production numbers, and two orchestras, on opposite sides of the room, alternating between Latin and Top-40 music.

Show times: Wed, Thurs, and Sun at 9pm; Fri–Sat at 8pm and 10pm. Jackets required.

Admission: $10.

LES VIOLINS SUPPER CLUB, 1751 Biscayne Blvd. (Downtown). Tel. 371-8668.

★ What Club Tropigala is to the North American "snowbirds," Les Violins is to the Latin community. Garish, lavish, and utterly formal, the entertainment here features glittery costumes, spectacular floor shows, and strolling violinists. Despite this, however, Les Violins is not fake or contrived. Rather, the club's intricately staged entertainment is performed with an entirely straight face. The dances amuse, and the sets are truly stunning.

Except for Cuban desserts and Spanish wines, the cuisine is strictly continental. Highly recommended.

Show times: Tues, Wed, and Sun at 7pm and 10:30pm; Thurs–Sat 7pm, 10:30pm, and 12:30am. Closed Mon. Jackets required.

Admission: $10.

SEVEN SEAS DINNER SHOW, at the Holiday Inn Newport Pier Resort, 16701 Collins Ave., Sunny Isles. Tel. 940-7440.

It's not exactly the South Seas, but it's Miami's only Polynesian dinner theater, complete with live music, hula girls, and fire dancers. This all-inclusive tropical luau features an all-you-can-eat three-course meal with a heavy Chinese influence, tax, tip, and a souvenir island necklace.

Show times: Wed–Sun 8:30pm.

Admission: $26–$28 for dinner and show.

MOVIES

Except for the annual Miami Film Festival (see "Miami Calendar of Events" in Chapter 2), foreign and independent screenings in the city are almost nonexistent. Most of Miami's libraries show classic films one day during the week (usually Wednesday), and are listed in the weekly *New Times,* and the *Miami Herald*'s Friday magazine section. Hollywood-oriented cinemas are commonplace, and are located in all the malls. Some of the larger, and better-located multiplexes include:

Bay Harbor 4 (tel. 866-2441), at 96th Street west of Collins Avenue in Miami Beach.

Cinema 10 (tel. 442-2299), in the Miracle Center, 3301 Coral Way, just east of Coral Gables.

Movies at The Falls (tel. 255-5200), U.S. 1 and SW 136th Street, in The Falls shopping center in Greater Miami South.

Omni 10, (tel. 358-2304), 1601 Biscayne Blvd., inside the Omni International Mall at 16th Street (Downtown).

CHAPTER 11

EXCURSIONS FROM MIAMI

1. **EVERGLADES NATIONAL PARK**
2. **CRUISING THE CARIBBEAN**
3. **KEY WEST**

Miami's scenic surroundings make a short excursion a great idea. Whether you'd like to tour Everglades National Park, hop aboard a Caribbean cruise, or just relax on a beach in Key West, all are easily accessible to you. For information about the Greater Miami area, contact the **Greater Miami Convention and Visitors Bureau,** 701 Brickell Ave., Miami, FL 33131 (tel. 305/539-3063 or toll free 800/283-2707). The offices are open Monday to Friday from 9am to 5:30pm.

1. EVERGLADES NATIONAL PARK

Encompassing over 2,000 square miles and 1.5 million acres, Everglades National Park covers the entire southern tip of Florida, and is one of America's most unusual regions. Unlike Yosemite or Grand Canyon national parks, the Everglades' awesome beauty is more subtle. In fact, it is not its geological grandeur that, in 1947, led lawmakers to preserve this remarkable place. Rather, the Everglades is a wildlife sanctuary, set aside for the protection of its delicate plant and animal life. Don't misunderstand, this park is gorgeous; but its beauty may not be immediately obvious. At first glance, the Glades appear only to be a river of saw grass dotted with islands of trees. But stand still and look around: You'll notice deer, otters, and great white egrets. Follow a rustle and a tiny tree frog appears. Hawks and herons flutter about, while baby—and bigger—alligators laze in the sun. You are in one of the world's most unusual jungles; the longer you stay, the more you perceive. But, beware of mosquitos! Wear protective clothing and don't forget your repellant.

INFORMATION

For general information, as well as specific details, you can also direct your inquiries to the Park Superintendent, Everglades National Park, P.O. Box 279, Homestead, FL 22020.

The **South Dade Visitors Information Center,** 160 U.S. 1, Florida City, FL 33034 (tel. 305/245-9180 or toll free 800/388-

9669), is located at the turnoff from U.S. 1 to the main entrance to the park. You can pick up information about the surrounding area plus a good map. Open daily from 8am to 6pm.

GETTING THERE

From Miami, there are two ways to approach the park, either from the east, through the Main Visitor Center, or from the north, via the Tamiami Trail (Hwy. 41).

The Main Visitor Center (tel. 305/242-7700) is located on the east side of the park, about 45 miles south of Downtown Miami. From Downtown Miami, take U.S. 1 South about 35 miles. Turn right (west) onto Route 9336 (follow the signs), and continue straight for about 10 miles to the park entrance. This is the park's official headquarters. A small building there houses audiovisual exhibits on the park's fragile ecosystems. It's open 8am to 5pm.

The Tamiami Trail (Hwy. 41), runs east-west from Downtown Miami to the Gulf of Mexico, and follows the northern edge of the Everglades into Big Cypress National Preserve. Along the way you will pass a number of concerns offering airboat and other rides through the saw grass of the Everglades.

WHAT TO SEE & DO

If you just have one day to tour the park, take the single road that winds its way for about 38 miles, from the Main Visitor Center at the park's entrance, to the Flamingo Visitor Center in the southwest corner of the state. This scenic drive provides a beautiful introduction to the park. Along the way you will pass through a half-dozen distinct ecosystems, including a dwarf cypress forest, endless saw grass, and dense mangroves. Well-marked winding trails and elevated board-walks are plentiful along the entire stretch; all contain informative signs.

At the Royal Palm Visitor Center, just beyond the main entrance, you'll come to two of the park's most famous paths; the Anhinga boardwalk, and the Gumbo Limbo Trail. You will see snakes, fish, alligators, and a cross section of the park's unusual offerings. The center itself is open from 8am to 4:30pm.

A visit to the Everglades through the park's northern entrance offers an extremely scenic, but slightly more superficial tour of the wetlands. However, approaching from this angle is recommended if you want to take advantage of the two excellent tours listed below. It is also shorter than the all-day trip to Flamingo (see above). To reach the park's northern edge, follow the scenic Tamiami Trail (Hwy. 41) for about 35 miles to Shark Valley, or the Miccosukee Indian Reservation, just beyond. Along the way you will see several signs advertising airboat rides and other tourist-oriented attractions.

In addition to a small visitor center and bookstore, Shark Valley (tel. 505/221-8455) offers an elevated boardwalk, hiking trails, bike rentals, and an excellent tram tour that delves 7.5 miles into the wilderness to a 50-foot observation tower. Built on the site of an old oil well, the tower gives visitors sweeping views of the park, including endless acres of saw grass. Tours run regularly, year-round from 9am to 4pm. Reservations are recommended from December to March. The cost is $7 for adults, $3.50 for children, and $6.25 for seniors.

At the Miccosukee Indian Village (tel. 305/223-8380), you can take a half-hour, high-speed airboat tour through the rushes. Birds scatter as the boats approach, and when you slow down, alligators and other animals appear. This thrilling "safari" through the Everglades is one you will not soon forget—highly recommended. Rides are offered daily from 9am to 5pm, and cost just $6.50.

IN FLAMINGO

The Everglades' main road, which begins at the Main Visitor Center, terminates in the tiny "town" of Flamingo. This is the jumping-off point for a number of sight-seeing excursions including the White Water Bay Cruise and the Florida Bay Cruise. Operated from the Flamingo Lodge Marina (tel. 305/253-2241), these boat tours cruise nearby estuaries and sandbars for an in-depth look at native plant and animal life. The White Water tour lasts about two hours and costs $10.50 for adults, and $5 for children ages 6 to 12. The Florida Bay Cruise, which goes out into open water, lasts an hour and a half, and costs $7.75 for adults, and $3.75 for children ages 6 to 12. Tours run regularly year-round and, although reservations are not required, they are suggested from December to March. Phone for tour times.

The Wilderness Tram Tour also departs from the Flamingo Lodge, and winds its way through mangrove forests and tropical rushes. The two-hour tour operates from November to April only, and is sometimes stalled due to flooding, or particularly heavy mosquito infestation. The cost is $7 for adults, $3.50 for children ages 6 to 12. Phone for tour times.

WHERE TO STAY

Since the Everglades is so close to Miami, most visitors return to their city hotel rooms at night. If you want to stay in the park, however, Flamingo is not only the best, it's the only place. **Camping** is a good option here, though in the summer a ton of mosquito repellent is required gear. There are 235 sites made for cars and tents, and RVs. There is no electricity and showers are cold. Permits cost $4 to $8 per site from November to April and it's free the rest of the year. Checkout time is 10am.

THE FLAMINGO LODGE MARINA & OUTPOST RESORT, P.O. Box 428, Flamingo, FL 33030. Tel. 305/253-2241. Fax 305/695-3921. 102 rms, 24 cottages. No-smoking rooms available. AE, DC, MC, V.

$ Rates: Nov–Apr, $69–$95 single/double; May–Oct, $50–$70 single/double; year-round cottages from $62.

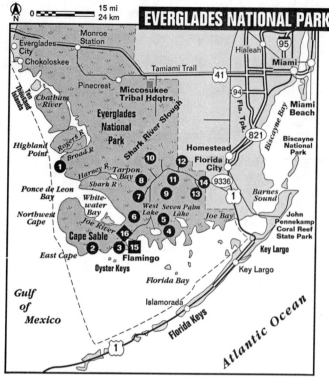

EVERGLADES NATIONAL PARK

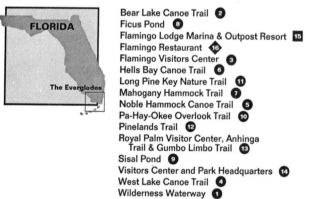

FLORIDA

The Everglades

Bear Lake Canoe Trail **2**
Ficus Pond **8**
Flamingo Lodge Marina & Outpost Resort **15**
Flamingo Restaurant **16**
Flamingo Visitors Center **3**
Hells Bay Canoe Trail **6**
Long Pine Key Nature Trail **11**
Mahogany Hammock Trail **7**
Noble Hammock Canoe Trail **5**
Pa-Hay-Okee Overlook Trail **10**
Pinelands Trail **12**
Royal Palm Visitor Center, Anhinga
   Trail & Gumbo Limbo Trail **13**
Sisal Pond **9**
Visitors Center and Park Headquarters **14**
West Lake Canoe Trail **4**
Wilderness Waterway **1**

An attractive, well-appointed, and spacious motel, the Flamingo is located right in the center of the action. It is also the only lodging to be found inside the Everglades park. Rooms are relatively simple and clean and overlook the Florida Bay. Lodge facilities include a restaurant and bar, freshwater swimming pool, gift shop, and coin laundry.

WHERE TO DINE

THE FLAMINGO RESTAURANT, in the Flamingo Visitor Center. Flamingo, FL 33030. Tel. 253-2241.
Cuisine: AMERICAN.
$ Prices: Main courses $10–$15. AE, MC, V.
Open: Nov–Apr for breakfast 7–10:30am, lunch 11:30am–2:30pm, dinner 5:30–9pm; May–Oct buffet dining 11:30am–9pm.

This is one of the best restaurants in South Florida, and the only one in the Everglades park area. The view from this multilevel eatery overlooking the Floriday Bay is spectacular. The menu features several meat and poultry dishes, but is noted for its well-prepared fresh fish selections.

2. CRUISING THE CARIBBEAN

Most people think that taking a cruise means spending thousands of dollars and booking a ship far in advance. It's true that some unusually big trips require serious advance planning, but most of the Caribbean-bound ships, sailing weekly out of the Port of Miami, are relatively inexpensive, can be booked without advance notice, and make for an excellent excursion.

Home to 22 cruise ships from all around the world, the Port of Miami is the world's busiest, with a passenger load of close to 3 million annually. The popularity of cruises shows no sign of tapering off, and the trend in ships is toward bigger, more luxurious liners. Usually all-inclusive, cruises offer exceptional value and unparalleled simplicity compared to other vacation options.

All of the shorter cruises are well equipped for gambling, and casinos open as soon as the ship clears U.S. waters; typically 45 minutes after the ship leaves port. Usually, four full-size meals are served daily, with portions so huge, they're impossible to finish. Games, movies, and other on-board activities ensure that you are always busy. Passengers can board up to two hours prior to departure for meals, games, and cocktails.

There are dozens of cruises to choose from, from a one-day excursion to a trip around the world. A full list of options can be obtained from the **Metro-Dade Seaport Department,** 1015 North America Way, Miami, FL 33132 (tel. 305/371-7678).

Most of the ships listed below offer 2- and 3-day excursions to the Bahamas. Cruise ships usually depart Miami on Friday night and return Monday morning. If you want more information, contact the **Bahamas Tourist Office,** 255 Alhambra Circle, Suite 425, Coral Gables, FL 33134 (tel. 442-4860). All passengers must travel with a passport or proof of citizenship for reentry into the United States.

CARNIVAL CRUISE LINES, 3655 NW 87th Ave., Miami, FL 33178. Tel. 305/599-2200 or toll free 800/327-9501.
Ship: *Fantasy.* **Itinerary:** 3 nights to Nassau. **Depart/Return:** Fri 4pm to Mon 7am. **Cost:** From $360.

One of the largest cruise ships in the world, the *Fantasy* made its debut in March 1990, amid wide critical attention. Several swimming pools, game rooms, and lounges surround a spectacular multistory foyer that has quickly made the *Fantasy* the centerpiece of Carnival's fast-growing fleet. The 70,000-ton ship can accommodate up to 2,600 passengers.

CHANDRIS FANTASY CRUISES, 4770 Biscayne Blvd., Miami, FL 33137. Tel. 305/262-5411 or toll free 800/437-3111.
Ship: *Britanis.* **Itinerary:** 2 nights to Nassau. **Depart/Return:** Fri 4:30pm to Sun 8am. **Cost:** From $220.

If you've never taken a cruise before, the *Britanis* is a good way to get acquainted with the waves. It's very inexpensive, the food is excellent, and even with a full load of 922 passengers, it doesn't seem crowded. All sailing is done at night, so you arrive at your destination well rested.

DOLPHIN CRUISE LINE, 901 South American Way, Miami, FL 33132. Tel. 305/358-5122 or toll free 800/222-1003.
Ship: *Dolphin IV.* **Itinerary:** 3 or 4 nights to Nassau and Blue Lagoon Island. **Depart/Return:** 3 nights—Fri 4:30pm to Mon 8am; 4 nights—Mon 4:30pm to Fri 8am. **Cost:** From $289.

One of the smallest ships sailing from Miami is the intimate 590-passenger *Dolphin IV,* which not only goes to Nassau but also to uncrowded Blue Lagoon Island, about 45 minutes away. The line often runs promotional price specials; call for details.

NORWEGIAN CRUISE LINE, 95 Merrick Way, Coral Gables, FL 33134. Tel. 305/445-0866 or toll free 800/327-7030.
Ship: *Sunward II.* **Itinerary:** 3 nights to Nassau, Key West, and Great Stirrup Cay. **Depart/Return:** Fri 4:30pm to Mon 8am. **Cost:** From $415.

The 676-passenger *Sunward II* spends a full day in both Nassau and on Great Stirrup Cay, the cruise line's private island resort. Like other Caribbean-bound ships, passengers are not required to disembark at any destination. You can stay on board for lunch, drinks, and games.

ROYAL CARIBBEAN CRUISE LINE, 1050 Caribbean Way, Miami, FL 33132. Tel. 305/539-6000 or toll free 800/327-6700.
Ship: *Nordic Empress.* **Itinerary:** 3 nights to Nassau and Coco Cay. **Depart/Return:** Fri 5pm to Mon 9am. **Cost:** From $515.
In 1990 Royal Caribbean entered the 3-night Caribbean market

with the brand-new *Nordic Empress*. Beautifully streamlined and stylized, this special ship is fully outfitted, and treats its 1,610 passengers to some of the world's swankiest seafaring. Coco Cay is the cruise line's private island, 5 hours from Nassau.

SEAESCAPE LTD., 1080 Port Blvd., Miami, FL 33132. Tel. 305/379-0000 or toll free 800/327-7400.
Ship: *Scandinavian Dawn.* **Itinerary:** 1-day cruise to Freeport or Bimini, or 1-night Cruise to Nowhere. **Depart/Return:** Freeport or Bimini daily 8:30am to 8:30 or 9:30pm; Cruise to Nowhere Fri 10:30pm to 3am. **Cost:** Freeport or Bimini $107; Nowhere $49, including port taxes.

SeaEscape's cruises arrive in the Bahamas by 2pm, and stay for about three hours. On the way is a bacchanalian orgy of eating, drinking, partying, and playing at the casino and on the dance floor. Hotel packages are available for passengers who want to stay on the islands overnight, and return the next day.

A Cruise to Nowhere is to Miamians what a trip to Atlantic City or Las Vegas is to people from New York or Los Angeles. Nonstop casinos, on-board entertainment, and lavish meals are as extravagant as any.

3. KEY WEST

Located about 150 miles from Miami, at the terminus of U.S. Highway 1, Key West is the most distant member of Florida's key chain. Accessible only by boat until 1912, when Henry Flagler extended his railroad to the end of the keys, Key West's relative isolation from the North American mainland has everything to do with the island's charm.

During the first half of the 19th century, many locals made their living as "wreckers"—helping themselves to the booty of ships overturned in the shallows offshore. Since that time, the key has been home to an untold number of outlaws, pirates, drifters, writers, musicians, and other eccentric types.

Today, in addition to artists and intellectuals, the island supports a healthy mix of Cubans and Caribbeans, and one of the largest gay populations in America. On Duval Street, smart boutiques stand next to divey old gin joints, and laid-back strollers fill the sidewalks. Key West is known for its terrific weather (about 10 degrees cooler than Miami during the height of summer), quaint 19th-century architecture, and a friendly, easygoing atmosphere.

GETTING THERE

One of the best things about Key West is the journey there. Airlines connect the island with Miami but, unless you're really pressed for time, driving is the way to go.

BY AIR

Several major airlines fly nonstop from Miami to Key West, and charge from $99 to $298 round-trip, depending on dates of travel and ticket restrictions. These include: **Continental** (tel. toll free 800/525-0280), and **USAir** (tel. toll free 800/428-4322).

Planes fly into **Key West International Airport,** South Roosevelt Boulevard (tel. 305/296-5439), on the southeastern corner of the island.

BY CAR

U.S. 1 skips over 42 bridges, and across 31 islands through some of the most beautiful terrain in the world. Separating the Gulf of Mexico from the Atlantic Ocean, much of the stretch is wide with water vistas, where on either side you can see as far as the horizon. At other times, the road is clogged with shopping centers, and billboards advertising restaurants, rest stops, and attractions. A good portion of U.S. 1 is a narrow two-lane highway. When it opens up to four lanes, regulars speed up to 80 miles per hour and more. The legal speed limit is 55 m.p.h., and on a good day you can make the trip from Miami in 4 hours. But don't rush. The scenery is beautiful, and there are plenty of places to stop along the way.

You should know that gasoline prices rise rapidly the farther south you go, but then descend slightly when you arrive on Key West. If you can, fill up in Miami.

Also along the way, you'll find that most addresses are given by mile marker (MM), a white number on the right side of the road that announces the distance from Key West.

INFORMATION

For information on attractions, accommodations, or entertainment, contact the **Florida Keys and Key West Visitors Bureau,** 416 Fleming St., Key West, FL 33040 (tel. 305/296-3811, or toll free 800/FLA-KEYS).

The **Greater Key West Chamber of Commerce,** 402 Wall St., Key West, FL 33041 (tel. 305/294-2587), also has information on area hotels, shops, and other businesses.

The local **American Express** office is located at 811 Peacock Plaza (tel. 294-3711).

SPECIAL EVENTS

Old Island Days refer to a calendar full of special events scheduled every year from December through April. These happenings, for the benefit of tourists and locals alike, usually occur on weekends and include garden tours, special readings, outdoor party events, and a myriad of other unusual activities. A full list of Old Island Days activities, along with their respective dates and times can be obtained from the Key West Chamber of Commerce, 402 Wall St., Box 984, Key West, FL 33040 (tel. 305/294-5988 or toll free 800/527-8539).

The **Arts Expo Craft Show,** (tel. 294-0431) usually on the last weekend of January, is a colorful explosion of local talent exhibiting and selling unique functional art.

At the beginning of February, the **Old Island Days Art Festival** gives local fine artists a chance to display their creations. The **Annual House and Garden Tours** are an island tradition, showing off some of the Key's best homes during the last two weekends in February. Contact the Chamber of Commerce (address above) for tour dates and ticket information.

Old Island Days continue in March with the **Annual Flagging of the Old Island Armada.** Dozens of private and commercial vessels parade in Key West's main channel, and flags are ceremoniously hoisted. Also in March is the **Key West Garden Club Flower Show** with its annual display of homegrown horticulture.

The **Conch Republic Celebration** is one of the year's biggest parties. In an attempt to catch illegal aliens and drug smugglers, in April 1982, the U.S. Border Patrol blocked the highway connecting Key West to the mainland. Island leaders, furious about being treated like foreigners, mockingly declared Key West an independent "Conch Republic." The annual celebrations in April are festive occasions.

The **Key West Fishing Tournament** (tel. 296-7586) is held each year in May on the first weekend of the fishing season. Fishers pulling in the biggest monsters are rewarded with fame and fortune.

The **Hemingway Days Festival** (tel. 294-4400) celebrates the life of Key West's most famous citizen. In addition to rewarding the island's best writers and storytellers, the July festival hosts an Ernest Hemingway look-alike contest, one of the weekend's most popular events. The **July Fourth Swim Around The Island** is one of the highlights of Key West's Independence Day celebrations. Look for beach parties, fireworks, along with the usual island shenanigans.

Fantasy Fest is Key West's best festival. Held during the week before Halloween, this Mardi Gras–style celebration includes costume parades, contests, toga parties, and Duval Street's biggest parade.

In November, the **Reef Relief's Cayo Festival** (tel. 294-3100) raises both money and consciousness for the protection of the Key's fragile coral reefs. Organized by a nonprofit organization, the festival features food, fun, and activities for all ages.

Christmas by the Sea, held the second week of December, includes a boat parade, and other warm-weather holiday celebrations. (tel. 294-5135). The **Festival of the Continents** (tel. 296-5000) starts on a weekend in December and continues every weekend through April. Culturally oriented events include English-language plays, international song and dance, and a host of other arts-oriented events.

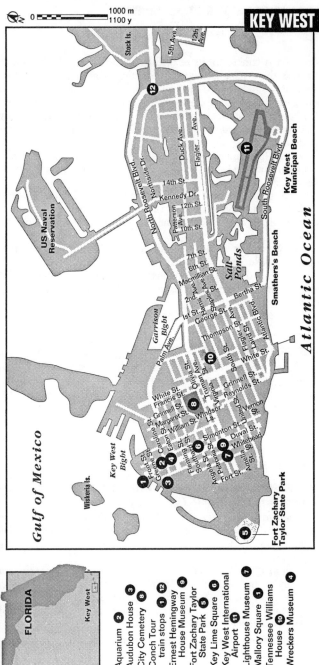

KEY WEST

0 — 1000 m
1100 y

Gulf of Mexico

Atlantic Ocean

US Naval Reservation

Key West Municipal Beach

Smathers's Beach

Salt Ponds

Garrison Bight

Key West Bight

Wisteria Is.

Stock Is.

Fort Zachary Taylor State Park

FLORIDA

Key West

Aquarium ②
Audubon House ③
City Cemetery ⑧
Conch Tour train stops ① ⑫
Ernest Hemingway House Museum ⑨
Fort Zachary Taylor State Park ⑤
Key Lime Square ⑥
Key West International Airport ⑪
Lighthouse Museum ⑦
Mallory Square ①
Tennessee Williams House ⑩
Wreckers Museum ④

WHAT TO SEE & DO

Key West is famous for its relaxed atmosphere. Literally the end of the road, this distant hideaway is one of the few areas in America that still deserves to be called the "wild west." Sure the island was tamed long ago by gourmet ice cream and chocolate-chip cookie shops, but Key West has reached legend status for the way its residents jealously guard the island's independent identity. Tales of old-time pirating and modern-day renegades abound. And natives, who call themselves "Conchs" (pronounced "conks"), have mockingly declared their secession from the United States, becoming the independent "Conch Republic."

Accordingly, the best thing to do on the island is to take a long stroll down Duval Street, and stop in at the many open-air bars. Meet some locals, have a few drinks, and end up at the Mallory Dock by sunset.

Key West is just 4 miles long and 2 miles wide, so getting around is easy. The "Old Town," centered around Duval Street, is the island's meeting ground and collective watering hole. It is also the location of some of this key's most interesting sites. Many of the surrounding streets are filled with some of America's most beautiful Victorian-style homes. While strolling around, try to visit some of the houses below.

AUDUBON HOUSE, 205 Whitehead St. Tel. 294-2116.

Named for the famous naturalist John James Audubon, who visited here in 1832, this restored three-story house features the master artist's original etchings and a large collection of lithographs.

The house also holds period furnishings and a collection of Dorothy Doughty's porcelain birds. A self-guided walking tour brochure of the lush tropical gardens is available.

Admission: $5 adults, $1 children 6–12.

Open: Daily 9:30am–5pm.

THE ERNEST HEMINGWAY HOUSE MUSEUM, 907 Whitehead St. Tel. 294-1575.

Home to Hemingway from 1931 to 1961, the author shared these quarters with 50-odd cats, and lived here while writing most of his greatest novels, including *Death in the Afternoon* and *For Whom the Bell Tolls*.

Built in 1851, this Spanish Colonial house was one of the first on the island to be fitted with indoor plumbing and a built-in fireplace. The pretty home was opened as a museum two years after Hemingway's death, and contains many personal possessions, as well as dozens of feline descendants.

Admission: $6 adults, $1.50 children under 12.

Open: Daily 9am–5pm.

A TOUR

Because Key West is so small, a tour of the island can be informative and fun. Touring is not intense, as there are no tight schedules to meet.

THE CONCH TRAIN TOUR. Tel. 294-5161.

The Conch Train is not a train at all, but a series of tram cars pulled by a "locomotive." These canopied cars, a familiar sight around Key West, offer a smart way to see the island. The tour passes about 60 local sites spread out over some 14 miles of road.

Reservations are not necessary. Trains depart every few minutes from 3850 North Roosevelt Boulevard (on U.S. 1, near the island bridge), and from Mallory Square (at the end of Duval Street). Tours run daily from 9am to 4pm, and cost $11 for adults, $5 for children under 16.

WHERE TO STAY

Key West is a popular vacation destination, so rooms are plentiful. Still, if you are traveling in the height of the season, advance reservations are a good idea. In general, accommodations options on the island are divided into two distinct categories: hotels and guesthouses. Both types of lodging are available in a wide range of price categories.

HOTELS

PIER HOUSE, 1 Duval St., Key West, FL 33040. Tel. 305/296-4600 or toll free 800/327-8340 (800/432-3414 in Fla.). Fax 305/296-7568. 142 rms, including 13 suites. A/C TV TEL

$ Rates: Nov–Mar $250–$350 single/double; the rest of the year $150–$225 single/double. Suites from $650. Extra person $10. Children free in parents' room. Packages available. AE, CB, DC, DISC, MC, V.

The recently renovated Pier House is one of South Florida's premier properties. Its excellent location, on the edge of the Old Town, makes it walkable to all the local restaurants and sights. But the hotel's spacious grounds and oceanfront setting shields you from the revelry.

One of this key's oldest landmarks, the Pier House is an important part of the island's history. Playwright Tennessee Williams was a frequent guest in the Pier House Restaurant, and singer/songwriter Jimmy Buffett got his start in the Roof Top bar. Today, the hotel's tiki-hut Beach Club bar is one of the area's most popular meeting places.

SOUTHERNMOST MOTEL, 1319 Duval St., Key West, FL 33040. Tel. 305/296-6577 or toll free 800/354-4455. Fax 305/294-8272. 127 rms. No-smoking rooms available. A/C TV TEL

$ Rates: Dec–Apr, $90–$165 single/double; the rest of the year, $60–$115 single/double. AE, MC, V.

At the other end of Duval Street, at the corner of South Street, is this kitschy motel with basic, but clean, rooms dressed in green and yellow. You can walk to everything from here, but if you want to stay put, there is a swimming pool and tanning area.

GUESTHOUSES

As quaint as the town itself, guesthouses are, for the most part, the most enjoyable way to experience the community of the keys. Accommodations vary, from simple rooms to elegant bed and breakfasts. Most are charming and cozy, and many are refurbished turn-of-the-century homes.

There are dozens of guesthouses on the island catering to different pocketbooks and lifestyles. Several houses are primarily geared toward gay travelers and are frank about their orientation. Don't be afraid to ask. For a full list of available accommodations, contact the Florida Keys and Key West Visitors Bureau, or the Key West Chamber of Commerce (see "Information," above).

THE CURRY MANSION INN, 115 Caroline St., Key West, FL 33040. Tel. 305/294-5349 or toll free 800/253-3466. Fax 305/294-4093. 20 rms. No-smoking rooms available. A/C TV TEL

$ Rates (including breakfast): Dec 22–May 1, $170–$190 single/double; June 2–Oct 1, $125–$140 single/double; the rest of the year, $140–$160 single/double. AE, MC, V.

A modern annex next to a house dating from 1899 is the site of this thoroughly charming B&B. Each of the well-decorated, carpeted rooms boasts its own individual identity, bursting with color, and maintained with care.

The inn's proprietors, Al and Edith Amsterdam, also own the historic house next door; most of which is open to the public. Guests are treated to complimentary cocktails, and are entitled to privileges at the Pier House Beach Club, just a block away.

WICKER GUESTHOUSE, 913 Duval St., Key West, FL 33040. Tel. 305/296-4275. 16 rms. A/C TV TEL

$ Rates: Dec–May, $60–$95 single/double; the rest of the year, $40–$85 single/double. Additional person $10. AE, MC, V.

Occupying three separate buildings overlooking busy Duval Street, the Wicker offers some of the best-priced accommodations on the island. Pretty porches outline the traditional "Conch" houses, though rooms are predictably sparse. This cozy B&B is a welcome option in tab-happy Key West.

WHERE TO DINE

When you start to get hungry, the Old Town is, again, a great place to be. Touristy restaurants abound, but, somehow, most of these eateries are really quite good, despite their orientation. A walk down

Duval Street reveals dozens of meaty choices for places to both eat and drink. Try to take this stroll before the stomach pangs set in, so you can choose a restaurant without duress.

THE BUTTERY, 1208 Simonton St. Tel. 294-0717.

Cuisine: CONTINENTAL. **Reservations:** Recommended.

$ Prices: Appetizers $7–$9, main courses, $16–$24. AE, CB, DC, MC, V.

Open: Nightly 6–11pm. **Closed:** 2 weeks in Sept.

One of the area's oldest and best-known establishments, The Buttery features a well-regarded continental cuisine with a French flair. Each of the restaurant's six dining rooms boasts its own flavor, but are united by a plethora of plants. Heavy creams douse tender steak filets, and local fruit sauces typically top the freshest of fish.

HALF SHELL RAW BAR, at the foot of Margaret St. Tel. 294-7496.

Cuisine: SEAFOOD.

$ Prices: Main courses $5–$10. No credit cards.

Open: Mon–Sat 11am–11pm, Sun noon–11pm.

This is the best place on the island for inexpensive, fresh-as-can-be seafood, in an authentic dockside setting. Decorated with "vanity" license plates from every state in the union, the Half Shell features a wide variety of freshly shucked shellfish, and daily catch selections. Beer is the drink of choice here, though other beverages and a full bar are available. Seating is either indoors, or out, on the small, but pretty deck overlooking the piers.

JIMMY BUFFETT'S MARGARITAVILLE CAFE, 500 Duval St. Tel. 292-1435.

Cuisine: AMERICAN.

$ Prices: Sandwiches $5–$6, fresh fish platter $10, margarita $4. AE, MC, V.

Open: Sun–Thurs 11am–2am, Fri–Sat 11am–4am.

This easygoing restaurant/bar is heavy on soups, salads, sandwiches, and local catches. A long bar runs the length of the place, and the attached gift shop can be seen through a glass window along one wall. Very touristy. Recommended.

INDEX

GENERAL INFORMATION

SIGHTS & ATTRACTIONS

MIAMI & ENVIRONS

EXCURSION AREAS

Note: An asterisk (*) indicates an author's favorite.

ACCOMMODATIONS

MIAMI & ENVIRONS

Key to Abbreviations: *B* = Budget; *CG* = Campground; *E* = Expensive; *GH* = Guesthouse; *M* = Moderate; *VE* = Very Expensive; *YH* = Youth hostel; *$* = Super-special value; * = An author's favorite.

EXCURSION AREAS

RESTAURANTS

MIAMI & ENVIRONS

Key to Abbreviations: *B* = Budget; *E* = Expensive; *I* = Inexpensive; *M* =
Moderate; *VE* = Very Expensive; *\$* = Super-special value; *** = An author's favorite.

MIAMI & ENVIRONS

EXCURSION AREAS

Now Save Money on All Your Travels by Joining
FROMMER'S ® TRAVEL BOOK CLUB
The World's Best Travel Guides at Membership Prices

FROMMER'S TRAVEL BOOK CLUB is your ticket to successful travel! Open up a world of travel information and simplify your travel planning when you join ranks with thousands of value-conscious travelers who are members of the FROMMER'S TRAVEL BOOK CLUB. Join today and you'll be entitled to all the privileges that come from belonging to the club that offers you travel guides for less to more than 100 destinations worldwide. Annual membership is only $25 (U.S.) or $35 (Canada and all foreign).

The Advantages of Membership

1. Your choice of three free FROMMER'S TRAVEL GUIDES. You can pick two from our FROMMER'S COUNTRY and REGIONAL GUIDES (listed under Comprehensive, $-A-Day, and Family) and one from our FROMMER'S CITY GUIDES (listed under City and City $-A-Day).
2. Your own subscription to **TRIPS & TRAVEL** quarterly newsletter.
3. You're entitled to a **30% discount** on your order of any additional books offered by FROMMER'S TRAVEL BOOK CLUB.
4. You're offered (at a small additional fee) our **Domestic Trip Routing Kits.**

Our quarterly newsletter **TRIPS & TRAVEL** offers practical information on the best buys in travel, the "hottest" vacation spots, the latest travel trends, world-class events and much, much more.

Our **Domestic Trip Routing Kits** are available for any North American destination. We'll send you a detailed map highlighting the best route to take to your destination—you can request direct or scenic routes.

Here's all you have to do to join:
Send in your membership fee of $25 ($35 Canada and foreign) with your name and address on the form below along with your selections as part of your membership package to FROMMER'S TRAVEL BOOK CLUB, P.O. Box 473, Mt. Morris, IL 61054-0473. Remember to check off 2 FROMMER'S COUNTRY and REGIONAL GUIDES and 1 FROMMER'S CITY GUIDE on the pages following.

If you would like to order additional books, please select the books you would like and send a check for the total amount (please add sales tax in the states noted below), plus $2 per book for shipping and handling ($3 per book for all foreign orders) to:

FROMMER'S TRAVEL BOOK CLUB
P.O. Box 473
Mt. Morris, IL 61054-0473
1-815-734-1104

[ ] YES. I want to take advantage of this opportunity to join FROMMER'S TRAVEL BOOK CLUB.
[ ] My check is enclosed. Dollar amount enclosed_____*
(all payments in U.S. funds only)

Name_____

Address_____

City_____ State_____ Zip_____

To ensure that all orders are processed efficiently, please apply sales tax in the following areas: CA, CT, FL, IL, NJ, NY, TN, WA, and CANADA.

*With membership, shipping and handling will be paid by FROMMER'S TRAVEL BOOK CLUB for the three free books you select as part of your membership. Please add $2 per book for shipping and handling for any additional books purchased ($3 per book for all foreign orders).

Allow 4-6 weeks for delivery. Prices of books, membership fee, and publication dates are subject to change without notice.

Please Send Me the Books Checked Below

FROMMER'S COMPREHENSIVE GUIDES
(Guides listing facilities from budget to deluxe, with emphasis on the medium-priced)

	Retail Price	Code		Retail Price	Code
☐ Acapulco/Ixtapa/Taxco 1993–94	$15.00	C120	☐ Jamaica/Barbados 1993–94	$15.00	C105
☐ Alaska 1990–91	$15.00	C001	☐ Japan 1992–93	$19.00	C020
☐ Arizona 1993–94	$18.00	C101	☐ Morocco 1992–93	$18.00	C021
☐ Australia 1992–93	$18.00	C002	☐ Nepal 1992–93	$18.00	C038
☐ Austria 1993–94	$19.00	C119	☐ New England 1993	$17.00	C114
☐ Austria/Hungary 1991–92	$15.00	C003	☐ New Mexico 1993–94	$15.00	C117
☐ Belgium/Holland/ Luxembourg 1993–94	$18.00	C106	☐ New York State 1992–93	$19.00	C025
☐ Bermuda/Bahamas 1992–93	$17.00	C005	☐ Northwest 1991–92	$17.00	C026
☐ Brazil, 3rd Edition	$20.00	C111	☐ Portugal 1992–93	$16.00	C027
☐ California 1993	$18.00	C112	☐ Puerto Rico 1993–94	$15.00	C103
☐ Canada 1992–93	$18.00	C009	☐ Puerto Vallarta/ Manzanillo/ Guadalajara 1992–93	$14.00	C028
☐ Caribbean 1993	$18.00	C102			
☐ Carolinas/Georgia 1992–93	$17.00	C034	☐ Scandinavia 1993–94	$19.00	C118
☐ Colorado 1993–94	$16.00	C100	☐ Scotland 1992–93	$16.00	C040
☐ Cruises 1993–94	$19.00	C107	☐ Skiing Europe 1989–90	$15.00	C030
☐ DE/MD/PA & NJ Shore 1992–93	$19.00	C012	☐ South Pacific 1992–93	$20.00	C031
☐ Egypt 1990–91	$15.00	C013	☐ Spain 1993–94	$19.00	C115
☐ England 1993	$18.00	C109	☐ Switzerland/ Liechtenstein 1992–93	$19.00	C032
☐ Florida 1993	$18.00	C104	☐ Thailand 1992–93	$20.00	C033
☐ France 1992–93	$20.00	C017	☐ U.S.A. 1993–94	$19.00	C116
☐ Germany 1993	$19.00	C108	☐ Virgin Islands 1992–93	$13.00	C036
☐ Italy 1993	$19.00	C113	☐ Virginia 1992–93	$14.00	C037
			☐ Yucatán 1993–94	$18.00	C110

FROMMER'S $-A-DAY GUIDES
(Guides to low-cost tourist accommodations and facilities)

	Retail Price	Code		Retail Price	Code
☐ Australia on $45 1993–94	$18.00	D102	☐ Israel on $45 1993–94	$18.00	D101
☐ Costa Rica/ Guatemala/Belize on $35 1993–94	$17.00	D108	☐ Mexico on $50 1993	$19.00	D105
			☐ New York on $70 1992–93	$16.00	D016
☐ Eastern Europe on $25 1991–92	$17.00	D005	☐ New Zealand on $45 1993–94	$18.00	D103
☐ England on $60 1993	$18.00	D107	☐ Scotland/Wales on $50 1992–93	$18.00	D019
☐ Europe on $45 1993	$19.00	D106			
☐ Greece on $45 1993–94	$19.00	D100	☐ South America on $40 1993–94	$19.00	D109
☐ Hawaii on $75 1993	$19.00	D104	☐ Turkey on $40 1992–93	$22.00	D023
☐ India on $40 1992–93	$20.00	D010	☐ Washington, D.C. on $40 1992–93	$17.00	D024
☐ Ireland on $40 1992–93	$17.00	D011			

FROMMER'S CITY $-A-DAY GUIDES
(Pocket-size guides with an emphasis on low-cost tourist accommodations and facilities)

	Retail Price	Code		Retail Price	Code
☐ Berlin on $40 1992–93	$12.00	D002	☐ Madrid on $50 1992–93	$13.00	D014
☐ Copenhagen on $50 1992–93	$12.00	D003	☐ Paris on $45 1992–93	$12.00	D018
☐ London on $45 1992–93	$12.00	D013	☐ Stockholm on $50 1992–93	$13.00	D022

FROMMER'S TOURING GUIDES
(Color-illustrated guides that include walking tours,
cultural and historic sights, and practical information)

	Retail Price	Code		Retail Price	Code
☐ Amsterdam	$11.00	T001	☐ New York	$11.00	T008
☐ Barcelona	$14.00	T015	☐ Rome	$11.00	T010
☐ Brazil	$11.00	T003	☐ Scotland	$10.00	T011
☐ Florence	$ 9.00	T005	☐ Sicily	$15.00	T017
☐ Hong Kong/Singapore/ Macau	$11.00	T006	☐ Thailand	$13.00	T012
			☐ Tokyo	$15.00	T016
☐ Kenya	$14.00	T018	☐ Venice	$ 9.00	T014
☐ London	$13.00	T007			

FROMMER'S FAMILY GUIDES

	Retail Price	Code		Retail Price	Code
☐ California with Kids	$17.00	F001	☐ San Francisco with Kids	$17.00	F004
☐ Los Angeles with Kids	$17.00	F002			
☐ New York City with Kids	$18.00	F003	☐ Washington, D.C. with Kids	$17.00	F005

FROMMER'S CITY GUIDES
(Pocket-size guides to sightseeing and tourist accommodations
and facilities in all price ranges)

	Retail Price	Code		Retail Price	Code
☐ Amsterdam 1993–94	$13.00	S110	☐ Minneapolis/St. Paul, 3rd Edition	$13.00	S119
☐ Athens, 9th Edition	$13.00	S114	☐ Montréal/Québec City 1993–94	$13.00	S125
☐ Atlanta 1993–94	$13.00	S112			
☐ Atlantic City/Cape May 1991–92	$ 9.00	S004	☐ New Orleans 1993–94	$13.00	S103
☐ Bangkok 1992–93	$13.00	S005	☐ New York 1993	$13.00	S120
☐ Barcelona/Majorca/ Minorca/Ibiza 1993–94	$13.00	S115	☐ Orlando 1993	$13.00	S101
			☐ Paris 1993–94	$13.00	S109
☐ Berlin 1993–94	$13.00	S116	☐ Philadelphia 1993–94	$13.00	S113
☐ Boston 1993–94	$13.00	S117	☐ Rio 1991–92	$ 9.00	S029
☐ Cancún/Cozumel/ Yucatán 1991–92	$ 9.00	S010	☐ Rome 1993–94	$13.00	S111
			☐ Salt Lake City 1991–92	$ 9.00	S031
☐ Chicago 1993–94	$13.00	S122			
☐ Denver/Boulder/ Colorado Springs 1990–91	$ 8.00	S012	☐ San Diego 1993–94	$13.00	S107
			☐ San Francisco 1993	$13.00	S104
			☐ Santa Fe/Taos/ Albuquerque 1993–94	$13.00	S108
☐ Dublin 1993–94	$13.00	S128			
☐ Hawaii 1992	$12.00	S014	☐ Seattle/Portland 1992–93	$12.00	S035
☐ Hong Kong 1992–93	$12.00	S015			
☐ Honolulu/Oahu 1993	$13.00	S106	☐ St. Louis/Kansas City 1993–94	$13.00	S127
☐ Las Vegas 1993–94	$13.00	S121			
☐ Lisbon/Madrid/Costa del Sol 1991–92	$ 9.00	S017	☐ Sydney 1993–94	$13.00	S129
			☐ Tampa/St. Petersburg 1993–94	$13.00	S105
☐ London 1993	$13.00	S100			
☐ Los Angeles 1993–94	$13.00	S123	☐ Tokyo 1992–93	$13.00	S039
☐ Madrid/Costa del Sol 1993–94	$13.00	S124	☐ Toronto 1993–94	$13.00	S126
			☐ Vancouver/Victoria 1990–91	$ 8.00	S041
☐ Mexico City/Acapulco 1991–92	$ 9.00	S020			
☐ Miami 1993–94	$13.00	S118	☐ Washington, D.C. 1993	$13.00	S102

Other Titles Available at Membership Prices

SPECIAL EDITIONS

	Retail Price	Code		Retail Price	Code
☐ Bed & Breakfast North America	$15.00	P002	☐ Where to Stay U.S.A.	$14.00	P015
☐ Caribbean Hideaways	$16.00	P005			
☐ Marilyn Wood's Wonderful Weekends (within a 250-mile radius of NYC)	$12.00	P017			

GAULT MILLAU'S "BEST OF" GUIDES
(The only guides that distinguish the truly superlative from the merely overrated)

	Retail Price	Code		Retail Price	Code
☐ Chicago	$16.00	G002	☐ New England	$16.00	G010
☐ Florida	$17.00	G003	☐ New Orleans	$17.00	G011
☐ France	$17.00	G004	☐ New York	$17.00	G012
☐ Germany	$18.00	G018	☐ Paris	$17.00	G013
☐ Hawaii	$17.00	G006	☐ San Francisco	$17.00	G014
☐ Hong Kong	$17.00	G007	☐ Thailand	$18.00	G019
☐ London	$17.00	G009	☐ Toronto	$17.00	G020
☐ Los Angeles	$17.00	G005	☐ Washington, D.C.	$17.00	G017

THE REAL GUIDES
(Opinionated, politically aware guides for youthful budget-minded travelers)

	Retail Price	Code		Retail Price	Code
☐ Able to Travel	$20.00	R112	☐ Kenya	$12.95	R015
☐ Amsterdam	$13.00	R100	☐ Mexico	$11.95	R016
☐ Barcelona	$13.00	R101	☐ Morocco	$14.00	R017
☐ Belgium/Holland/ Luxembourg	$16.00	R031	☐ Nepal	$14.00	R018
			☐ New York	$13.00	R019
☐ Berlin	$11.95	R002	☐ Paris	$13.00	R020
☐ Brazil	$13.95	R003	☐ Peru	$12.95	R021
☐ California & the West Coast	$17.00	R121	☐ Poland	$13.95	R022
			☐ Portugal	$15.00	R023
☐ Canada	$15.00	R103	☐ Prague	$15.00	R113
☐ Czechoslovakia	$14.00	R005	☐ San Francisco & the Bay Area	$11.95	R024
☐ Egypt	$19.00	R105			
☐ Europe	$18.00	R122	☐ Scandinavia	$14.95	R025
☐ Florida	$14.00	R006	☐ Spain	$16.00	R026
☐ France	$18.00	R106	☐ Thailand	$17.00	R119
☐ Germany	$18.00	R107	☐ Tunisia	$17.00	R115
☐ Greece	$18.00	R108	☐ Turkey	$13.95	R027
☐ Guatemala/Belize	$14.00	R010	☐ U.S.A.	$18.00	R117
☐ Hong Kong/Macau	$11.95	R011	☐ Venice	$11.95	R028
☐ Hungary	$14.00	R118	☐ Women Travel	$12.95	R029
☐ Ireland	$17.00	R120	☐ Yugoslavia	$12.95	R030
☐ Italy	$13.95	R014			